THE CULINARY INSTITUTE OF AMERICA®

POULTRY

Thomas Schneller

IDENTIFICATION · FABRICATION · UTILIZATION

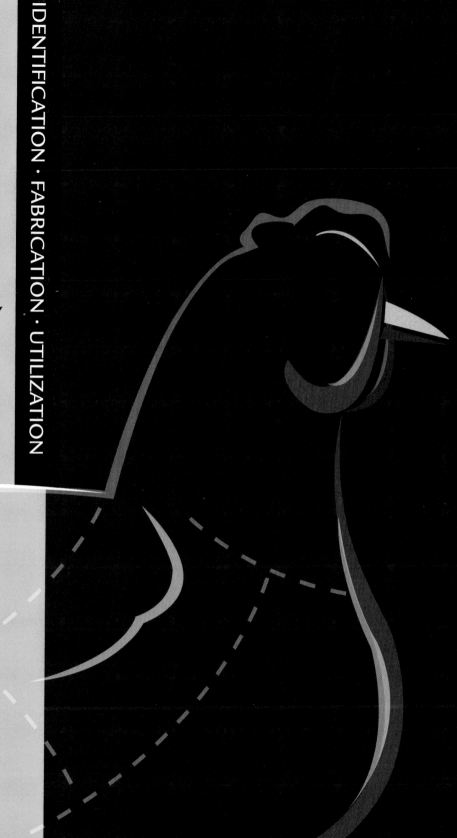

KITCHEN PRO SERIES

Join us on the web at

culinary.delmar.com

THE CULINARY INSTITUTE OF AMERICA®

IDENTIFICATION · FABRICATION · UTILIZATION

POULTRY

Thomas Schneller

DELMAR
CENGAGE Learning™

Australia · Brazil · Japan · Korea · Mexico · Singapore · Spain · United Kingdom · United States

KITCHEN PRO SERIES

KitchenPro Series: Guide to Poultry Identification, Fabrication, and Utilization
Thomas Schneller

Vice President, Career and Professional Editorial: Dave Garza

Director of Learning Solutions: Sandy Clark

Acquisitions Editor: James Gish

Managing Editor: Larry Main

Product Manager: Nicole Calisi

Editorial Assistant: Sarah Timm

Vice President, Career and Professional Marketing: Jennifer McAvey

Marketing Director: Wendy Mapstone

Marketing Manager: Kristin McNary

Marketing Coordinator: Scott Chrysler

Production Director: Wendy Troeger

Senior Content Project Manager: Glenn Castle

Art Director: Bethany Casey

Technology Project Manager: Chrstopher Catalina

Production Technology Analyst: Thomas Stover

The Culinary Institute of America

President: Dr. Tim Ryan '77

Vice-President, Dean of Culinary Education: Mark Erickson

Senior Director, Educational Enterprises: Susan Cussen

Director of Publishing: Nathalie Fischer

Editorial Project Manager: Lisa Lahey 00'

Editorial Assistant: Shelly Malgee '08

Editorial Assistant: Erin Jeanne McDowell '08

Photography:

Keith Ferris, Photographer

Ben Fink, Photographer

For product information and technology assistance, contact us at
Professional & Career Group Customer Support, 1-800-648-7450

For permission to use material from this text or product,
submit all requests online at **cengage.com/permissions**
Further permissions questions can be e-mailed to
permissionrequest@cengage.com.

Library of Congress Control Number: 2009932784

ISBN-13: 978-1-4354-0038-2

ISBN-10: 1-4354-0038-0

Delmar
5 Maxwell Drive
Clifton Park, NY 12065-2919
USA

Cengage Learning products are represented in Canada by Nelson Education, Ltd.

For your lifelong learning solutions, visit **delmar.cengage.com**

Visit our corporate website at **cengage.com**

Printed in the United States of America
1 2 3 4 5 12 11 10 09

Contents

RECIPE CONTENTS viii

ABOUT THE CIA ix

AUTHOR BIOGRAPHY xii

ACKNOWLEDGEMENTS xiii

1 POULTRY 3

Poultry Animals' Role in Farm Life 4
History of Poultry Production 4
The Modern Poultry Industry 5
Avian Flu 8
Basic Poultry Food Safety 8
Packaging and Storage 10
Cooking Safety 10
Poultry Grading and Evaluation 11
Classifications of Poultry 11
Poultry Muscle Fibers 12
Natural Poultry 13

2 CHICKEN 15

Domestication of Chicken 16
Chicken Production 16
Chicken Feed 18
Breeds and Varieties of Chicken 20
Classes of Chicken 24
Foodservice Market Forms 24
Purchasing Specifications 26
Chicken Processing 33

3 DUCK 55

History of Duck   56
Domestication of Ducks   56
Duck Feed   58
By-Product Feathers   59
Domestic Breeds of Duck   60
Classes of Duck   65
Purchasing Specifications   65
Duck Fabrication   72
Foie Gras   83

4 GOOSE 87

History of the Goose   88
Modern Goose Production   91
By-Product of Geese   91
Breeds of Geese   92
Classes of Geese   93
Purchasing Specifications   94
Goose Fabrication   97

5 TURKEY 107

History of the Turkey   108
Modern Turkey Production   109
Turkey Feed   109
Breeds of Turkey   111
Classes of Turkey   115
Purchasing Specifics   116
Turkey Fabrication   122

6 GAME BIRDS 137

History of Game Birds   138
Game Birds   139
Fabrication of Game Birds   151

7 POULTRY NUTRITION 165

Offal from Poultry   167
Nutrition Charts   168

8 EGGS 179

History 179
Large-Scale Egg Production 180
Free Ranged vs Pasture-Raised Eggs 182
Organic Eggs 183
Candling 184
Chicken Egg Grading and Sizing 184
Storage and Freshness 189
Packaging 190
Food Safety 192
Nutrition 192
Eggs as Food 195

9 POULTRY RECIPES 201

READINGS AND RESOURCES 244

GLOSSARY 245

APPENDIX 248

INDEX 252

PHOTO CREDITS 261

CIA CONVERSION CHARTS 262

Recipe Contents

Basic Chicken Stock   202

Basic Poultry Brine for Enhancing Moisture   203

Basic Poultry Brine for Curing and Smoking   204

Frenched Chicken Breast with Fresh Basil Sauce   205

Apple-Walnut Stuffed Cornish Game Hens   207

Columbian Chicken Sancocho   211

Chicken Paprikash   212

Easy Slice Roast Turkey   213

Turkey Pastrami   217

Roast Goose Grand Marnier   218

Smoked Goose Breast with Hoisin Glaze   221

Duck Magret with Sauce Cassis   225

Barbequed Duck Legs   226

Spanish Griddled Quail   227

Pecan-Stuffed Pheasant   229

Duck Saucisse (Sausage)   233

Peppered Ostrich Fillets with Duck Steak Fries   235

Foie Gras Fig Newton   237

Pan Seared Squab Au Jus   241

ABOUT THE CIA

THE WORLD'S PREMIER CULINARY COLLEGE

The Culinary Institute of America (CIA) is the recognized leader in culinary education for undergraduate students, foodservice and hospitality professionals, and food enthusiasts. The college awards bachelor's and associate degrees, as well as certificates and continuing education units, and is accredited by the prestigious Middle States Commission on Higher Education.

Founded in 1946 in downtown New Haven, CT to provide culinary training for World War II veterans, the college moved to its present location in Hyde Park, NY in 1972. In 1995, the CIA added a branch campus in the heart of California's Napa Valley—The Culinary Institute of America at Greystone. The CIA continued to grow, and in 2008, established a second branch campus, this time in San Antonio, TX. That same year, the CIA at Astor Center opened in New York City.

From its humble beginnings more than 60 years ago with just 50 students, the CIA today enrolls more than 2,700 students in its degree programs, approximately 3,000 in its programs for foodservice and hospitality industry professionals, and more than 4,500 in its courses for food enthusiasts.

LEADING THE WAY

Throughout its history, The Culinary Institute of America has played a pivotal role in shaping the future of foodservice and hospitality. This is due in large part to the caliber of people who make up the CIA community—its faculty, staff, students, and alumni—and their passion for the culinary arts and dedication to the advancement of the profession.

Headed by the visionary leadership of President Tim Ryan '77, the CIA education team has at its core the largest concentration of American Culinary Federation—Certified Master Chefs (including Dr. Ryan) of any college. The Culinary Institute of America faculty, more than 130 members strong, brings a vast breadth and depth of foodservice industry experience and insight to the CIA kitchens, classrooms, and research facilities. They've worked in some of the world's finest establishments, earned industry awards and professional certifications, and emerged victorious from countless international culinary competitions. And they continue to make their mark on the industry, through the students they teach, books they author, and leadership initiatives they champion.

The influence of the CIA in the food world can also be attributed to the efforts and achievements of our more than 37,000 successful alumni. Our graduates are leaders in virtually every segment of the industry and bring the professionalism and commitment to excellence they learned at the CIA to bear in everything they do.

UNPARALLELED EDUCATION

DEGREE PROGRAMS

The CIA's bachelor's and associate degree programs in culinary arts and baking and pastry arts feature more than 1,300 hours of hands-on learning in the college's kitchens, bakeshops, and student-staffed restaurants along with an 18-week externship at one of more than 1,200 top restaurant, hotel, and resort locations around the world. The bachelor's degree programs also include a broad range of liberal arts and business management courses to prepare students for future leadership positions.

CERTIFICATE PROGRAMS

The college's certificate programs in culinary arts and baking and pastry arts are designed both for students interested in an entry-level position in the food world and those already working in the foodservice industry who wants to advance their careers. A third offering, the Accelerated Culinary Arts Certificate Program (ACAP), provides graduates of baccalaureate programs in hospitality management, food science, nutrition, and closely related fields with a solid foundation in the culinary arts and the career advancement opportunities that go along with it.

PROFESSIONAL DEVELOPMENT PROGRAMS AND INDUSTRY SERVICES

The CIA offers food and wine professionals a variety of programs to help them keep their skills sharp and stay abreast of industry trends. Courses in cooking, baking, pastry, wine, and management are complemented by stimulating conferences and seminars, online culinary R&D courses, and multimedia training materials. Industry professionals can also deepen their knowledge and earn valuable ProChef® and professional wine certification credentials at several levels of proficiency.

The college's Industry Solutions Group, headed by a seasoned team of Certified Master Chefs, offers foodservice businesses a rich menu of custom programs and consulting services in areas such as R&D, flavor exploration, menu development, and health and wellness.

FOOD ENTHUSIAST PROGRAMS

Food enthusiasts can get a taste of the CIA educational experience during the college's popular Boot Camp intensives in Hyde Park, as well as demonstration and hands-on courses at the new CIA at Astor Center in New York City. At the Greystone campus, CIA Sophisticated Palate™ programs feature hands-on instruction and exclusive, behind-the-scenes excursions to Napa Valley growers and purveyors.

CIA LOCATIONS

MAIN CAMPUS—HYDE PARK, NY

Bachelor's and associate degree programs, professional development programs, food enthusiast programs

The CIA's main campus in New York's scenic Hudson River Valley offers everything an aspiring or professional culinarian could want. Students benefit from truly exceptional facilities that include 41 professionally equipped kitchens and bakeshops; five award-winning, student-staffed restaurants; culinary demonstration theaters; a dedicated wine lecture hall; a center for the study of Italian food and wine; a nutrition center; a 79,000-volume library; and a storeroom filled to brimming with the finest ingredients, including many sourced from the bounty of the Hudson Valley.

THE CIA AT GREYSTONE—ST. HELENA, CA

Associate degree program, professional development programs, certificate programs, food enthusiast programs

Rich with legendary vineyards and renowned restaurants, California's Napa Valley offers students a truly inspiring culinary learning environment. At the center of it all is the CIA at Greystone—a campus like no other, with dedicated centers for flavor development, professional wine studies, and menu research and development; a 15,000-square-foot teaching kitchen space; demonstration theaters; and the Ivy Award-winning Wine Spectator Greystone Restaurant.

THE CIA, SAN ANTONIO—SAN ANTONIO, TX

Certificate program, professional development programs

A new education and research initiative for the college, the CIA, San Antonio is located on the site of the former Pearl Brewery and features a newly renovated 5,500-square-foot facility equipped with a state-of-the-art teaching kitchen. Plans for the 22-acre site include transforming it into an urban village complete with restaurants, shops, art galleries, an open-air *mercado,* an events facility, and expanded CIA facilities, including a demonstration theater and skills kitchen.

THE CIA AT ASTOR CENTER—NEW YORK, NY

Professional development programs, food enthusiast programs

The CIA's newest educational venue is located in the NoHo section of New York's Greenwich Village, convenient for foodservice professionals and foodies alike. At The Culinary Institute of America at Astor Center, students enjoy courses on some of the most popular and important topics in food and wine today, in brand-new facilities that include a 36-seat, state-of-the-art demonstration theater; a professional teaching kitchen for 16 students; and a multipurpose event space.

AUTHOR BIOGRAPHY

Chef Schneller started working with meat at the age of 14 in his family's business. He is by all definitions of the word a "butcher". With over 30 years of meat cutting experience and having taught the meat class at the acclaimed Culinary Institute of America for the past 10 years, Chef Schneller brings a high level of understanding to this book. Chef Schneller also owned and operated his own restaurant and catering business for 11 years, has worked in a variety of restaurant positions including back and front of the house and has an understanding of foodservice. As Chef Schneller continues teaching at the Institute, he is focused on acquiring more knowledge in all aspects of the meat industry.

ACKNOWLEDGEMENTS

The research for this book dates back to my early days as a butcher in my father's shop in Kingston, N.Y. Whole, freshly processed chickens from Maine would arrive in wooden crates topped with ice. They were fresh and plump. My father would rave about them and show me that they had no spots or other defects. They came with little tags claiming Penobscot as the origin. We would sell some whole and cut others to order as requested by our customers.

Another poultry memory was boning whole geese and ducks for fabricating into patespâtes and terrines. Boning whole turkeys and tying them into roasts, slow cooking them with thyme, sage, and bacon strips over the top was another task we did weekly. This became our sliced turkey cold cuts. During holiday times we would carry a large assortment of specialty birds such as fat capons, Muscovy ducks, and assorted game birds. All of this contributed to my understanding of poultry.

Beyond our store, poultry was part of my upbringing. Grandma's chicken Paprikash, various roasts and stews prepared by my mother and grandfather, and eggs collected from a neighbor's chickens all connected me with what is poultry.

Upon arriving at the Culinary Institute of America, I furthered my education by touring various poultry plants and conferring with our purveyors, multitudes of chefs, colleagues, and students. I can only say that this college continues to amaze and teach me every day and I can only thank all of my acquaintances here for these many opportunities. My students continue to drive me to bring them more and more information and they are the original inspiration for this book.

I would like to thank the editing staff at the CIA for helping me to achieve this goal, especially Lisa Lahey and Shelly Malgee. Their work with the concepts and design of this project were truly appreciated. Lisa was the encouraging force behind this and other projects.

This book would not be possible without the work of two photographers, Ben Fink and Keith Ferris. Poultry is not pretty, yet they succeed in holding our attention to the page through their fine craftsmanship. Thanks to both!

Thanks to the CIA meat storeroom staff for getting all of my various poultry items in house and then making sure they were all used within our school. Almost all of the poultry shot in this book were kept cold during filming and were used as part of our curriculum.

A few students helped with the set up and recipes for the book. My teaching assistant at the time, Tracy Malechek, was extremely helpful in helping creating the squab photo, the fun Foie Gras Fig Newton, and finding friends to help with the other recipes. Tracey's work on this project and her overall interest in great food was wholeheartedly appreciated. She will do great things!

Included in this book are some photos that I was thankful to have permission to use. Cynthia Crawford (Fig 5.1 Wild turkeys grazing) Susan Quilty (Fig 4.3 Goose attacking) Eric Swisher of Five Turkeys Farm (Fig 5.2 Turkeys grazing on a farm) Chore-Time Brock International (Fig 2.2 Chicken feed bins) Terry and Lisa Kilmer at Gray Horse Farm (Figures 20–23 in the egg chapter)

And last, but certainly not least, I would like to thank my wife, Patricia, and my children, Max and Mary, for they make a well-roasted chicken with apples and herbs complete.

Thomas K. Schneller

1

POULTRY

The poultry industry as we know it today is a relatively modern phenomenon. When we think of the term *poultry* what comes to mind? Of course domestic chicken, but also duck, goose, and turkey are part of the definition. In early agrarian societies we find poultry as a fixture on the farm. The picture of the crowing rooster waking the farm as the sun comes up is embedded in even the most urban mindset. When we look at the farm of old we see the animals all playing some important role; the cow and goat as a source of milk or meat, the sheep for its wool, the horse for transportation and pulling the plow, the pig as meat and a recycler of waste food. The chicken, duck, and goose all were raised primarily for their eggs and eventually, meat.

POULTRY ANIMALS' ROLE IN FARM LIFE

On the farm the poultry animals played other important roles beyond a source of food protein. The chickens were used to control insect populations. Chickens will eat many pests found in a garden and if allowed to roam the barnyard they will eat ticks and larvae that could infest other animals. Poultry, like pigs, were kept to consume any excess or waste grain on the farm. After a harvest poultry animals were allowed to glean the fields where they ate any missed grain and also added fertilizer as they roamed. Poultry were part of the synergy of the farm. Poultry also acted as an alarm system. The honking of a goose or cackling of chickens in the night would indicate to the farmer that a predator is in their midst. The early morning rooster would wake the farmer to another day. Geese were used by crop farmers as "weeders" sent into fields between rows to pluck out unwanted weeds. And, as anyone who has gotten too close to one knows, they can be as ferocious as any guard dog.

Feathers and down were used as a source of insulation for clothing and beds. A "down" pillow and blanket reduced the need for heat in the farmhouse on cold winter nights. Poultry played a large part in the symbiotic relationships of the farm.

Eggs were probably the first human-animal food. Early hunters and gatherers stole eggs from nests for a quality source of protein. They hunted birds for meat and the fact that they had no way to store meats meant that poultry items were generally just the right size to be consumed in one sitting.

HISTORY OF POULTRY PRODUCTION

The domestication of poultry began around 3000 B.C. Chickens were first domesticated from the Red Jungle Fowl in India and Southeast Asia. There are many depictions of domestic duck and geese in ancient Egypt. During the height of Egyptian prosperity in ancient times, geese were fed to the point of engorgement creating early versions of the "foiegras" or fattened liver. Writings on how to prepare ducks with salt speak of early preservation methods.

Early Chinese civilizations show signs of domestication of poultry around 1400 B.C. The rooster appears in Chinese mythology and it was believed mythical roosters signaled earthly roosters to crow. The Rooster appears on the Chinese zodiac. The last "Year of the Rooster" was in 2005. Poultry was and is an integral part of Chinese food culture. Legendary tales of poultry are found in many western writings also. The famous character "Chanticleer the Rooster" created by Geoffrey Chaucer in his *Canterbury Tales* written in the late fourteenth century, tells of the proud rooster who dominates the farm. Many tales of poultry exist. "Chicken Little" tells of the poultry animals of the farm being duped by the wily fox. Prokofiev's famous "Peter and the Wolf" musical story casts the haunting oboe as the duck.

In Europe, emerging from the Dark Ages, we find butchers specialized in poultry. Farmers' markets were established in all villages and towns throughout Europe and poulterers were a common site. They sold eggs as well as live or slaughtered poultry. Eggs were a major part of the poultry business and still play a part today. The English established the Smithfield market on the edge of London and every Friday a large assortment of livestock and poultry items were sold. The Smithfield market was in existence around 1100 A.D. and was granted "Market Rights" in 1327 A.D.

In the late 1400s and early 1500s explorations led by the European countries began a joining of continents through trade and conquest. Part of the reason for traveling the globe was to find spice routes to the Orient. In so doing the explorers encountered many lands inhabited with indigenous peoples who often were hunting, or raising domestically, a variety of birds. The meaty North American wild turkey was introduced to the rest of the world. Species of Indian and Asian fowl were transported back to Europe where they were often crossbred with other breeds. Today there is evidence that Polynesians brought the first chickens to South America around the late 1300s, about 100 years before Columbus. No doubt resourceful early mariners brought domesticated poultry on long journeys due to their ability to be cooped and survive and for the eggs the birds produced. The poultry industry changed as humans came into the industrial age. Chicken in particular gradually grew from a primarily egg industry into a major meat source. Other poultry such as turkey grew in popularity. Farmers began to mechanize and had modern materials to work with. The ability to maintain larger flocks and increase egg production actually meant that poultry became less expensive compared to other meats. Grains became cheaper and many poultry operators grew. Before 1900, a typical poultry farm had no more than 200 to 300 birds. This was all a small farmer could manage. The developments by geneticists and nutritionists improved flocks rapidly and by the early 1900s poultry farms had numbers in the thousands. In a book written in 1910, *Profitable Poultry Production* by M.G. Kains, it describes the foundation for modern poultry production. The beginnings of the "long" house as opposed to multiple small units, introduction of modern mesh wire, and descriptions of nutritional guidelines were all designed to modernize poultry production. Most of the chicken production was still focused on eggs at this time. During World War II a change began in the U.S. poultry industry. Chickens were grown for meat alone and eggs became a separate industry. Raising birds as meat only meant you could do away with all of the worries of egg production and storage. Integrated systems were established where the producer was no longer simply the farmer. At this point we find the producers owning the feed mill, the incubators, the chicken houses, the processing plants, and distribution. By the late 1930s John Tyson, who previously had been a transporter of chicken, purchased his own feed mill. Later John Tyson purchased incubators to hatch the birds and by 1947 Tyson began its rise to the dominant poultry/meat company it is today. One of the biggest innovations that Tyson introduced was his experimentations with crossbreeding to develop a faster growing, meatier bird. By 1950, Tyson was selling 96,000 broilers a week!

THE MODERN POULTRY INDUSTRY

Today poultry production is growing worldwide. Trade agreements and global markets now allow poultry products to be sold as any other commodity item, subjecting them to price fluctuations and supply and demand issues. Prices for poultry have gradually risen over the past few years as higher feed costs are factored. Production continues to be high. U.S. chicken production for 2007 was estimated at 35.9 billion pounds and turkey production was up to an estimated 5.8 billion pounds. The chicken industry worldwide produced over 71 million tons in 2005 and production continues to grow.

THE 15 LEADING CHICKEN PRODUCERS (thousands of tons—eviscerated)					
	1985	1990	1995	2000	2005
United States	6,407	8,667	11,486	13,944	15,869
China	1,474	2,692	6,097	9,075	10,196
EU-25	5,132	5,625	6,703	7,883	8,894
United Kingdom	715	790	1,077	1,214	1,331
France	938	1,049	1,232	1,242	1,122
Spain	796	807	904	965	1,047
Poland	249	301	347	560	980
Brazil	1,490	2,356	4,050	5,980	8,668
Mexico	551	750	1283	1825	2436
India	161	342	578	1,080	1,900
Japan	1,425	1,462	1,317	1,255	1,338
Indonesia	346	560	961	904	1,400
Russian Federation			859	754	1,345
Canada	505	555	720	880	981
Thailand	393	575	910	1,091	950

(*Continues*)

(*Continued*)

	1985	1990	1995	2000	2005
Turkey	273	401	490	643	936
South Africa	339	572	641	868	978
Malaysia	239	377	712	690	913
Iran	235	380	637	803	825
World TOTAL	27,840	35,805	46,987	59,430	71,851

Source: Food and Agriculture Organization (FAO)

Systems for growing poultry more efficiently have allowed many countries to export their excess around the world. Brazil is now the number one exporter of broiler chickens.

A typical large volume chicken processor in the United States can process up to 250,000 birds a day. This process has become highly automated with machines that are now able to break down the carcass without much hands-on skill required. This factor is another reason poultry has stayed very inexpensive.

Chicken and turkey are by far the dominant production fowl but duck and geese are also found in large quantities throughout the world. World production of water fowl has increased over the past ten years. China is the leading producer of ducks followed by France, India, Thailand, and Vietnam. For geese, again China is the largest and then Eastern European countries, Ukraine, Hungary, then Egypt, Taiwan. Many of the southeast Asian countries are traditional poultry farming societies. The cuisines of these countries reflect this fact.

Europe also produces large amounts of water-fowl poultry. France has long been known for its hearty dishes created from the goose or duck.

The United States and Canada produce a fair amount of duck and geese but these meats tend to be less popular with the majority selling in seasonal waves. Retail stores will see most of their yearling duck and goose sales around the winter holidays. The mid- to upscale food service industry, more specifically the sit-down restaurants, tend to sell more duck than the in casual take away or fast food establishments.

AVIAN FLU

One factor affecting poultry production worldwide is the emergence of the "Bird Flu." This disease affects a variety of birds including those in the wild. Bird flu is a very general term. There are thousands of strains of flu that have circulated in bird populations for many years. The highly pathogenic variety, H5N1, has been the cause of serious concern over the past few years. This flu, which can be spread from flock to flock by water or air, is able to spread through populations of birds very quickly. Some instances where humans have come into close contact with the infected birds have resulted in severe flu symptoms from which there is no real defense. The flu will actually cause a very healthy person's immune system to overreact to this previously unseen strain causing the person's vital organs to shut down. Over 200 people worldwide have died from the disease.

Outbreaks in 2003 caused the government in Vietnam to cull thousands of birds and use a vaccine to guard against it. All over Asia poultry operations were affected and immunizing all flocks especially in more rural areas has proven difficult. The H5N1 flu has spread from Southeast Asia into China, India, Iran, Egypt, Turkey, Japan, Russia, all of Europe and England. Outbreaks have been somewhat seasonal with most occurring in the winter. The fact that much of the large poultry production is now done in large indoor or outdoor grow-out pens means these animals are more susceptible to an outbreak. They are in close quarters where the flu is easily transmitted and most are very young animals that do not have a chance to develop any resistance. Older wild fowl tend to be much more resistant and may not even show symptoms. Certain fowl, such as swans, tend to be more susceptible to the disease than wild ducks. Unregulated transfer of poultry across borders is considered a major contributor to the spread of the disease.

Conflicting research points in two directions. One says this is an imminent danger where the flu will mutate into a human form easily passed from one person to another and a pandemic human outbreak is possible. Other research claims that bird flu would need to mutate dramatically, which could weaken the strain making it less harmful. Either way, the World Health Organization (WHO) and many government agencies are watching the situation carefully.

BASIC POULTRY FOOD SAFETY

Poultry meats are considered highly susceptible to pathogens due to the high water content of the lean muscle and the fact that many poultry items are water chilled. Care must be taken when handling poultry products and the risk of a variety of food borne illnesses must be taken very seriously. Salmonella, Escherichia coli (*E. coli*), *Staphylococcus areoles,* Campylobacter, and Listeria are examples of serious food borne illnesses that can affect any consumer, especially young children, the elderly, and those with compromised immune systems. Basic guidelines implemented by the United States Department of Agriculture (USDA) and the Food Safety and Inspection Service will help to ensure safety.

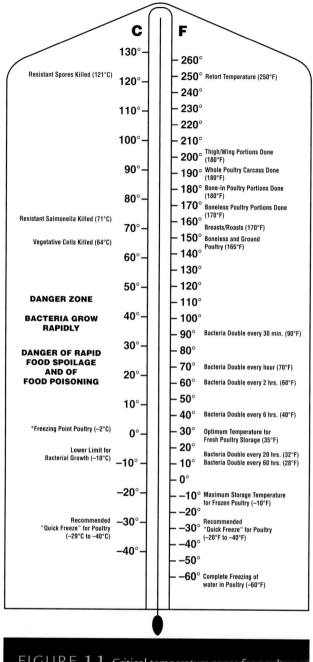

C **F**

- 130° — 260°
Resistant Spores Killed (121°C) — 120° — 250° Retort Temperature (250°F)
— 240°
- 110° — 230°
— 220°
- 100° — 210°
— 200° Thigh/Wing Portions Done (180°F)
- 90° — 190° Whole Poultry Carcass Done (180°F)
— 180° Bone-in Poultry Portions Done (180°F)
- 80° — 170° Boneless Poultry Portions Done (170°F)
Resistant Salmonella Killed (71°C) — 160° Breasts/Roasts (170°F)
- 70° — 150° Boneless and Ground Poultry (165°F)
Vegetative Cells Killed (64°C) — 140°
- 60° — 130°
— 120°
- 50° — 110°
DANGER ZONE — 100°
BACTERIA GROW - 40° — 90° Bacteria Double every 30 min. (90°F)
RAPIDLY — 80°
- 30° — 70° Bacteria Double every hour (70°F)
DANGER OF RAPID
FOOD SPOILAGE - 20° — 60° Bacteria Double every 2 hrs. (60°F)
AND OF
FOOD POISONING — 50°
- 10° — 40° Bacteria Double every 6 hrs. (40°F)
*Freezing Point Poultry (−2°C) - 0° — 30° Optimum Temperature for Fresh Poultry Storage (35°F)
— 20°
Lower Limit for — 10° Bacteria Double every 20 hrs. (32°F)
Bacterial Growth (−10°C) - −10° Bacteria Double every 60 hrs. (28°F)
— 0°
- −20° — −10° Maximum Storage Temperature for Frozen Poultry (−10°F)
— −20°
Recommended - −30° — −30° Recommended "Quick Freeze" for Poultry (−20°F to −40°F)
"Quick Freeze" for Poultry (−29°C to −40°C) — −40°
- −40° — −50°
— −60° Complete Freezing of water in Poultry (−60°F)

FIGURE 1.1 Critical temperature zones for poultry.

Source: United States Department of Agriculture (USDA)

USDA INSPECTION

All poultry must be inspected upon slaughter, according to USDA guidelines and regulations. According to the Food and Drug Administration's regulation, the "Poultry Products Inspection Act" states all poultry meats sold commercially must be deemed wholesome and unadulterated, properly marked, labeled, and

FIGURE **1.2**
Typical USDA
poultry inspection
label.

packaged. Inspection is most important during the slaughter phase. Poultry need to be slaughtered and chilled relatively rapidly compared to other meats. The USDA has implemented the use of Hazard Analysis Critical Control Points (HACCP) regulations for poultry plants. This is a system of the industry identifying critical control points such as time and temperatures, general cleaning procedure and self checking them. Data is recorded and reviewed by USDA inspectors. USDA inspectors may be on site or they can stop by unannounced depending on the size of the operation. If all inspection requirements are met the processor can stamp the product tag, bag, or box.

PACKAGING AND STORAGE

Traditionally poultry was packaged in wooden crates topped with fresh crushed ice. This practice actually kept the meat very fresh. The problem was the fact that the melting ice created a huge mess and allowed any bacteria present in one crate to be spread throughout all the others. Packaging progressed to what is known as MAP or Modified Atmospheric Packaging. This packaging is a loose bag surrounding the poultry. A modified atmosphere containing higher amounts of CO_2 or nitrogen is pumped into the bag slowing bacteria growth. Some companies still use the ice method whereas others have gone to MAP only. Poultry items last 10 to 14 days topped with ice or in Modified Atmospheric Packaging. Many processors use a quick chill system today which brings the temperature down to around 26°F/−3°C which slightly freezes the item. Sometimes this results in retained water. Be sure ice is drained properly and does not contaminate floors or other shelves.

Frozen poultry is brought down to −20°F/−29°C very rapidly, which minimizes cellular degradation. Freezing in-house can damage some poultry because the cells may get damaged by the larger ice crystals that form during a slow freeze. Many restaurants utilize frozen product with little or no effect on quality. Thawing poultry should be done slowly in the walk-in cooler over a couple days or in a clean sink with fresh cool running water (60°F/16°C or colder).

Always remember raw poultry items need to be stored separately from other meats and produce items. Placing poultry on the bottom shelf or on a rack designed to capture any ice runoff is very important. Salmonella and Campylobacter, two serious pathogens, are found on a large amount of fresh poultry items.

COOKING SAFETY

Poultry items require an internal cooked temperature of 160°F/71°C according to the USDA guidelines. It is well known by customers that chicken and turkey need to be cooked thoroughly. Be sure to test product with an accurate thermometer.

Some poultry items, duck in particular, may be preferred undercooked to 130° to 145°F/54° to 63°C. Although this is against USDA guidelines, many restaurants choose to cook duck to this temperature range. If doing so, a disclaimer on the menu may be a good option. Talk to your local health department official to see whether they have any guidelines for this. Use only very fresh or frozen product.

POULTRY GRADING AND EVALUATION

The purpose for grading poultry is to assign value and so the purchaser is guaranteed a level of quality without having to physically inspect each bird. Poultry are divided into classes. Classes will divide poultry by size, age, sometimes gender and breed.

Only certain classes, those that will result in a high value, are typically graded. Grading will consist of two types, ready-to-cook whole poultry carcasses or poultry products such as ready-to-cook legs or breasts. Typically the USDA will grade poultry for larger processors. The cost of grading is paid for by the processor and only federally licensed graders can apply the USDA stamp.

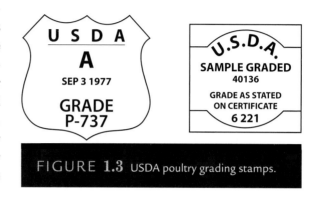

FIGURE **1.3** USDA poultry grading stamps.

The following factors are evaluated during grading:

- Conformation or meat to bone ratio
- Fleshing
- Fat covering
- Skin covering or exposed flesh
- Defeathering or pin bones
- Discolorations
- Disjointed or broken bones
- Missing parts
- Freezer burn or defects
- Other considerations for grading boneless parts or other processed poultry product
  - Bone fragments, tendons, or cartilage
  - Bruising or blood splash in the meat

CLASSIFICATIONS OF POULTRY

When growing poultry on a commercial scale there are different classifications and breeds that are considered, the *hens* or older breeding females and the males or *rooster* kept as breeding stock. The young birds are the offspring of the other two and these are what are typically sold as graded poultry. The term *young* is applied by some processors to geese, duck, turkey, and chickens.

In this book we break down each poultry item into chapters and discuss the classifications of each.

TYPE	CHICKEN	DUCK	GOOSE	TURKEY	GUINEA FOWL	PIGEON	PARTRIDGE	PHEASANT	QUAIL	OSTRICH	EMU
BASIC POULTRY CLASSIFICATIONS											
Classification	Broiler/fryer	Duckling	Young	Young	Baby	Squab					
	Capon	Roasting	Mature	Tom/hen	Mature	Mature pigeon	No classifications	No classifications	No classifications	No classifications	No classifications
	Cornish hen	Mature									
	Fowl										
	Rooster										
	Poussin										

POULTRY MUSCLE FIBERS

How is poultry meat different than other species? All muscle is made of basic components, water, protein, fat, and connective tissues. Poultry items tend to be much higher in water than other meats. The look of beef is a deep red color and large muscle fibers whereas poultry has very fine fibers. There are two basic categories of domestic fowl, migratory and non-migratory. Migratory birds, even though they have been domesticated for many years, still have a muscle structure that would allow them to fly for long distances and the ability to build large reserves of fat. Examples are ducks and geese. Both have dark breast meat and more of a protein, myoglobin. This protein works with iron to bring oxygen to the muscle cells. It is the presence of a lot of myoglobin that gives dark meat birds a stronger flavor.

Non-migratory birds, such as chickens, turkeys, and pheasants, are primarily land birds and do not fly for any great distances. These birds have all been genetically selected over the years and modified to grow faster with more breast meat. Traditionally they would have light and dark meat of about equal proportions. The "white meat" in these birds meant the bird could rapidly turn stores of carbohydrates into energy. They would do so to avoid danger and rapidly fly up from predators. With modifications the breast meat is now much larger than in a normal bird.

Muscle fibers change as a bird matures. It no longer has the ability to stay as moist when cooked. An old "hen" cooks out "dry" and very tough if cooked in a dry method. These items need to be stewed slowly.

Poultry meat is affected by its diet. Flavor and color can be altered by changing the feed. Adding large amounts of beta-carotene can produce a yellow meat and fat. Birds that are allowed to forage on wild feedstuffs will have much more flavor than those fed a single or combination grain diet. The downside is the foraged birds require much more space and time to mature depending on the farm. Modern chicken production using a grain diet is very efficient. It takes about 8 pounds of grain to produce a 4-pound broiler and they are typically at market weight in only 6 weeks time. An older style chicken that is on forage may take 3 months to reach the same weight. The choice is up to the purchaser. Some niche market producers are offering foraged birds but they tend to be expensive. There are also companies that combine the two methods to achieve a more marketable bird.

NATURAL POULTRY

The term *natural* on a label of poultry is an indicator that the poultry was not enhanced with any extra chemical additives that would either preserve it or retain extra water. Natural does not necessarily have anything to do with the way the bird was raised when alive. There are ingredients such as salt, certain flavorings, and broth that can be added to a poultry item and it can still be deemed natural.

FREE RANGE/PASTURE RAISED

Many poultry birds are raised in relatively close quarters and indoors in large grow out houses. As previously stated this is a highly efficient system. There are also companies offering free ranged poultry. What is the definition of free range poultry? Basically the term "free range" indicates the birds have access to the outdoors and are allowed to roam within a larger but confined space.

Pasture raised indicates the birds are getting at least 20 percent of their feed from forage. These are two different styles but can overlap. Marketing of this type of poultry has expanded rapidly over the past few years in some sectors of the food service industry. Chefs may seek to upscale a poultry dish and add more flavor and these products allow that.

ANTIBIOTIC FREE

Along with free range and pastured poultry there are also birds that are raised in the typical grow out houses but are not fed any antibiotics. This trend away from antibiotic use is becoming more prevalent due to customer demand. Customers are worried about resistant strains of bacteria that may have come about due to the pre-emptive use of antibiotics in the industry. Another trend is to use a different antibiotic than humans typically use, reducing the risk of a crossover superbacteria.

CHICKEN

The word *chicken* originates from the Old English "cycen." Typically a chicken was meant as a young chicken and not an older egg-laying hen or mature male rooster.

The chicken originates from wild jungle fowl. The Red Jungle Fowl or the species *Gallus gallus,* was thought to be the wild ancestor to all modern chicken but recent genetic research done by Uppsala University in Sweden, shows the Grey Jungle Fowl, *Gallus sonneratii,* is also included in the gene pool. These birds are in the family *Phasianidae* relating it to pheasant, turkey, quail, and peacock among others. They are all primarily ground dwelling, non-migratory birds. The primary habitat for the Red Jungle Fowl is from India eastward into southern China and through the tropical southern Asian countries on the continent and down into Indochina to Sumatra, Java, and Bali. The Grey Jungle Fowl is found primarily in India. Both of these birds were hunted for meat and feathers. The male birds possess bright plumage that was used for decorative dress.

The genome of the chicken was mapped in 2004 enabling scientists to better understand the genetic variations in breeds and the possibility of isolating birds for better meat or egg production. The research, conducted by the Washington University School of Medicine, St. Louis, MO, enables chicken to be selected, genetically, for traits that improve yield and to resist diseases.

DOMESTICATION OF CHICKEN

The domestication of chicken or the Red Jungle Fowl, is believed to have occurred in Southeast Asia in Thailand and Vietnam around 8,000 years ago. Paleontologists have discovered sites in southern China that date back 7,500 years. Very early sites were also found in India and Pakistan where the crossbreeding with the Grey Jungle Fowl is believed to have occurred. Different than most other ancient species, both of these birds can still be found in the wild. The jungle fowl of today are in danger of becoming extinct due to habitat loss and hunting.

The domestication of chickens stems from two main theories, first the fowl was a scavenger of human areas. It will eat insects and worms found in waste, extra grains left around a village, and it thrives in semi-open forest, which would bode well for clearings created by early humans. The birds are natural flocking animals and it may be that early humans captured flocks to harvest eggs.

Another aspect for more recent domestication is cock fighting. Tribes often held aggressive roosters for fighting and traded birds for sport with other tribes. In Harappa, an ancient city located in present-day Pakistan, tribes domesticated fowl for fighting around 4,000 years ago. This civilization was one of the earliest organized civilizations in the world, located in the Indus Valley and had a population of more than 50,000 people. The Harappan Tribe had villages throughout eastern India and Pakistan. Trading among villages probably included roosters and conducted fights for entertainment. The end result would be crossbreeding poultry to create bigger, more aggressive birds.

Years later, when trade routes from the Indus Valley extended west, the chicken was brought to ancient Greece and later Rome. Roman recipes for chicken include fattening the bird and then soaking it in milk before cooking.

The chicken is found in many religious writings. There are mentions of chicken in the bible. The Jewish tradition of kapparos involves chicken. The Chinese have the chicken on the Zodiac. Those born under the sign of the rooster are thought to be very quick minded and almost to have a sixth sense. The African Yoruban tribe's creation myth has the chicken playing a major role in how all land on earth was created. The chicken was sent from heaven to scratch the sand deposited on earth. Wherever the chicken scratched, land formed. Over and over chickens and references to roosters and hens are part of folk tales.

CHICKEN PRODUCTION

Most farmers in the 1800s had an assortment of animals including chickens. Originally chicken was grown in the United States as a source of eggs. The farmers grew what they needed for their own existence. If there were extra eggs, farmers sold them in market places. As farming practices improved with mechanization, greater crop yields resulted. This enabled larger layer houses to produce eggs for the cities and distributors. The invention of refrigeration allowed eggs to be stored and transported.

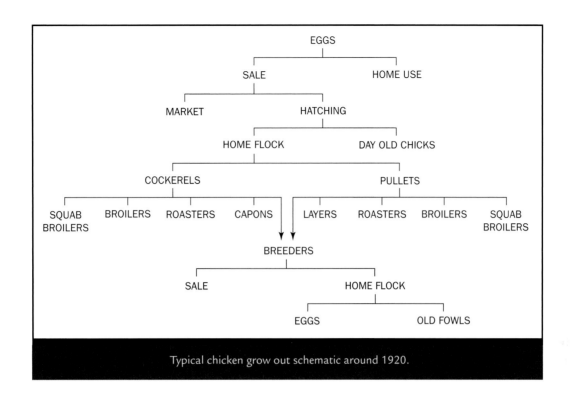

EGGS

SALE   HOME USE

MARKET   HATCHING

HOME FLOCK   DAY OLD CHICKS

COCKERELS   PULLETS

SQUAB BROILERS   BROILERS   ROASTERS   CAPONS   LAYERS   ROASTERS   BROILERS   SQUAB BROILERS

BREEDERS

SALE   HOME FLOCK

EGGS   OLD FOWLS

Typical chicken grow out schematic around 1920.

Eating chicken was considered a specialty item. The chicken was typically only eaten on a holiday or if a laying hen stopped producing. This type of chicken, considered a by-product of the egg industry, was tough and rather dry as a meat, requiring a moist cooking method such as stewing. During the industrial revolution, around 1850, farmers began growing hybrid birds that served well as laying hens and then were also good for meat. By the early 1900s grain production increased, creating surpluses that could be feasibly fed to poultry. In the years following, farmers began large-scale chicken production. The advent of the "grow out" house where chickens were raised in close proximity to one another and fed an intensive grain diet to grow them rapidly changed the type of chicken meat available. Today grow out houses containing about 30,000 birds each.

Farms grew from having a hundred egg layers to a farm holding thousands of meat birds on site.

Growers started buying hatched chicks rather than allowing hens and roosters to mate. This enabled the farmer to focus on growing rather than egg production. Egg production was done in "Layer Hen" houses where thousands of layer hens produced eggs that were hatched in huge incubators as opposed to nesting birds. This greatly increased the amount of birds available. By the 1940s chicken production had gained a larger meat market share and has increased ever since. Statistics provided by the United States Department of Agriculture (USDA) state that by 1940 an average wage earner had to work a half hour to afford one pound of chicken. By the 1950s chicken production began to increase rapidly. Between 1960 and 1964, 6.9 billion pounds of ready-to-cook poultry were produced. From 1965 to 1969, 9.1 billion pounds were

produced. During the 1960s chicken production began to consolidate. About one third of all poultry was produced by twenty companies. In the late 1990s in the United States beef and chicken were competing for "the most consumed meat per capita" status. Each year the amount of chicken consumed would rise as beef stayed static.

By the 1990s production increased to 35 billion pounds annually. Today we find chicken consumption at an all-time high. Per capita consumption is at around 85 pounds and over 48 billion pounds of broilers were produced in total. Mergers and acquisitions created more domination and centralization in the industry. Tyson Corporation emerged as the number one producer of chicken.

CHICKEN FEED

During the growth of the chicken meat industry, growing efficiency also increased. Many of the chicken producers developed totally integrated systems. This model has the processor owning the feed milling and formulation, incubation and hatching, grow out houses and finally harvest, processing and distribution. In the 1950s it took around 8 pounds of chicken feed to produce 1 pound of salable meat. Today that total is about 2 pounds of feed to 1 pound of meat. Growth is now at around 6 to 7 weeks for a broiler whereas during the 1920s it took at least 16 weeks. Breeds and feed types were scientifically formed by many of the agricultural colleges worldwide.

Here are two typical feeds for derived for broilers:

Rice bran and polishings	32.5 percent
Grain sorghum	30.0 percent
Soybean meal, solvent process	17.0 percent
Meat and bone meal	15.0 percent
Molasses	4.0 percent
Salt	0.5 percent
Vitamin-trace mineral supplement	1.0 percent

Source: http://www.bcca.org/services/lists/noble-creation/poultry.html

19% Broiler Grower

1,015 lb	Shelled corn
625 lb.	Roasted soybeans
100 lb.	Oats
100 lb.	Alfalfa meal
75 lb.	Fish meal, 60%
25 lb.	Aragonite (calcium)
60 lb.	Poultry nutri-balancer
2,000 lb.	Total

Source: *Understanding Poultry Meat and Egg Production* by Dr. H.R. Bird. (ISBN: 0-86619-212-3)

Producers will formulate the feed to grow the chicken with a specific outcome. The usual goal is to gain weight and muscle mass as fast as possible, maintain an appealing color and shape, and minimize the amount of excess fat. Feed can change the color of a chicken's skin. Birds fed a diet containing lutein, a beta-carotene, will create a yellow skin and fat that is often considered a quality feature even though it minimally changes flavor.

The presence of animal by-product in some feeds has created a controversy with some consumers. Some producers are growing chickens on an entirely vegetarian diet. There are arguments for feeding chicken some animal protein. They are by nature, omnivores and will consume animal proteins if left to truly free-range. A chicken is a scavenger and will consume a number of bugs, worms, spiders, and even peck on carrion if allowed to. The question of animal protein added to diet may be one of what kind of animal protein is added.

The pharmaceutical industry often partners with chicken producers to increase production and decrease mortality rates. Chicken broilers may be fed a medicated feed mixture that contains pre-emptive antibiotics and antimicrobials. These products are used to avoid a number of bacterial infections such as Salmonella and forms of *Escherichia coli*. These keep the birds healthy during their rapid growth. The use and overuse of antibiotics has been disputed by some scientists. The idea that the overuse of antibiotics, especially those that are similar to those given to humans, creates resistant strains of bacteria has changed the way some companies are now feeding. Some companies are now using "probiotics" such as various lactic acid bacteria which establish a good flora in the digestive system, maintaining health. The dramatic market increase of "antibiotic-free" poultry shows consumers are willing to pay extra not to have them included.

Another controversial antimicrobial added to some feeds is Roxarsone-4-hydroxy-3-nitrobenzenearsonic acid. Roxarsone is a common arsenic-based additive used in some chicken feed today. This product contains organic arsenic. In its organic form it does not pose a health hazard but often, inside the chicken, it is converted to an inorganic form. According to the Environmental Protection Agency (EPA), long-term exposure to inorganic arsenic can cause bladder, lung, skin, kidney, and colon cancer, and have immunological, neurological, and endocrine effects. Low-level exposures can lead to diabetes. Also when chicken waste is spread on fields, the organic arsenic can convert to inorganic arsenic and contaminate ground water. Arsenates were first added into chicken feed in the 1950s as broiler production increased. The European Union banned the use of arsenates in 1999 and the Tyson and Fosters poultry companies stopped using it in 2004.

FIGURE 2.1 Automated feed system.

FIGURE 2.2 Decorative feather fan.

BREEDS AND VARIETIES OF CHICKEN

Chickens, as previously stated, are related to wild Jungle Fowl. As humans domesticated chickens they created numerous new breeds. Very early domestication seems to be often focused on "game" birds or birds used for fighting. Game cocks were roosters that had an ability to destroy an opponent. These were highly aggressive and their meat quality was probably very low. In the late 1600s and early 1700s science began to understand breeding and defining breeds. Breeds were created for different purposes and a focus on egg production began.

Another breed group was chosen for feathers. Throughout history colorful feathers of all poultry were used for fans and hat and clothing decorations. Ceremonial garb often included feathers. Certain feathers were desired to make fishing flies. Pillows and bedding in colder climates were made from feathers. Wealthy people would use duck or goose down but poorer folks used chicken feathers. With over 9 billion chickens processed each year in the United States, we find feather technology spreading into a large variety of industrial productions. Feathers can be made into a quality paper, hard reinforcements in plastics, and more.

Show birds were another type of chicken selected for their uniqueness in shape and feathers. Many of these birds were the same as the "feather" birds but these were prized for their decorative value while alive. These chickens have unique plumage and featuring bright colors and extreme length of feathers. Today we find show birds being bred for the many county and state fairs around the country. Purebred show birds are expensive and have become a commodity similar to other unique birds or pets.

Egg production was the predominant chicken industry by the 1800s and egg layers were bred to produce larger and larger eggs or more volume.

FIGURE 2.3 Large meat breed chicken.

A focus on meat or hybrid breeds began in the mid-1880s. Birds that could be sold as layer hens or meat birds became common.

Strictly meat breeds were a more recent phenomenon. Chickens were developed with the goal of rapidly raising meat with the least amount of grain. Breeds were created to grow well in confinement barns. Aggressiveness was bred out and the focus placed on gain and breast weight was bred in. Birds were no longer chosen for their ability to forage or survive in a more free-ranging barnyard.

FIGURE **2.4** Modern chicken grow-out house.

Definition of a *breed* is a bird that possesses a set of physical features that when mated with another like bird, can be successfully passed on to the offspring. Within a breed are varieties. A *variety* is basically a sub-division of a breed. These may have the basic characteristics of the breed but may have some differentiation such as longer feathers or coloration. A *strain* is when an entity or company breeds a variety for a specific characteristic or purpose. The focus is on the entire flock as opposed to individual birds. A company may develop a strain of broiler chicken by taking two breeds, hybridizing and watching the result over the whole flock. The modern development of breeds and individual birds was primarily from 1875 to 1925. After this time, as modern meat production began, poultry farmers focused on strains of breeds. Today's meat poultry is a result of only a very few breeds with many multiple proprietary strains.

TYPICAL BREEDS

There are over 350 different breeds of chicken worldwide. This publication will focus on those most typical. The meat poultry industry has developed many strains and varieties derived from these basic original breeds. Some more recently developed strains may be patented to a specific company and flocks are controlled and may not be available to others.

There are hundreds of breeds that are no longer viable for commercial production. These "heritage" breeds may take too long to grow or may not have the meat to bone ratio that is profitable. Unfortunately some of the heritage breeds are not produced and their numbers are dwindling. Many of these birds are raised as show birds for fairs and hobbyists. Heritage birds often have unique and more complex flavors that some chefs are seeking. There are some efforts by small niche market producers to re-introduce unique breeds at higher prices.

CHICKEN BREED AND VARIETIES

CHICKEN BREED AND VARIETIES	USES
AMERICAN	
Delaware	Cross breed between Plymouth Rock and New Hampshire, excellent meat breed, broilers
Dominique	Early American heritage breed, slow growing, rare today, excellent forager
California Poulet Blue	New breed, excellent meat flavor, limited availability, specialty
Jersey Giant	Very large, good as a roaster, slow growing, not produced commercially
New Hampshire	Developed from Rhode Island Reds, quick growing, good brown egg production
Plymouth Rock (many varieties, White Rock most popular)	Docile, good for meat and eggs, often crossed with Cornish to make the most popular meat breed
Rhode Island Red	Good egg production, popular for exhibition and home chickens
Wyandotte (many varieties)	Non-aggressive, dual purpose
ASIATIC BREEDS	
Brahmans	Large dual purpose, good for roaster class birds or large fowl
Cochin	Large, soft feathers, not used in large scale production today, once very popular
Langshans	Chinese breed, dual purpose, egg and meat

(Continues)

CHICKEN BREED AND VARIETIES	USES
ENGLISH	
Dorking	Ancient breed brought to England by the Romans, rare today
Cornish	Very popular meat breed. Often crossed with Rock, wide breast meat
Sussex	Old breed, dual purpose
Orpington (many varieties)	Egg layer, large, crossed with other breeds
MEDITERRANEAN	
Leghorn (very many varieties)	Most prolific egg layer, revolutionized the egg industry, used as "fowl" for meat
Minorca	Large, egg layer, some meat production
Andalusian	Blue colored bird, egg layer
CONTINENTAL	
Hamburg	Old breed originated in Holland
Poulet de Bresse	French breed known for flavor
Polish (many varieties)	Very old breed, many used as show birds
SOUTH AMERICAN	
Aruacana	Lays bluish eggs, small, tailless

CLASSES OF CHICKEN

Chicken is divided into specific classes that are defined by the North American Meat Processors Association. Chickens are classified by size and age. The *broiler* chicken dominates the industry and most whole chicken and commercial parts are from broilers. The term *fryer* chicken typically meant a larger broiler but today we find the terms *broiler* and *fryer* meaning the same thing.

CLASSES OF CHICKEN			
NAME	DESCRIPTION	SIZE	AGE
Poussin	Small, sold whole, with giblets	1–1.5 lbs	3–4 weeks
Cornish Game Hen	Small, sold whole, with giblets	1–2 lbs	4–5 weeks
Broiler/Fryer	Mid-sized, sold whole, split, parts, boneless parts, with or without giblets	2.5–4.5 lbs	6–10 weeks
Roaster	Large, sold whole, large parts, boneless parts, with giblets	5–9 lbs	9–12 weeks
Capon	Large, castrated male, sold whole, with giblets	5–9 lbs	9–12 weeks
Hen/Stewing Fowl	Large, female egg layer, sold whole, with giblets	4.5–7 lbs	More than 10 months old
Rooster	Large, male, sold whole, untypical	4–8 lbs	More than 10 months old

FOODSERVICE MARKET FORMS

There is a very large variety of foodservice items available in the marketplace today. There are hundreds of options presented by chicken processors and they vary from company to company.

BASIC PACKAGING OPTIONS

Bulk—Items bagged together as bulk meat or birds.

CVP—Items put in a loose vacuum-sealed bag.

Individually wrapped—Each bird has its own bag and label.

Individually portion packaged in container—Item is placed in a tray cup.

MAP—Modified Atmospheric Packaging. Loose vacuum bag typically with a high CO_2 gas flush.

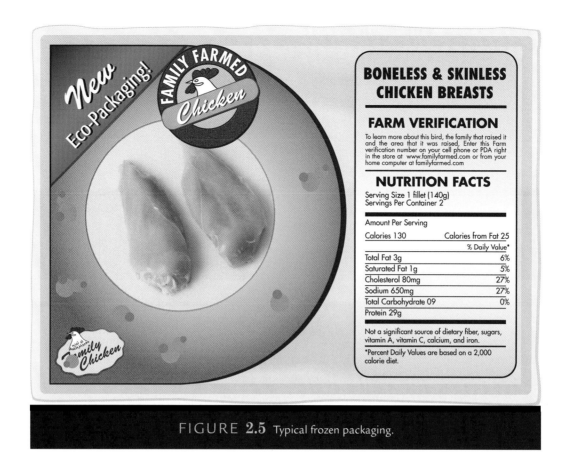

FIGURE **2.5** Typical frozen packaging.

CONDITION

Fresh/chilled—Unfrozen but is typically quick chilled to 26°F/–3°C which lightly freezes the outside.

Frozen, Bulk—Items brought down to 0°F/–18°C in a bulk package.

IQF—Individually quick frozen. Items are flash frozen as individual items and then bulk packaged.

Iced—Bulk item topped with ice, requires proper drainage.

Irradiated—The poultry is exposed to either electronic beam or gamma radiation, disrupting the DNA in any pathogen, basically sterilizing the product. Also known as *cold pasteurization*. Must be labeled accordingly.

ADDITIVES

Injected—A water-based flavor or water retention agent is added to the bird or meat.

ISP—Isolated Soy Protein added.

Enhanced—Pumped with a solution to guarantee moistness.

Basted—Enhanced with moisture agent only.

Marinated—Enhanced with moisture and flavor agent.

RTC—Ready to cook.

Seasoned—Flavor added including spice mixtures.

Breaded and Battered—Coated with either bread crumbs or batter to be baked or fried.

Combination—More than one of the categories above included.

NUTRITION FACTS

Serving Size 1 fillet (140g)
Serving Per Container 2

Amount Per Serving

Calories 130	Calories from Fat 25
	% Daily Value*
Total Fat 3g	6%
Saturated Fat 1g	5%
Cholesterol 80mg	27%
Sodium 650mg	27%
Total Carbohydrate 0g	0%
Protein 29g	

Not a significant source of dietary, fiber, sugars, vitamin A, vitamin C, calcium and iron.

*Percent Daily Values are based on a 2,000 calorie diet.

FIGURE **2.6** Typical package nutrition label.

PURCHASING SPECIFICATIONS

When purchasing chicken items it is important to establish proper specifications with the vendor. Understanding average weights and requesting logical sizes ensures a consistent portion. Typical package sizes and counts per bag and box are listed. These are general specs for fresh chicken and can change from processor to processor. Every processor has some items they choose to package differently.

CHICKEN PURCHASING AND USAGE SPECIFICATIONS				
ITEM AND NAMP NUMBER	DESCRIPTION/ FABRICATION	SUGGESTED COOKING METHOD/ APPLICATION	AVG. SUGGESTED WEIGHT LBS.	TYPICAL PACKAGE SPECS
Broiler/fryer P1000	Whole bird, sold with giblets, typically cut into parts.	Dry cook, broil, grill, roast, pan sear, fry	Sold from 2.5–4.5 lbs in ¼ or ½ lb. increments	10 per case or 16 per case, bulk package or individually wrapped
Broiler/fryer P1002	Whole bird, WOG (without giblets)	Same as above	Same as above	Same as above
Roaster P1100	Whole Bird, with giblets, can be cut as large parts	Roasting whole, dry cook parts	5–9 lbs	6 per case, individually wrapped
Capon P1200	Whole bird, sold with giblets	Roasting whole, carving	6–9 lbs	6 per case
Fowl/Stewing Hen P1300	Whole bird, sold with giblets	Stewing, slow cooking, soup, pulled meat	5–8 lbs	6 per case, bulk packaged or individually wrapped
Poussin P1400	Whole bird, sold with giblets	Roasting whole	1–1.5 lbs	12 per case
Rock Cornish Hen P1500	Whole bird, sold with giblets	Roasting whole, semi-boneless	1–2 lbs	24 per case, individually wrapped
Broiler, 8 pc. (2 breast, 2 wings, 2 drumsticks, 2 thighs) P1005	Cut, sold without giblets	Dry cook, fry, BBQ, broil	3–3.5 lbs	16 per case, bulk
Broiler, 10 pc. Same as 8 pc but breast cut in half P1007	Cut, sold without giblets	Dry cook, fry, BBQ, broil	3–3.5 lbs	16 per case, bulk

(Continues)

There are multitudes of processed chicken products not included in this list due to the massive amounts available.

The North American Meat Processor's Meat Buyer's Guide has established a standard number code system for meat purchasing.

(*Continued*)

ITEM AND NAMP NUMBER	DESCRIPTION/ FABRICATION	SUGGESTED COOKING METHOD/ APPLICATION	AVG. SUGGESTED WEIGHT LBS.	TYPICAL PACKAGE SPECS
Broiler halves P1008	Split, sold without giblets	Dry cook, broil, BBQ	3–4 lbs	12 or 16 per case, bulk
Broiler quarters P1009	Legs and breast, sold without giblets	Dry cook, broil, BBQ, fry	3–4 lbs	12 or 16 per case, bulk
Broiler breast, bone-in with ribs or without ribs P1012, P1013	Whole unsplit breast, with wishbone	Dry cook,	1.5–2 lbs each (P1013 has a better yield)	24 per case
Broiler Airline breast P1016	Boneless except for drumette wing portion	Dry cook, broil, sauté, grill	6–9 oz each pc	Four 10-lb. bags per case
Broiler breast, skin-on, with rib meat	Unsplit boneless breast with a small amount of extra rib meat	Dry cook, broil, sauté, grill	12–18 oz each double breast	Four 10-lb. bags per case
Broiler breast, skinless, with rib meat	Unsplit boneless breast with a small amount of extra rib meat	Dry cook, broil, sauté, grill	10–16 oz each double breast	Four 10-lb. bags per case or individual portion tray packs
Roaster breast	Unsplit boneless breast with a small amount of extra rib meat	Dry cook, broil, sauté, grill	16–24 oz each double breast	Four 10-lb. bags per case
Broiler cutlets	Split and trimmed breast with "tender" taken out	Dry cook, sauté, grill, broil, breaded	4–6 oz each	Four 10-lb bags per case
Broiler tender	Small center section of breast	Dry cook, breaded, grill, sauté	2 oz each	Four 10-lb bags

(*Continues*)

ITEM AND NAMP NUMBER	DESCRIPTION/ FABRICATION	SUGGESTED COOKING METHOD/ APPLICATION	AVG. SUGGESTED WEIGHT LBS.	TYPICAL PACKAGE SPECS
Broiler leg quarters with back bone P1030	Thigh and drumstick attached	Dry cook, moist cook	8–10 oz each	Bulk 20- or 40-lb case
Broiler leg, back bone removed P1031	Thigh and drumstick attached	Dry cook, moist cook	6–8 oz each	Bulk 20- or 40-lb case
Broiler thigh (bone-in skin-on or boneless, skinless)	Thigh section	Dry or moist cook	4–6 oz each	Four 10-lb bags
Broiler drumstick, bone-in only P1035	Shank section	Dry or moist cook	4–6 oz each	40 lb bulk
Broiler wings P1036, P1037, P1038 (larger roaster wings available as well)	Sold as whole wing or as drumette, flat only	Dry cook, moist cook, deep fat fry	2 oz each	Four 10-lb bags

(Continues)

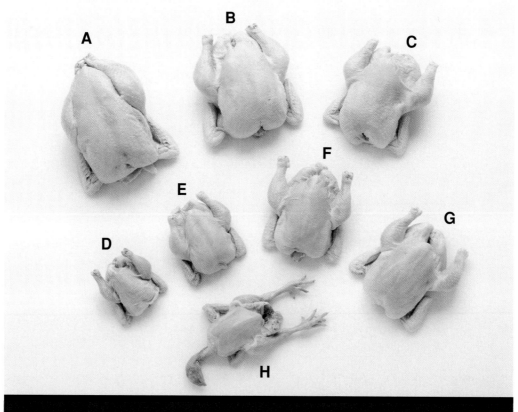

FIGURE **2.7** A: Capon; B: Roaster; C: Stewing hen; D: 1 lb Cornish game hen; E: 2 lb Cornish game hen; F: 3½ lb broiler; G: 3½ to 4 lb broiler; H: poussin.

ITEM AND NAMP NUMBER	DESCRIPTION/ FABRICATION	SUGGESTED COOKING METHOD/ APPLICATION	AVG. SUGGESTED WEIGHT LBS.	TYPICAL PACKAGE SPECS
Livers P1045	—	Sauté, pate, mousse, flavor agent	1–2 oz each	5-lb tubs
Necks P1042	—	Soup, stock, BBQ	3–4 oz each	40 lb bulk
Gizzards P1044	—	Soup, stock, sauces	2 oz each	5–lb tubs
Hearts P1052	—	Skewers, soup, sauces	1 oz each	5–lb tubs
Bones, whole carcass, or backs	—	Soup stock		40 lb bulk
Feet	—	Soup stock		40 lb bulk

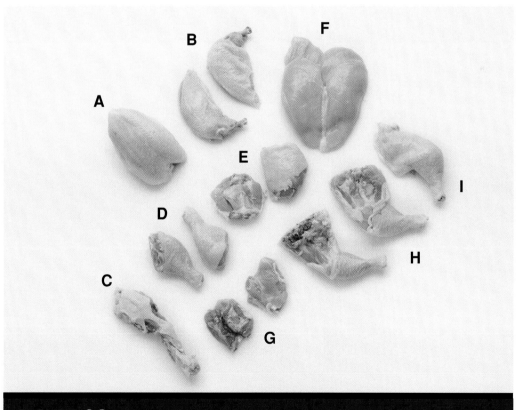

FIGURE 2.8 A: Whole breast, bone-in, unsplit with rib meat; B: Frenched or airline breasts; C: Back; D: Drumsticks; E: Bone-in thighs with skin on; F: Boneless, skinless breast, unsplit; G: Boneless thigh meat; H: Leg quarter with back; I: Legs back-off.

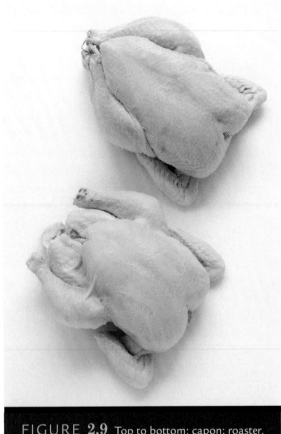

FIGURE **2.9** Top to bottom: capon; roaster.

FIGURE **2.10** Stewing hen.

FIGURE **2.11** Poussin Asian-style.

FIGURE **2.12** Cornish game hen.

Processed chicken products can be categorized into raw and precooked products. Raw products may be water added, preseasoned, vegetable protein-added breaded or coated. Various chicken sausages are also available. All of these items need to be cooked before serving. Items can be sold fresh or frozen.

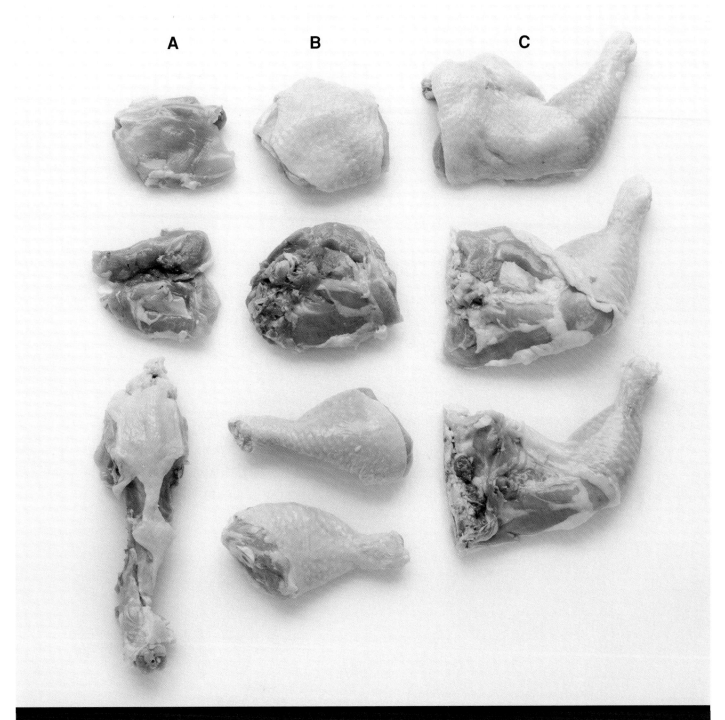

FIGURE **2.13** Left column, top to bottom, A: Boneless, skinless thighs, back. Middle column, top to bottom, B: Bone-in, skin-on thigh, drumsticks. Right column, top to bottom, C: Leg quarters with no back attached, leg quarter with back on.

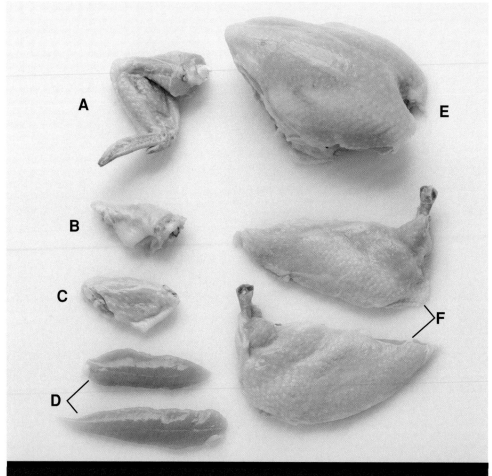

FIGURE 2.14 A: Whole wing with tip; B: Wing drumette; C: Wing flap; D: Tenderloins; E: Double breast, bone-in; F: Frenched or airline breasts.

FIGURE 2.15 Boneless, skinless chicken breast.

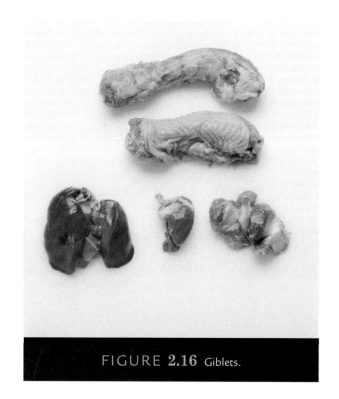

FIGURE 2.16 Giblets.

Precooked products are basically heat and serve. Examples are precooked seasoned portion cut breasts, pulled or cubed cooked chicken meat, smoke roasted or BBQ whole or cut birds.

CHICKEN PROCESSING

Chicken processing is highly automated today. The small size and uniformity of the broiler chicken enables engineers to create machinery that can rapidly process the chicken into parts. A large modern producer can fabricate more than 250,000 birds a day. The process begins at the farm. Birds are gathered and placed into crates and then trucked to the plant. Grow-out farms tend to be located relatively close to the processor to minimize travel stress.

Upon reaching the plant, birds are placed on a darkened loading dock. Red lights similar to a dark room are used and the darkness keeps the birds in a sedated state. Birds are then placed upside down in foot shackles on an assembly line. An electric shock is administered and then the bird is bled. This process is very rapid. Then the chickens are dipped in hot water to loosen feathers, transported through a defeathering machine, and then eviscerated. Entrails are looked at by USDA inspectors and separated. The chickens are then chilled, either by ice bath or air chill rooms. Once chilled they can be lightly frozen, brought down to 25°F/–4°C. Chickens are then disjointed and boned using a highly automated system that removes the legs, wings, breasts, etc. The bones can be sold or used for stock creation. Some companies take bones and place them in an Advanced Meat Recovery (AMR) system. AMR systems basically extract all the protein from the bones by centrifuge. This product can be used as an ingredient in processed products.

CHICKEN FABRICATION

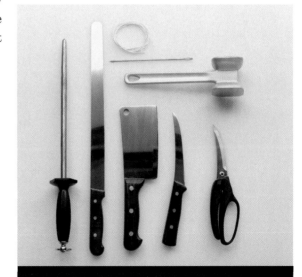

TRUSSING

Trussing or tying a poultry item is done for a number of reasons, the foremost being trussing will enable even cooking throughout, maintaining more moisture. It also helps shape the bird for presentation making it look fuller or plump by pushing up the breast meat. Trussing secures the opening at the back of the bird, ensuring any stuffing stays inside. When a bird is tied it is stable so it can be placed on a rotisserie.

There are many ways to truss a chicken. A chef may have been taught a specific method and insist that their way is the best. This publication will demonstrate two different trusses but realize there are many more variations.

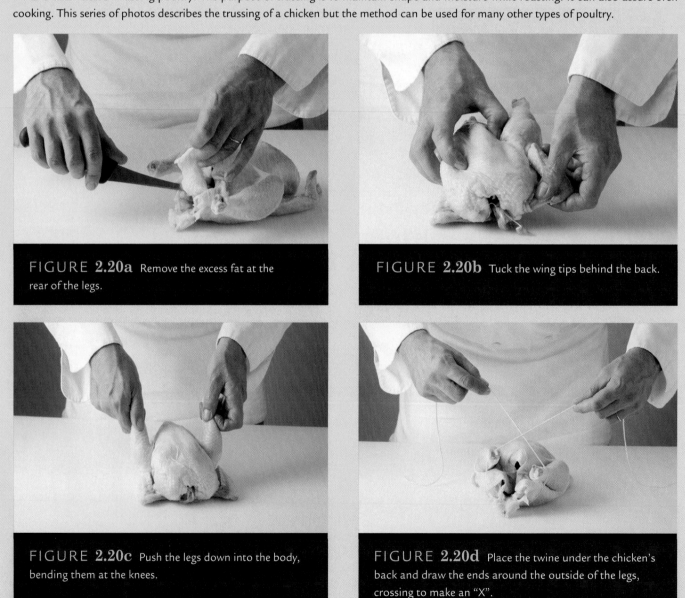

FIGURE **2.20** Trussing poultry. The purpose of trussing is to maintain shape and moisture while roasting. It can also assure even cooking. This series of photos describes the trussing of a chicken but the method can be used for many other types of poultry.

FIGURE **2.20a** Remove the excess fat at the rear of the legs.

FIGURE **2.20b** Tuck the wing tips behind the back.

FIGURE **2.20c** Push the legs down into the body, bending them at the knees.

FIGURE **2.20d** Place the twine under the chicken's back and draw the ends around the outside of the legs, crossing to make an "X".

(Continues)

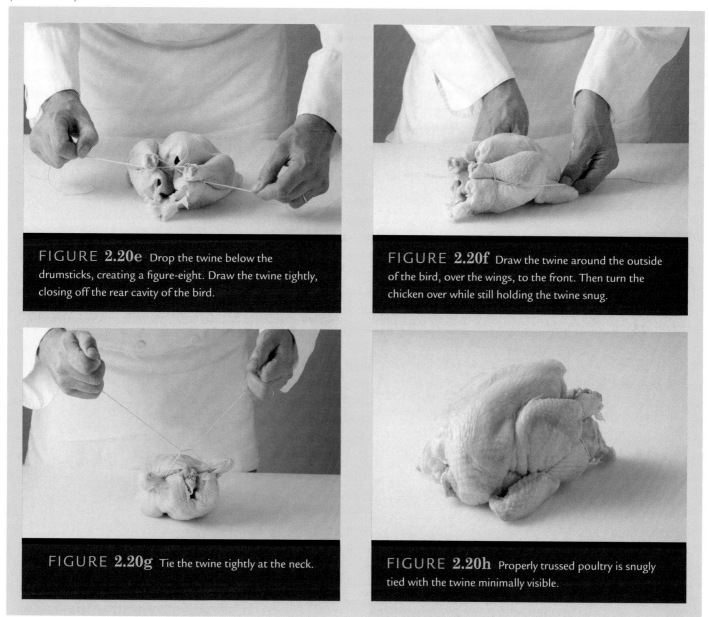

FIGURE **2.20e** Drop the twine below the drumsticks, creating a figure-eight. Draw the twine tightly, closing off the rear cavity of the bird.

FIGURE **2.20f** Draw the twine around the outside of the bird, over the wings, to the front. Then turn the chicken over while still holding the twine snug.

FIGURE **2.20g** Tie the twine tightly at the neck.

FIGURE **2.20h** Properly trussed poultry is snugly tied with the twine minimally visible.

CUTTING AN EIGHT- OR TEN-PIECE CHICKEN

An eight piece is often used for breaded, fried chicken and other bone-in presentations. A ten piece is the same basic fabrication with the breast further cut to give smaller, quick-cooking pieces. For this fabrication the chef will need only a small boning knife. The back will be removed but not counted as a section due to the fact that almost all the meat will be removed if done correctly.

FIGURE **2.21** Cutting a chicken (or other poultry item) into parts requires a short, stiff boning knife. The fabrications listed here are for breaking down a whole chicken but the techniques can be used for individual parts as well. Valuable techniques such as splitting the breast or disjointing the legs are included in this section.

FIGURE **2.21a** Remove the wings by pulling the tip away from the breast and cutting at the wing socket. Be careful not to cut too deeply into the breast meat.

FIGURE **2.21b** To remove legs, cut between the leg and the breast, pinching the skin to allow for enough skin to remain to keep the breast covered after the leg is removed. Be sure to cut through all membranes to base of leg.

FIGURE **2.21c** Pop the legs out of their sockets without breaking the back.

FIGURE **2.21d** Poultry has a small but flavorful muscle on its back that can be included as part of the leg. The oysters are found in the center of the back; find the oyster and cut around the muscle, loosening the leg.

FIGURE **2.21e** Finish removing the leg by cutting through the socket and continuing toward the tail.

FIGURE **2.21f** Removing the backbone requires a very stiff, sharp knife. In the center of the chicken's back there are two long flat bones running the length of the back and set about 1 inch/3 cm apart. While holding the tail, cut out the backbone.

(Continues)

FIGURE **2.21g** Cut through the ribs using a fair amount of force, always staying between the two flat back bones.

FIGURE **2.21h** To split the breast, first score the center of the keel bone.

FIGURE **2.21i** Break open the breast along the sides of the keel bone. Use your thumb to loosen the membrane from the keel.

FIGURE **2.21j** Pull out the keel bone.

FIGURE **2.21k** Remove the wishbone fragments from the front of the breast.

FIGURE **2.21l** Split the breast down the center, and trim away any excess connective tissues and fat.

(*Continues*)

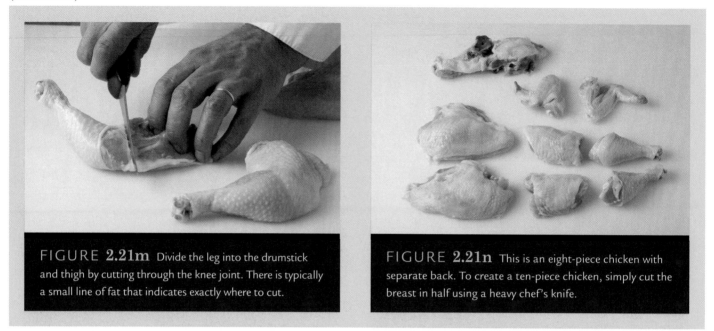

FIGURE **2.21m** Divide the leg into the drumstick and thigh by cutting through the knee joint. There is typically a small line of fat that indicates exactly where to cut.

FIGURE **2.21n** This is an eight-piece chicken with separate back. To create a ten-piece chicken, simply cut the breast in half using a heavy chef's knife.

BONELESS BREAST

The boneless chicken breast is used in a myriad of dishes. This item is sautéed, pan-seared, grilled, broiled, breaded and fried, pounded thin for stuffing or rolling. The possibilities are endless. Most chefs today choose to purchase this item already boned due to its inexpensive availability. Fabricating this item in-house may make sense if the by-product legs and bones can be used for other dishes or if purchasing from a small local niche market producer that only sells whole birds.

There are two basic methods when fabricating boneless breasts:

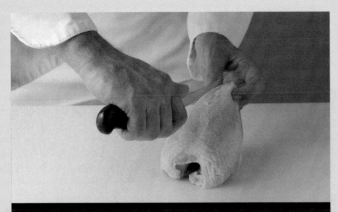

FIGURE **2.22a** Cut down the center of the keel bone from the back toward the wishbone.

FIGURE **2.22b** Push your thumb through the first cut to loosen the meat from keel bone.

FIGURE **2.22c** Cut along the wishbone and begin to pull meat off the rib cage.

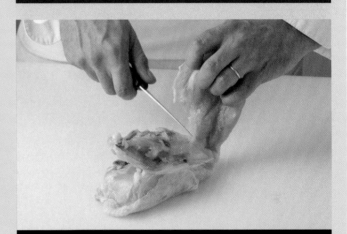

FIGURE **2.22d** Complete pulling all the meat off the ribs.

FIGURE **2.22e** Trim any excess fat and skin.

FIGURE **2.22f** The yield from a full chicken breast.

FIGURE **2.23** Method 2: The chicken breast can also be boned by removing the meat in reverse order from Method 1. This method can have a better yield but requires more knife skill.

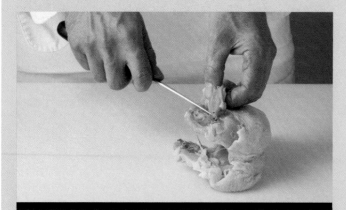

FIGURE **2.23a** Lay the breast on its side and peel the meat away from the flat bones along the back.

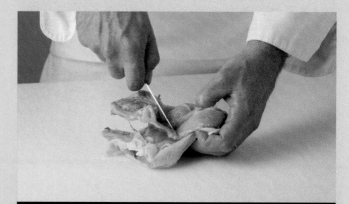

FIGURE **2.23b** Cut toward the keel bone, peeling the meat off the rib cage.

FIGURE **2.23c** Cut around the wish bone and remove it.

FIGURE **2.23d** Repeat the preceding steps for the opposite side, always peeling the meat toward the keel bone.

FIGURE **2.23e** Finish by cutting the breast away from the center of the keel bone without piercing skin.

FIGURE **2.23f** The yield from a full chicken breast using Method 2. This method allows the breast to be cooked whole without splitting.

FIGURE **2.24** Preparing a chicken breast for cutlets or quick sauté requires the exterior skin to be removed and pounding the breast to ensure even cooking.

FIGURE **2.24a** Carefully peel away the skin.

FIGURE **2.24b** If desired, the chicken "tender" can be pulled away for a separate use. This step is optional.

FIGURE **2.24c** Remove excess fat and sinews.

FIGURE **2.24d** Flatten the breast using a mallet and plastic wrap. Always flatten away from ready-to-eat foods, because small particles of poultry can fly if you are pounding rapidly or if the poultry isn't covered correctly.

AIRLINE BREAST

A variation of this is the "airline" breast which has a portion of the wing attached. The wing section provides an esthetic look and also maintains moisture. The end of the bone is often frenched to enhance the look. The "supreme" is basically the breast with the wing section attached and the skin removed.

FIGURE **2.25** The airline chicken breast is also known as the frenched breast or chicken "supreme." These can be purchased prefabricated, but they can be expensive, and often the ends of the wings are not cleaned well so further fabrication is still required. It also makes sense to fabricate frenched breasts from whole chickens.

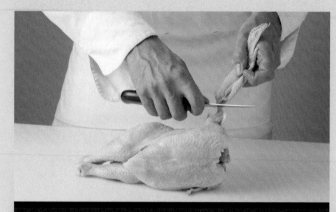

FIGURE **2.25a** First make a circular cut around the first wing bone just below the "elbow" joint. Do not cut through the joint.

FIGURE **2.25b** With a rapid snapping motion, pull the wing away at the joint.

FIGURE **2.25c** Clean off the end of the frenched wing and push the meat down, cleaning the bone. From this point, use the previously described techniques to disjoint the chicken, which can be cooked bone-in or semi-boneless. When boning the breast, be sure to leave the wing intact.

FRENCHING WINGS

Wings are inexpensive and often sold in casual dining establishments. The creation of the "Hot Wing" began in Buffalo, New York in the 1960s. Today it is recognized broadly and many restaurants serve a large variety of wings. Wings are divided into the tip, the flat, and the drumette. The "flat" section has a two-bone structure. This section can be frenched down to create a wing "lollipop."

FIGURE **2.26a** Cut off the wing tip through the joint.

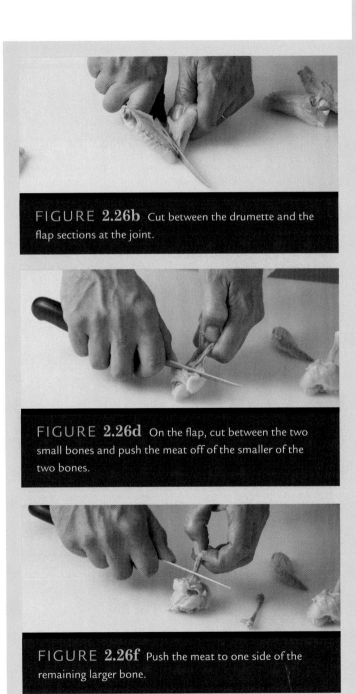

FIGURE **2.26b** Cut between the drumette and the flap sections at the joint.

FIGURE **2.26c** Push the meat off the thin side of the drumette and trim the ends of the bones.

FIGURE **2.26d** On the flap, cut between the two small bones and push the meat off of the smaller of the two bones.

FIGURE **2.26e** Cut away the smaller bone.

FIGURE **2.26f** Push the meat to one side of the remaining larger bone.

FIGURE **2.26g** Trim the ends so that the wings can stand up for presentation.

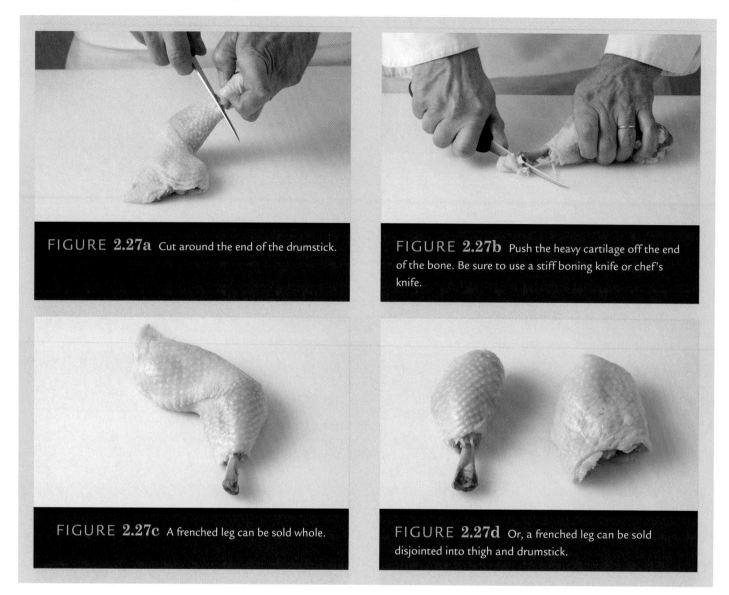

FIGURE **2.27a** Cut around the end of the drumstick.

FIGURE **2.27b** Push the heavy cartilage off the end of the bone. Be sure to use a stiff boning knife or chef's knife.

FIGURE **2.27c** A frenched leg can be sold whole.

FIGURE **2.27d** Or, a frenched leg can be sold disjointed into thigh and drumstick.

BONING LEGS

The chicken leg is probably the least expensive of all poultry cuts. Marketing the leg can be very profitable. The leg can be boned for use as loose meat for cubes or ground. Another technique is to hollow bone the leg for stuffing.

The leg contains a shank and femur bone. Boning it is a simple task that most prep cooks can master in minutes.

Open Style

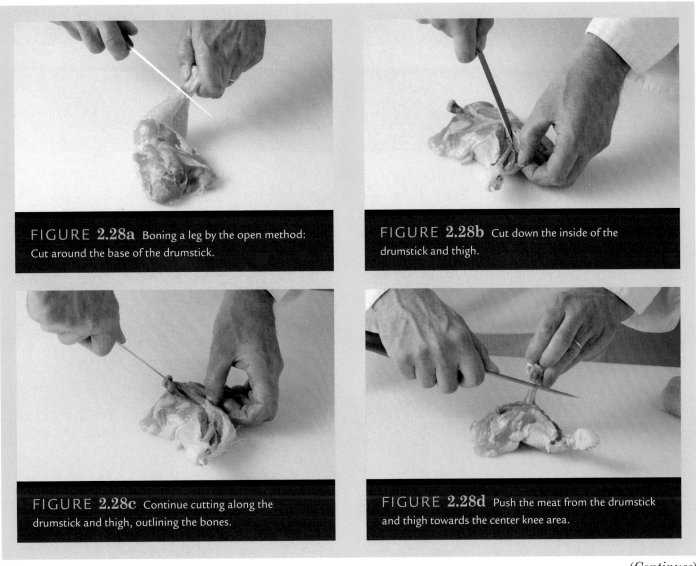

FIGURE **2.28a** Boning a leg by the open method: Cut around the base of the drumstick.

FIGURE **2.28b** Cut down the inside of the drumstick and thigh.

FIGURE **2.28c** Continue cutting along the drumstick and thigh, outlining the bones.

FIGURE **2.28d** Push the meat from the drumstick and thigh towards the center knee area.

(Continues)

(Continued)

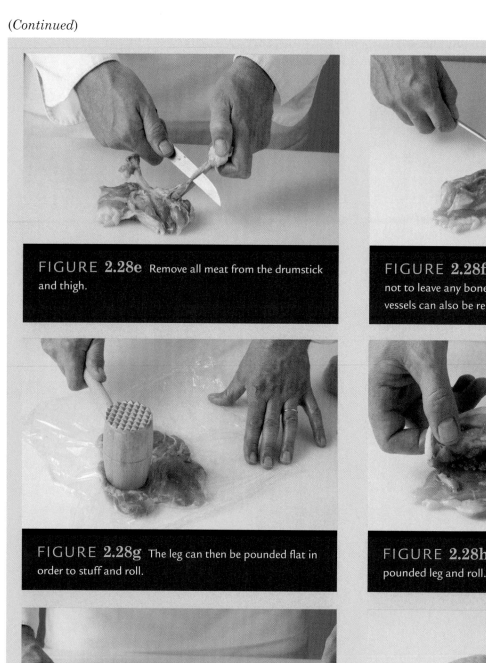

FIGURE **2.28e** Remove all meat from the drumstick and thigh.

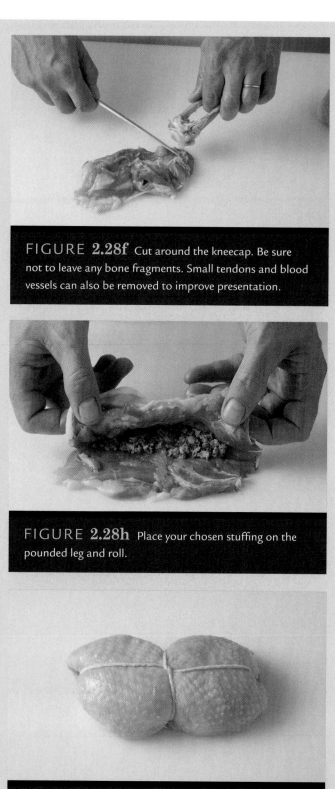

FIGURE **2.28f** Cut around the kneecap. Be sure not to leave any bone fragments. Small tendons and blood vessels can also be removed to improve presentation.

FIGURE **2.28g** The leg can then be pounded flat in order to stuff and roll.

FIGURE **2.28h** Place your chosen stuffing on the pounded leg and roll.

FIGURE **2.28i** Tie the leg using a crisscross "paupiette" knot.

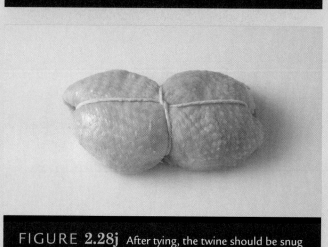

FIGURE **2.28j** After tying, the twine should be snug and neat.

Hollow Boning

FIGURE **2.29** The hollow boning method is like turning the leg inside out. It requires a steady knife and patience to learn.

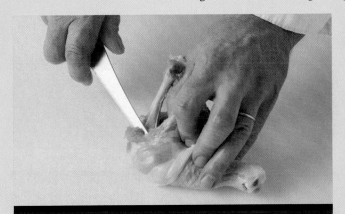

FIGURE **2.29a** Starting from the thigh end, push the meat toward the knee joint.

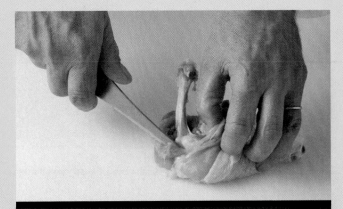

FIGURE **2.29b** Carefully cut around the knee, minimizing cuts.

FIGURE **2.29c** Start pushing the meat down the drumstick bone.

FIGURE **2.29d** Push the meat all the way down to the end of the drumstick bone.

FIGURE **2.29e** Clip off the exposed bone, leaving the small end piece intact.

FIGURE **2.29f** Turn the leg skin-side out. It is now ready for stuffing.

FLAT BONING FOR GALANTINE

The chicken can be boned to preserve its skin and use it to stuff the entire bird to make a galantine. This technique can also be used for any stuffing application. Some of the steps are similar to other fabrications.

FIGURE **2.30a** Cut wing away at first joint.

FIGURE **2.30b** Cut straight down the center of the chicken's back. Peel the meat away from one side of the rib cage, starting from the breast and working toward the leg.

FIGURE **2.30c** Cut through the leg socket.

FIGURE **2.30d** Without piercing the skin, cut down the rest of the rib cage, through the arm socket, and down to the keel bone.

FIGURE **2.30e** Repeat the preceding steps on the other side of the chicken, then cut around the wish bone.

FIGURE **2.30f** Cut away the carcass at the keel bone.

(Continues)

FIGURE **2.30g** Bone out the legs without removing the exterior skin.

FIGURE **2.30h** Bone out the wings.

FIGURE **2.30i** Carefully pull the meat off the skin without tearing it.

FIGURE **2.30j** Trim the skin to a rectangular shape.

FIGURE **2.30k** Flatten the breast meat and lay them evenly over the skin. Create a forcemeat out of the legs. (There are a variety of mixtures and recipes for forcemeats that can include many garnishes and spice combinations. The one pictured is made with chicken legs, herbs, salt, eggs, cream, bread crumbs, and a little ice.)

FIGURE **2.30l** Carefully roll the chicken into a cylinder.

(*Continues*)

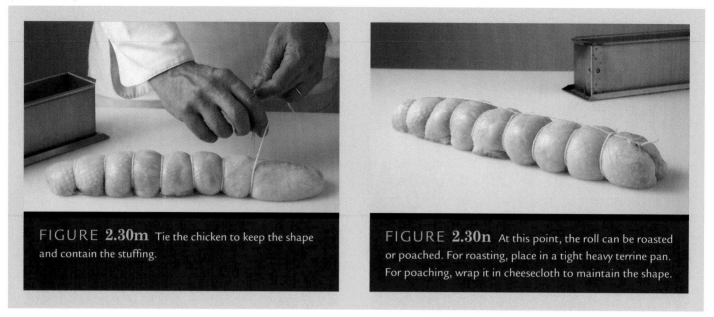

FIGURE **2.30m** Tie the chicken to keep the shape and contain the stuffing.

FIGURE **2.30n** At this point, the roll can be roasted or poached. For roasting, place in a tight heavy terrine pan. For poaching, wrap it in cheesecloth to maintain the shape.

GLOVE BONING A CHICKEN

Glove boning is a technique of boning the chicken without cutting through the skin. This technique enables the chef to stuff a small chicken or Cornish hen and serve it whole.

FIGURE **2.31** Glove boning a chicken requires a fairly high level of skill. You are basically cutting the skin and meat off the carcass without cutting through the skin. Cuts made along the backbone must be done especially carefully.

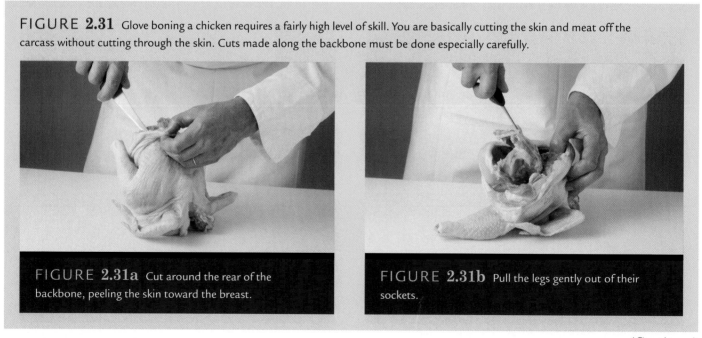

FIGURE **2.31a** Cut around the rear of the backbone, peeling the skin toward the breast.

FIGURE **2.31b** Pull the legs gently out of their sockets.

(*Continues*)

(*Continued*)

FIGURE **2.31c** Gently push the meat off the center of the back, exposing the two long, flat bones but stopping about ¾ of the way to the front.

FIGURE **2.31d** From the front of the chicken, find the wishbone and outline it with your knife.

FIGURE **2.31e** Remove the wishbone.

FIGURE **2.31f** Carefully push the meat off the flat back bones, working from the front of the neck area and connecting to the previous cuts made from the back.

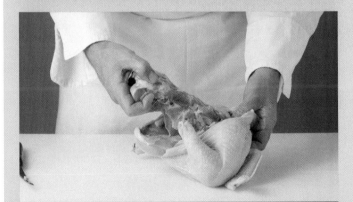

FIGURE **2.31g** The skin should now be loosened from the back. Push the legs over the neck, taking care not to tear the skin.

FIGURE **2.31h** Finish cutting down both sides of the rib cage, meeting at the keel bone. Carefully cut away the carcass at the keel bone.

(*Continues*)

(*Continued*)

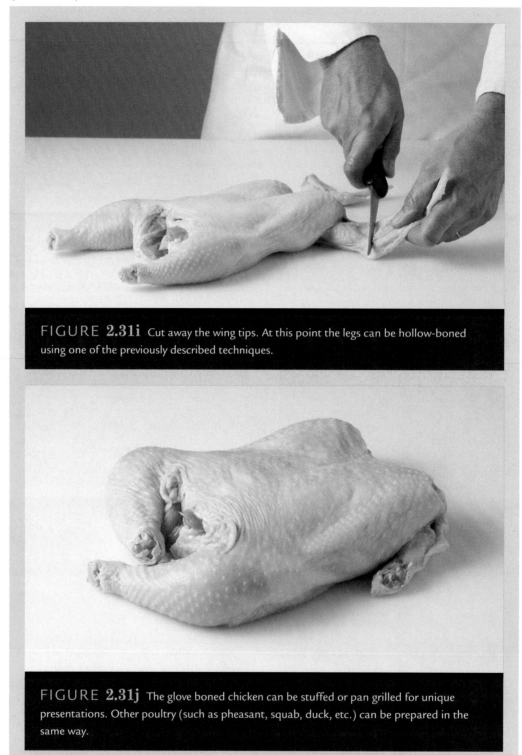

FIGURE **2.31i** Cut away the wing tips. At this point the legs can be hollow-boned using one of the previously described techniques.

FIGURE **2.31j** The glove boned chicken can be stuffed or pan grilled for unique presentations. Other poultry (such as pheasant, squab, duck, etc.) can be prepared in the same way.

DUCK

In the culinary world the duck plays a very important and prominent role. Its meat is flavorful and rich. It is often slow roasted to achieve a tender poultry that reminds many of holidays and special occasions. Its fat is considered a valuable by-product used as a cooking agent. The roast duck and its fat renderings supply many memorable dining occasions.

Contrary to the traditional slow roast, duck breast can be grilled or seared to a medium rare like a fine steak. Cooking a boneless duck breast in this fashion has transformed it from a carving item on holiday dinner tables to a "cook to order" item found in many restaurants. Chefs are presenting duck in many new and creative ways.

Being a red meat, duck lends itself to a wide variety of spicing and flavoring without its flavor getting lost. Today chefs curing it as a prosciutto-style ham or smoking it like bacon. These presentations enable variety on the menu.

Cooked duck was preserved before the invention of refrigeration by cooking it slowly in its own rendered fat, known in France as *confit* or simply translated as "preserves." Beyond the meat from duck, its fat is considered a culinary prize. Frying simple potatoes in duck fat produces a flavor that is nothing but appealing. Leaving a light pleasant aftertaste, duck fat can be used for frying even dessert items such as yeast doughnuts. In some cultures duck fat is spread on bread, similar to butter, and eaten plain.

Beyond the fat and meat is the liver. The fattened liver or *foie gras*, is a highly prized ingredient revered by many chefs and culinarians. Duck is not found hidden on the menu, it is often front and center, a culinary star item with a devoted following.

HISTORY OF DUCK

Most domestic ducks are related to the wild Mallard. The wild duck, which is in the family *Anatidae* that includes swan and geese, is a migratory bird that was domesticated about 3,000 years ago in China. Pottery and early writings depicting domestication scenes were discovered in southern China and during the early Han dynasty, China became the major center of domestication.

Ancient Egyptians had captured ducks and fed them to fatten their livers and improve their meat, similar to modern *foie gras* production. This process is known as *gavage* where the animal is fed large amounts over a short amount of time to mimic the natural fattening season before migration.

European domestication came much later. The Greeks and Romans may have captured wild ducks and fattened them but did not truly domesticate breeds. Not until medieval times do we find ducks truly domesticated and bred.

The Mallard bird's natural habitat extends from Europe, Asia, North and South America, and Africa. Ducks will migrate to Greenland and northern reaches of Russia and Scandinavia in the summer months. It has been introduced to Australia and New Zealand and there are now wild populations there. The wild duck migrates many thousands of miles each year and has the ability to store large amounts of fat to be used as fuel during the long journey. Being an ample flyer, with the ability to fly up to 40 miles per hour, means the duck's muscles need a lot of oxygen. Their meat is higher in pigmentation from myoglobin, the protein responsible for keeping oxygen flowing to the muscle cells. Myoglobin gives duck its darker red meat color. The fact that duck has a darker color and lots of fat accumulation explains its rich flavor.

Another duck in the Anatidae family is the Muscovy, also known as the *Barbary*. This larger duck is native to Central and South America and is not migratory and not nearly the flyer that its Mallard cousin is. It is primarily found in ponds and freshwater streams from the southern United States down through Mexico and into South America, mainly in warm areas. American indigenous peoples had already domesticated the Muscovy by the time the Spanish arrived. The Spanish brought the Muscovy to the Caribbean and West Africa where it thrived.

DOMESTICATION OF DUCKS

Domestication of ducks changed the meat content and coloration to better suit human needs. Duck eggs were also harvested and many ducks were raised for their ability to produce large "clutches" of eggs. Ducks can reproduce rapidly. In the wild a duck will create a ground nest in low grass or shrubs and lay anywhere from 9 to 15 eggs. The female will incubate them for about 4 weeks. Once they hatch the mother duck will bring the fledglings to water and they are often seen following in a row, learning to feed on water plants and small animals.

Before the late nineteenth century most ducks in the United States were either domesticated wild Canvasback Mallards or European breeds brought with settlers.

These ducks were relatively slow growing and were brooding ducks, reproducing naturally in pairs. The Pekin or Asian White duck was imported to Long Island and San Francisco in the 1870s as a meat duck and modern duck farming began.

Modern domestic meat-breed ducks are artificially inseminated and eggs are collected and incubated. Ducks are raised rapidly and reach market weight in 6 to 7 weeks. Most ducks are fed a formulated diet of corn and minerals in large indoor or outdoor pens. Primarily ducks are raised in three general locations in the United States, Long Island, NY, California, and Indiana. At one point Long Island ducks were considered the standard by which quality was compared.

Due to pressures from developers and the increasing size of New York City's suburbs, many of the duck farms on Long Island were bought out throughout the 1950s and 1960s. Some shifted operations to Indiana where corn and land were readily available. Today we find the two largest producers of duck are Maple Leaf Duck Farms, located in Milford, Indiana and Culver Duck, in Middlebury, Indiana. These two companies both have roots in Long Island but moved out due to the attractive locations found in Indiana at the time.

Long Island duck farms grew rapidly in the 1800s similar to the chicken industry. The introduction of the fast-growing Pekin duck and the explosion in population in New York City enabled duck farms to grow in size and volume by the 1900s. The invention of the incubator also increased volume and by the early 1890s farms were producing tens of thousands of ducks for market. By the 1940s this number was well into the millions. Duck farms on Long Island had grown to the point where many streams and tributaries had been occupied and pollution was becoming a problem. The very city that consumed most of the ducks was now starting to consume the duck farms themselves. Developers and residential housing began pressuring duck farms to control excessive waste and odor and feed prices began to rise leading to the demise of many small farms.

Today we find only two large farms left on Long Island, Jurgielewicz Duck Farm and Crescent Duck Farm. These are the last remaining vestiges of the once thriving industry along the southern coast. Today luxury homes sit on the old farm lands and there are no signs of the huge industry other than a few large farm houses.

In 1901, the Reichardt family began raising Pekin ducks in San Francisco. This was the beginning of large-scale production of Asian-style ducks for the markets on the West Coast. This farm is one of oldest continuously run family duck farms in the country catering primarily to the West Coast market. In the 1950s the farm was moved to Petaluma and continues to produce ducks for the Asian markets and for many of the chefs in the Bay Area.

Sonoma County also has the Sonoma County Poultry—Liberty Ducks farm owned by a family member of the Reichardts. This farm is more of a specialty grower featuring a larger version of the Pekin that is grown longer for more flavor. The growing of a very high quality slightly more mature duck results in a flavor that is different than the traditional Asian-style Pekin duck. Although still tender, the more mature ducks tend to have more complex flavor that chefs desire.

Woodland Duck Farms was a major producer for southern California but has been purchased recently by Maple Leaf Farms of Indiana.

Moulard Ducks are grown in a few locations for foie gras production. In New York, Hudson Valley Foie Gras and La Belle Poultry grow New York Style foie gras. In Quebec, Canada, and in France we find the largest producer is Rougie, producing a French style. California also grows foie gras in Sonoma County but legislation may be regulating it out of business. All of these produce Moulard duck meat as well as the liver.

In Europe the Pekin duck is also mass produced by a number of different companies and co-ops. A fair amount of heritage breeds are still being produced that have different flavors. These breeds, as previously stated, take longer to mature making them less economically desirable but having a richer flavor.

Duck production in Asia is varied and complex. There are thousands upon thousands of small and large farms producing numerous breeds. Duck remains a very popular meat and many specialty duck farms are still operating. More large commercial operations now exist using the specifically bred or hybrid Pekin ducks for rapid meat production. Even many small farmers are using Pekin which is the number one produced duck in China, Korea, Thailand, Vietnam, Malaysia, and the Philippines. Duck production worldwide grew rapidly during the 1980s and 1990s with the Asian markets more than doubling their production.

One recent factor in duck, and all poultry production for that matter, is the outbreak of avian flu strains. In some cases farmers had to eliminate all of their flock to stop the spread of the disease. The advent of dangerous avian flu into waterfowl stocks has caused some slowing of the rapid growth of duck production in China and southeast Asia. Feed costs in large production operations as opposed to small forage-type farms have also hampered growth.

DUCK FEED

Most commercially produced ducks are raised either in large outdoor pens or indoors in large open sheds. They are fed a diet of primarily corn with other grains mixed in. Typically some soy bean is mixed into the feed for protein. Faster growing commercial ducks require a lot of protein and are fed a diet specifically formulated with vitamins, proteins, and carbohydrates to ensure a rapid growth rate. Most ducks are fed an all-vegetarian diet even though they are omnivores in the wild. They can forage for snails, frogs, and small fish if allowed to. Ducks are hardy and do not require a pre-emptive antibiotic to remain healthy, therefore most carry the antibiotic-free label. Sometimes baby ducklings may have Salmonellosis and may require exposure to a sulfa antibiotic for a short period. Growth promotants or steroids are illegal for any poultry product and are never used on ducks. Free range ducks are those that are allowed access to the outdoors. They are not necessarily range or forage fed though.

BY-PRODUCT FEATHERS

Another aspect of the duck industry is the by-product feathers. The feather and down industry was a major part of the success of the early duck farms. Feather picking and processing for pillows, bedding, coats, and more was considered a high end job paying more than many other manual labor tasks by the end of the 1800s. The duck feather industry continues to be viable today but has become highly mechanized. Duck feathers and quality *down* are found in superior bedding and coats and it has been nearly impossible to artificially create a substitute for the softness and lightness of a quality down pillow.

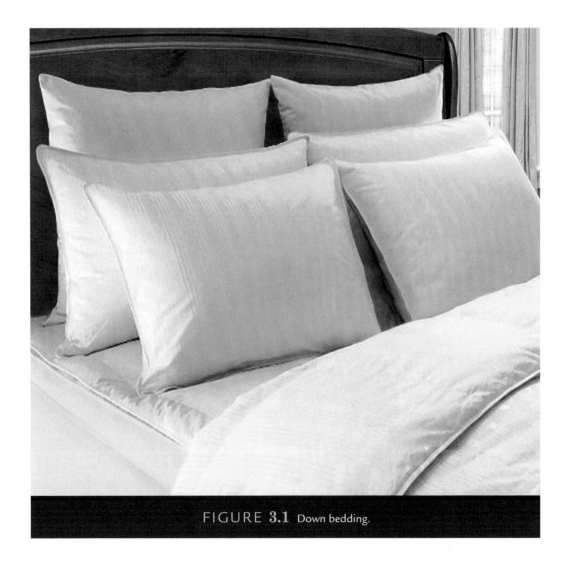

FIGURE **3.1** Down bedding.

DOMESTIC BREEDS OF DUCK

The breeds derived from Mallard and Muscovy ducks are the only two commercially available species. Almost all domestic ducks stem from either of them.

The male duck is known as *drake* and a female duck is known simply as *duck* or *hen* depending on the farmer. The term *duck* traditionally meant a female duck but today is either sex. A *duckling* is a term used for a young duck up to –6 to 8 weeks old. This is a market term used often for meat ducks.

FIGURE **3.2** White Pekin.

FIGURE **3.3** Duclair.

This list represents only a small portion of all the breeds and sub-breeds found around the world. There are many ducks that are created by farms, companies, or university research that are cross-breeds that may be patented.

PEKIN

The Pekin duck is the single most popular duck raised for meat worldwide. Originating in Asia, the Pekin was brought to the United States in the 1870s and rapidly dominated the duck market. Pekins are fast growing and can be ready for market in just 6 weeks. They are white and relatively small, averaging 3 to 8 pounds processed. They are fed primarily a corn-based diet when raised commercially.

DUCLAIR

The Duclair originated in Normandy and is prized for its flavor. This is not mass produced and not well known outside of its original area but efforts are being made to introduce it to the U.S. market as a niche item. It is black with a white vest and has a distinctive slightly wild flavor without being too strong. It has a large breast meat and small legs resulting in a good yield. Some chefs are dry aging the bird to create a unique beef-like flavor.

MALLARD

Wild breed that is raised as a specialty item and is not common. Their yield is generally poor but they have a unique, stronger flavor. Depending on the diet they can become exceedingly greasy or fatty which some find unpalatable. Suggestions about aging or marinating can enhance palatability. Never purchase a true wild duck from a hunter. This is illegal. Another wild breed similar to the Mallard is the Canvasback. It too is rarely found commercially produced.

FIGURE **3.4** Mallard.

ROUEN

Originating in France this name refers to a few breeds from the Rouen area in Normandy. These ducks were used for meat and plumage. It is about the size of a large Pekin duck and has less fat typically. The flavor is considered superior but it takes a little longer to get to market size therefore its popularity with farmers has lessened. Grown today as a niche market item, it is highly desired by some chefs.

FIGURE **3.5** Rouen.

MUSCOVY

Also known as the Barbary duck. This large duck originated in South America and is thought to be one of the world's earliest domesticated ducks. It is not in the same family as the Mallard therefore it looks somewhat different with an almost goose-like appearance. The Muscovy has a good yield and rich flavor. It is a very hearty bird and can be aggressive. Due to its heartiness it is often cross-bred with a Pekin and fed to produce foie gras or the fattened liver. This combination is known as a Moulard duck and, like a mule, it cannot reproduce therefore a Moulard is not a true breed.

FIGURE **3.6** Muscovy.

DUCK BREED WEIGHT CLASSIFICATIONS

HEAVY WEIGHT DUCK CLASS

Silver Appleyard Ducks	Silver Muscovy Ducks
Black Muscovy Ducks	Saxony Ducks
Blue Muscovy Ducks	

MEDIUM WEIGHT DUCK CLASS

Black Ancona Ducks	Silver Ancona Ducks
Blue Ancona Ducks	Tri-Colored Ancona Ducks
Chocolate Ancona Ducks	Black Cayuga Ducks
Lavender Ancona Ducks	

LIGHT WEIGHT DUCK CLASS

Khaki Campbell Ducks	Black Runner Ducks (sometimes called Indian Runner)
Bibbed Dutch Hook Bill Ducks	Blue Runner Ducks
Dusky Dutch Hook Bill Ducks	Blue Fawn Runner Ducks
White Dutch Hook Bill Ducks	Chocolate Runner Ducks
Black Magpie Ducks	Dusky Runner Ducks
Blue Magpie Ducks	Emery Penciled Runner Ducks

(Continues)

(Continued)

LIGHT WEIGHT DUCK CLASS

Faery Fawn Runner Ducks

Silver Runner Ducks

Fawn & White Runner Ducks

Trout Runner Ducks

Gray (Mallard) Runner Ducks

White Runner Ducks

Khaki Runner Ducks

Silver Welsh Harlequin Ducks

Penciled Runner Ducks

Golden Welsh Harlequin Ducks

Saxony Runner Ducks

BANTAM DUCK CLASS

Miniature Silver Appleyard Ducks
(sometimes called Mini Appleyard, Bantam
Appleyard, or Silver Bantam)

Miniature Overberg Ducks

Bluehead Australian Spotted Ducks

Black Silky Ducks

Greenhead Australian Spotted Ducks

Dusky Silky Ducks

Silverhead Australian Spotted Ducks

Gray (Mallard colored) Silky Ducks

Black East Indie Ducks (sometimes called
East India or East Indian)

Snowy Silky Ducks

Blue East Indie Ducks

White Silky Ducks

Bibbed Mallard Ducks

FIGURE **3.7** Teal.

FIGURE **3.8** Aylesbury.

TEAL

The Teal is a wild duck that may be found commercially but is similar to the Mallard. When wild it travels great distances and can acquire a lot of fat right before migration. It is a relatively small duck with a poor yield and can have tougher, somewhat gamey meat depending on the source.

AYLESBURY

This duck originated in Aylesbury, England. It is a pure white duck with a good meat flavor. During the early to mid-1800s it was the dominant breed in England. With the importation of the Asian Pekin, the Aylesbury was often crossbred so finding purebred birds today is extremely rare.

SUB-BREEDS OF DUCKS

There are hundreds of sub-breeds of duck that can be found worldwide. When farms and farmers could not intermingle due to geographic separation, before modern transportation, specialty breeds of ducks unique to individual areas were common. We find these "heritage" breeds becoming a rarity and often maintained by an association or group of farmers. Below is a large list of ducks preserved by the Holderread Waterfowl Preservation Farm in Corvallis, Oregon. These ducks are considered endangered not because of overharvesting but due to the fact that the poultry industry is focused on production and uniformity. Some chefs are looking for unique breeds and farms to separate themselves from the norm and to provide a different taste. Many of these breeds take longer to mature making them much more expensive.

CLASSES OF DUCK

Duck is divided into three basic classifications depending on age and size. The *duckling* is the most common and easily found commercially available. The *roasting* duck is a bit larger and more mature but not considered a mature breeding duck. It is basically an oversized duckling. A *mature* duck is a breeding duck that has been kept for egg laying and reproduction.

DUCK CLASSIFICATIONS			
NAME	DESCRIPTION	SIZE	AGE
Duckling	Typical duck, roasted whole or split, or as parts	3–6 lbs	6 weeks
Roasting Duck	Larger duck, young but full sized	5–8 lbs	10–16 weeks
Mature	Older duck used for breeding, typically braised or slow cooked	6–10 lbs	16+ weeks, usually over 6 months old

PURCHASING SPECIFICATIONS

Ducks are purchased fresh or frozen. If fresh, they have a shelf life of about 4 or 5 days. If frozen they are typically blast frozen at the plant and should remain at 0° to –20°F/–18° to –29°C. Freezing duck does not adversely affect the quality if stored and handled correctly.

Typically ducks are individually bagged if sold whole. They can also be purchased in a large variety of portion cut configurations such as quarters and boneless parts. The boneless breast from a Moulard duck is known as a *Magret*.

The following guide gives packaging specifics. Not all duck producers follow a standard packaging count or size so be sure to ask your purveyor for specifics when purchasing.

DUCK PURCHASING AND USAGE SPECIFICATIONS

ITEM AND NAMP NUMBER	DESCRIPTION/ FABRICATION	SUGGESTED COOKING METHOD/ APPLICATION	AVG. SUGGESTED WEIGHT LBS	TYPICAL PACKAGE SPECS
Duckling P3000 P3001 w/giblets P3002 w/o giblets	Whole bird, usually sold with giblets	Dry cook, roast whole or half, cut for parts	3–6 lbs	6 per case individually wrapped or 12 per case iced
Duckling Buddhist style	Whole bird, with head and feet attached	Cooked whole for Peking style duck	4–7 lbs	6 per case
Roasting duck P3100	Whole bird, sold with giblets	Slow roast whole or half, large parts	5–8 lbs	6 per case
Mature duck P3200	Sold whole, low quality, high in flavor	Processed, braising, slow cooking, sausage	6–8 lbs	varies
Moulard duck, foie gras duck	Sold whole or as large parts	Roast, grill breast as magret, confit legs	6–9 lbs	varies
Duckling quarters P3009	Two breast halves and two legs with all back and rib bones	Dry cook, roast, broil, grill	3–6 lbs	varies
Duckling breast, bone-in P3012	Bone-in, unsplit	Roast whole or fabricate into boneless breast	1.5 lbs each	12 per case
Duckling breast, boneless P3013	Boneless, skin-on or skin-off	Pan sear, broil, grill, cut skin to release fat	¾ lb each full breast	2 breast per pack, 6 packs per case
Moulard breast, boneless (magret)	Large, skin-on	Pan sear, broil, grill, cure for "prosciutto"	1.5 lbs each	1 full breast per bag, sold by the pound individually

(Continues)

(Continued)

ITEM AND NAMP NUMBER	DESCRIPTION/ FABRICATION	SUGGESTED COOKING METHOD/ APPLICATION	AVG. SUGGESTED WEIGHT LBS	TYPICAL PACKAGE SPECS
Duckling legs P3031 P3032 Also, drumstick and thigh sold separately	Bone-in or semi-boneless, (both have back bones removed)	Roast, grill, stuff, pulled meat, confit	½ lb each	36–40 pieces per case 17+ lbs each case
Moulard duck legs	Bone-in, back bones removed	Roast, grill, stuff, confit	¾ lb each	6 per bag
Duck wings P3036	Wing tips removed	Slow cook, BBQ, glaze	1–2 oz each	Sold in bulk
Duck liver P3045	Dark red color, sold in bulk, may require removal of sinews	Pate, terrines, mousse, sausages	1–2 oz each	5-lb tubs
Foie gras liver (French or NY style) P3046	Fattened liver from a Moulard duck	Sear whole, grill, terrines, mousse, pate, torchon	1–2 lbs each	1 per pack
Foie gras butter	Pieces of liver that are too small for grading	Mousse, grinds, sauce, spreads, forcemeats, custard	Loose pieces	varies
Duck paws (feet) P3048	Feet with webbing	Stock, sauces, dim sum	Loose pieces	Sold in bulk 25 lbs, weights vary
Duck tongue P3050	Small individual tongues	Used for soup, slow cooked	Loose pieces	Sold in bulk, varies
Duck fat, fresh or rendered	Fresh needs to be cooked slowly to remove impurities	Fry, sauté, flavor agent, confit	Bulk pack	Rendered—5-lb tubs Fresh—10-lb box

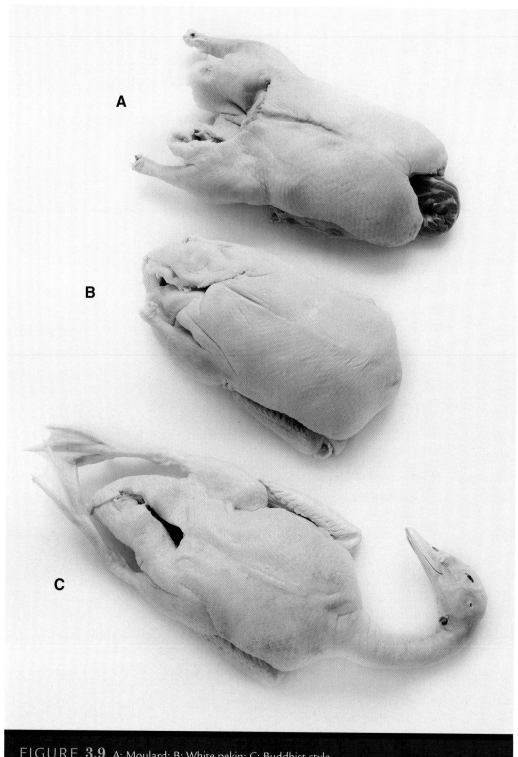

FIGURE **3.9** A: Moulard; B: White pekin; C: Buddhist style.

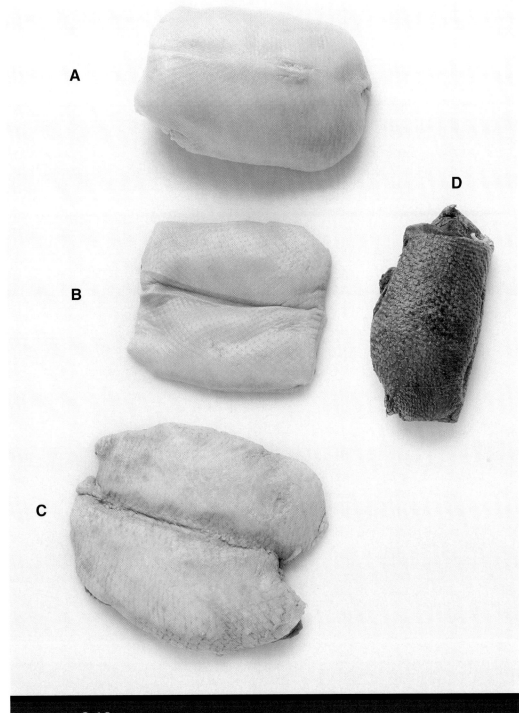

FIGURE **3.10** A: Bone-in pekin breast; B: White pekin breast; C: Moulard breast; D: Smoked duck breast.

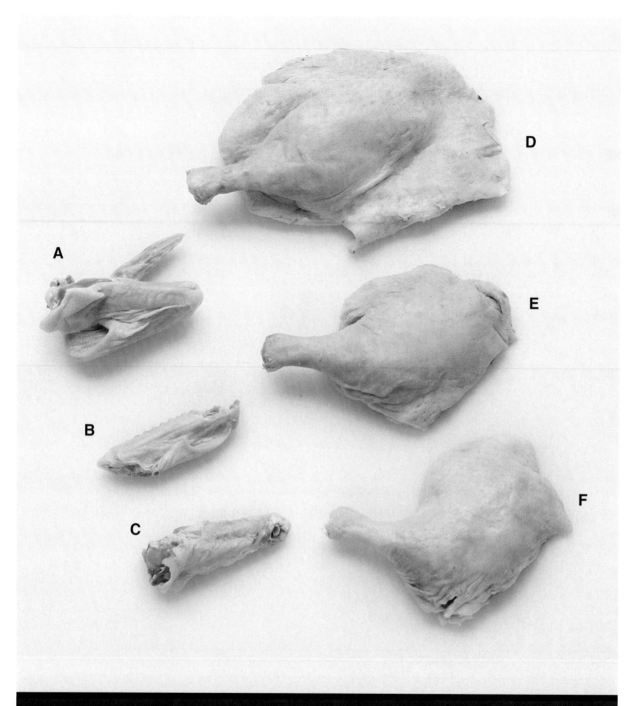

FIGURE **3.11** A: Whole wing; B: Wing flap; C: Wing drumette; D: Muscovy leg; E: Moulard leg; F: Pekin leg.

FIGURE **3.12** Duck leg confit.

FIGURE **3.13** Top to bottom: raw fat; rendered fat.

FIGURE **3.14** Duck giblets.

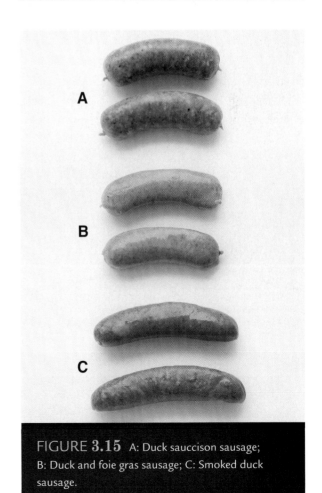

FIGURE **3.15** A: Duck sauccison sausage; B: Duck and foie gras sausage; C: Smoked duck sausage.

DUCK FABRICATION
DUCK SAUSAGE

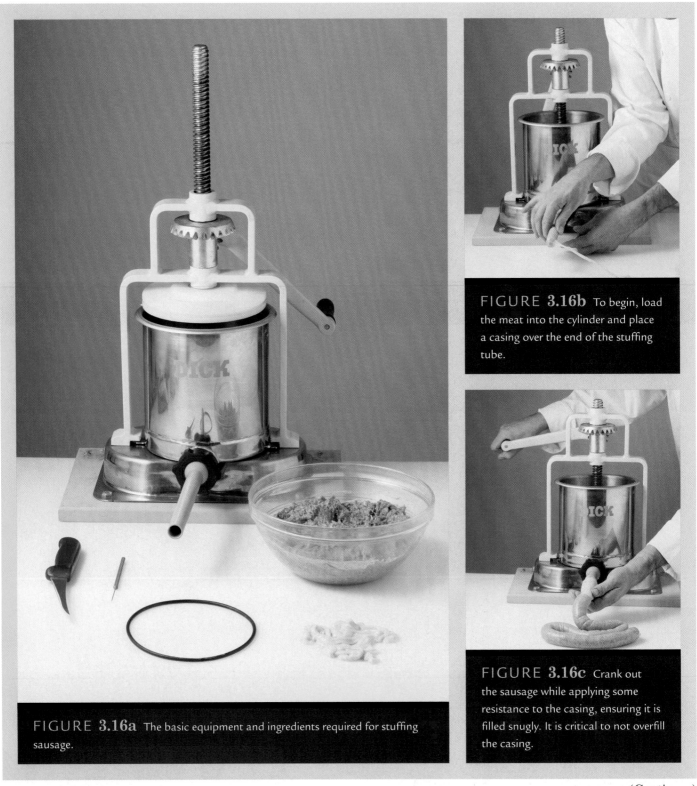

FIGURE **3.16a** The basic equipment and ingredients required for stuffing sausage.

FIGURE **3.16b** To begin, load the meat into the cylinder and place a casing over the end of the stuffing tube.

FIGURE **3.16c** Crank out the sausage while applying some resistance to the casing, ensuring it is filled snugly. It is critical to not overfill the casing.

(Continues)

(*Continued*)

FIGURE **3.16d** Tease the sausage to release any air pockets.

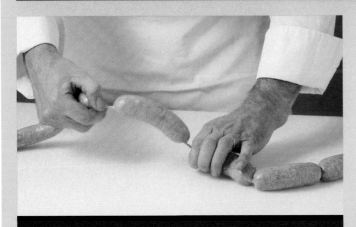

FIGURE **3.16e** Pinch the sausage and twist it into portions of the desired length.

FIGURE **3.16f** Finished sausage links. Allow links to set and dry out for about 24 hours before cooking.

TRUSSING

Trussing a duck for roasting can be done identically to the methods used for any other poultry. Following the step-by-step procedure show in the Chicken chapter will create a properly trussed duck. Unlike the chicken, the duck has a longer torso and squat legs. String positioning may be slightly different. The duck also has a large amount of fat which may accumulate on the rear of the bird. Be careful to remove much of the excess fat. Reserve it for rendering!

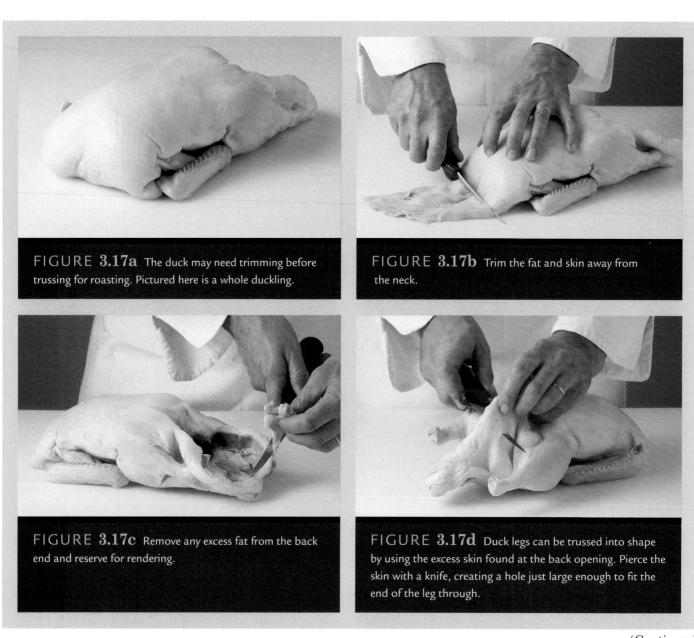

FIGURE **3.17a** The duck may need trimming before trussing for roasting. Pictured here is a whole duckling.

FIGURE **3.17b** Trim the fat and skin away from the neck.

FIGURE **3.17c** Remove any excess fat from the back end and reserve for rendering.

FIGURE **3.17d** Duck legs can be trussed into shape by using the excess skin found at the back opening. Pierce the skin with a knife, creating a hole just large enough to fit the end of the leg through.

(Continues)

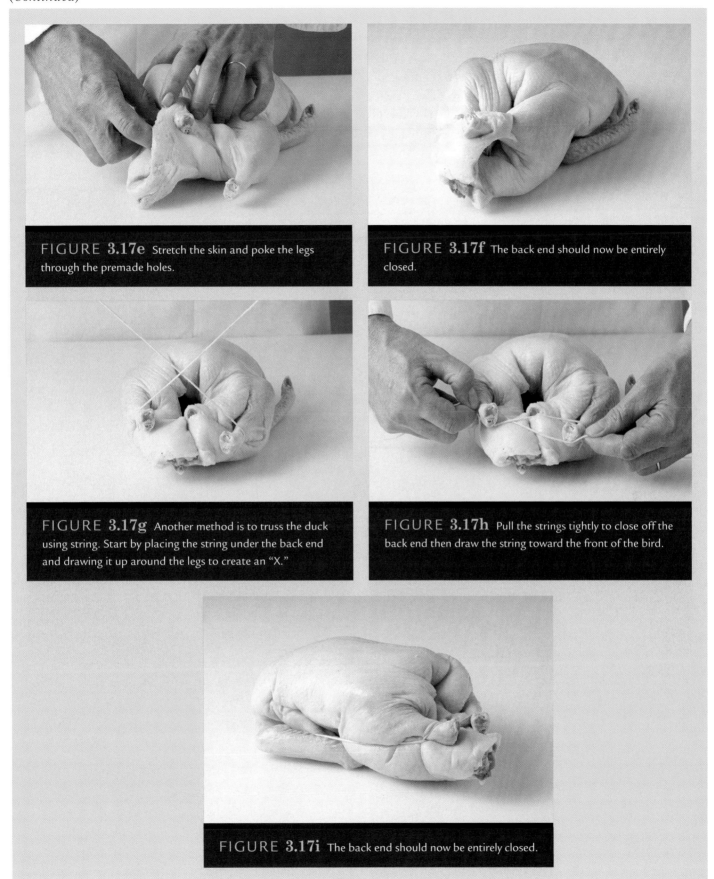

FIGURE **3.17e** Stretch the skin and poke the legs through the premade holes.

FIGURE **3.17f** The back end should now be entirely closed.

FIGURE **3.17g** Another method is to truss the duck using string. Start by placing the string under the back end and drawing it up around the legs to create an "X."

FIGURE **3.17h** Pull the strings tightly to close off the back end then draw the string toward the front of the bird.

FIGURE **3.17i** The back end should now be entirely closed.

SPLITTING A DUCK

Dividing a duck into halves for roasting is a typical fabrication. Stand the duck on its front end and cut along both sides of the back bone, removing it. This cut requires a stiff boning knife or poultry shears and the cut is made through rib bones which requires a fair amount of force. Once the back is removed, score into the keel bone and break the duck open revealing the keel bone. Run fingers along each side until you are able to pull out the keel bone. Finish by cutting through the center of the breast.

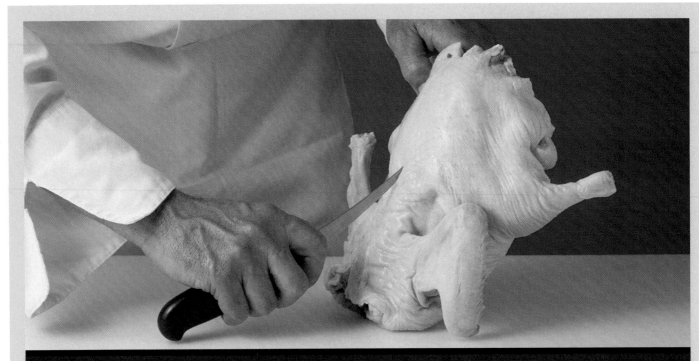

FIGURE **3.18a** Score down the back, identifying the center bone structure.

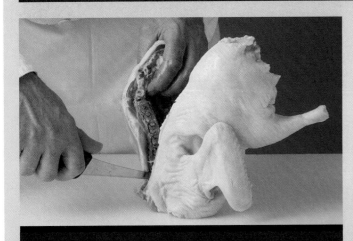

FIGURE **3.18b** Starting from the tail, cut down one side of the tail and through the back rib bones, always being sure to stay within the flat back bones.

FIGURE **3.18c** Pull up on the tail and cut along the other side of the back, removing the entire backbone. This cut will require some strength, but be sure not to crush the bird while cutting.

(Continues)

FIGURE **3.18d** Score the keel bone in the center of the duck.

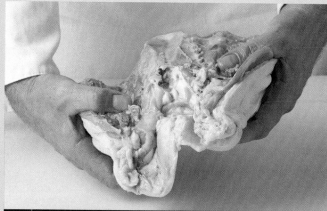

FIGURE **3.18e** Break open the keel bone and pop it up using your thumbs.

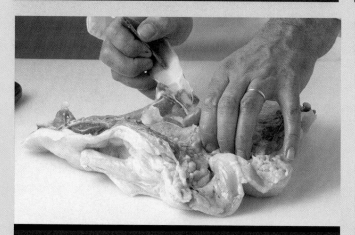

FIGURE **3.18f** Pull out the keel bone with one rapid motion.

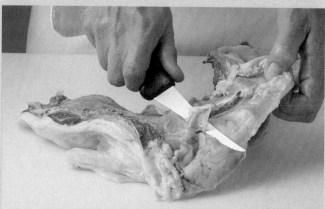

FIGURE **3.18g** Remove the wishbone from the front of the breast.

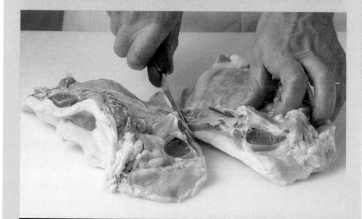

FIGURE **3.18h** Finish cutting through the duck, creating the two separate halves.

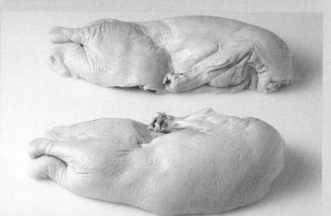

FIGURE **3.18i** Each duck half can now be roasted or grilled. The rib cage can also be removed after roasting for a semi-boneless presentation.

BONING A DUCK BREAST

Using the same basic technique for boning a chicken breast, the duck breast is easily boned. The breast is much longer and thinner than the chicken breast and has a lot more fat cover. Duck breast can also be fabricated as an airline or frenched breast, similar to chicken. Be sure to trim away extra fat cover once boned.

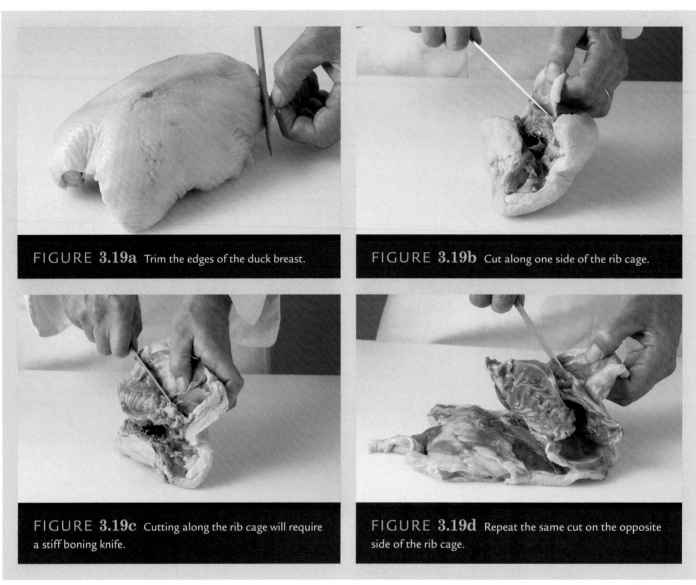

FIGURE **3.19a** Trim the edges of the duck breast.

FIGURE **3.19b** Cut along one side of the rib cage.

FIGURE **3.19c** Cutting along the rib cage will require a stiff boning knife.

FIGURE **3.19d** Repeat the same cut on the opposite side of the rib cage.

(Continues)

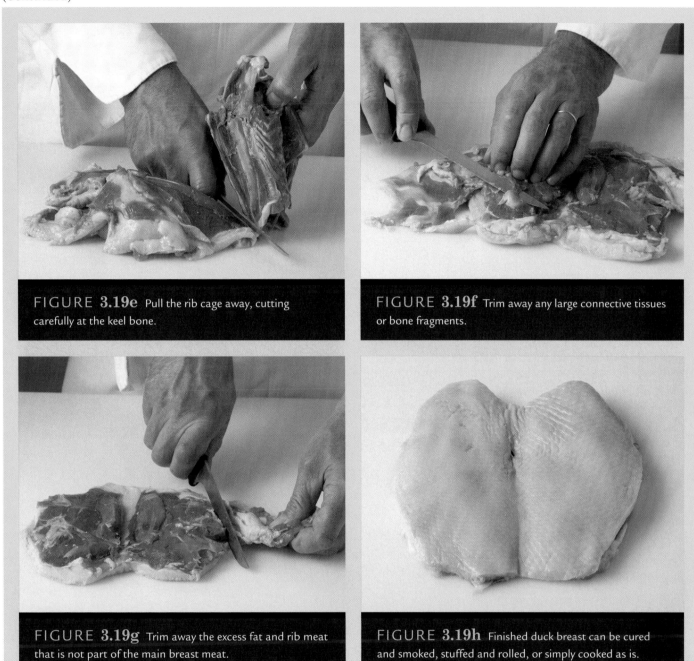

FIGURE **3.19e** Pull the rib cage away, cutting carefully at the keel bone.

FIGURE **3.19f** Trim away any large connective tissues or bone fragments.

FIGURE **3.19g** Trim away the excess fat and rib meat that is not part of the main breast meat.

FIGURE **3.19h** Finished duck breast can be cured and smoked, stuffed and rolled, or simply cooked as is.

CUTTING BREAST FOR SEARING

When searing a duck breast it is important to score the breast to release excess fat. The skin should be scored in an exacting pattern to give a nice presentation and to render the fat evenly.

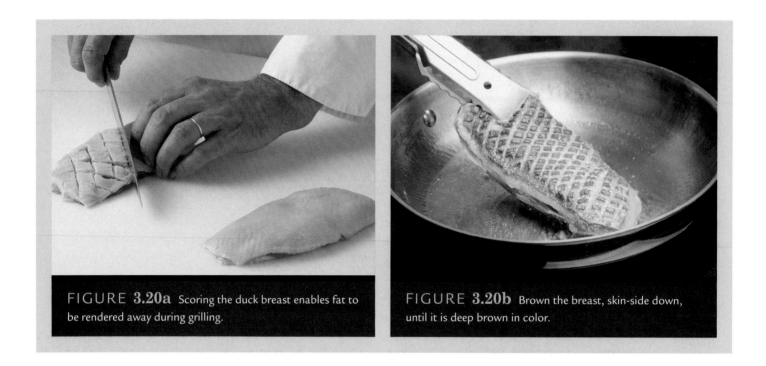

FIGURE **3.20a** Scoring the duck breast enables fat to be rendered away during grilling.

FIGURE **3.20b** Brown the breast, skin-side down, until it is deep brown in color.

BONING A DUCK LEG FOR STUFFING

Hollow boning a duck leg enables the chef to stuff it with a forcemeat or a variety of other ingredients. Use the same technique as for hollow boning of chicken legs. Once boned, secure the stuffed leg with twine or toothpicks.

RENDERING DUCK FAT

Rendering fresh duck fat cleans out all the moisture and impurities leaving a lard-like fat that can be used for frying, sautéing, or cooking confit. To render fresh fat you can either grind it first or chop it fine with a knife. Slightly freezing the fat enables it to be cut more easily.

FIGURE **3.21a** To render, chop the excess fat and cook over low to medium heat.

FIGURE **3.21b** Pour off the rendered fat and reserve for cooking. Collect any of the leftover "crisps."

FIGURE **3.21c** The "crisps" can be salted and used as a garnish or flavor agent.

DEVEINING A FOIE GRAS LIVER

The foie gras engorged liver is very solid but has some veins that run through its center. The liver should be worked on in a cold area or in small batches to avoid over-heating. The fat content is similar to butter and the liver will literally melt in your hands. Using a small knife open the inside of the liver to expose the veins. Gently pull out veins using a tweezers or small pliers. The veins add to toughness and must be removed. The liver can then be rolled to shape it before cooking.

FIGURE **3.22a** Duck foie gras before deveining.

FIGURE **3.22b** Open the liver from the bottom, gently exposing any of the interior blood vessels.

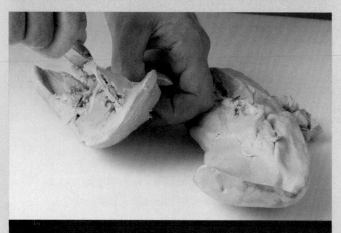

FIGURE **3.22c** Using small pliers or tweezers, gently pull away the blood vessels.

FIGURE **3.22d** The liver can be soaked in lightly salted milk to remove any discoloration.

FIGURE **3.22e** The foie gras can be placed in plastic wrap and rolled to create an even, cylindrical shape.

FIGURE **3.22f** Rolled foie gras can be poached whole or sliced into searing portions.

FOIE GRAS

The specialty duck industry has grown in the past few decades. Ducks are raised for their livers as opposed to just as a meat item. Foie gras, the engorged, fattened liver of the duck or goose, is produced in locations in France, Eastern Europe, China, United States, and Canada. The practice is banned in a dozen other European countries due to pressure from animal rights organizations. The sale of it was banned in the city of Chicago but that ban has since been lifted. Foie gras is considered an absolute delicacy by many chefs and culinarians.

The fattening of a duck or goose is known as *gavage* with the end result being an engorged liver known as *foie gras*. This process takes advantage of the natural ability for migratory birds to gorge themselves before flight. Ducks have been fattened for quality since early Egypt, some 5,000 years ago. Stone carvings depict ducks and cranes being fattened before slaughter. The early Greek and Roman civilizations also fattened ducks and geese with figs and fruits.

In Jewish law the use of pork fat is forbidden therefore the fattening of a duck or goose would provide the excess fat needed for flavor and cooking. This also meant that the liver would grow and enlarge with fat. By the 1500s Jewish communities in Eastern Europe were growing fattened waterfowl and word spread about the rich livers they produced.

In the 1780s the French farmers were raising foie and the tradition is continued today. France continues to dominate the world foie gras market with about 75 to 80 percent of the share. Other countries that produce it are Hungary, Bulgaria, Spain, China, Belgium, United States, and Canada. World production is about 60 million pounds annually.

The process of gavage starts with the breed of duck. A Moulard or "Mule" duck is used. This is a cross between a female Pekin and a male Muscovy. The offspring are sterile, therefore the "mule" name. The ducks are raised to adulthood, to around 12 weeks on free ranging farms. Then they are confined and fed heavily twice a day for either 2 or 4 weeks depending on the method. The French method used by Rougie, the world's largest producer, feeds the duck with a triggered tube and a mash made primarily of corn. This feeding is done twice a day for about 12 days. The other method, known as the New York method used by Hudson Valley Foie Gras and LaBelle Poultry, uses a corn and soy pellet that is funneled into the animal. This method takes about 28 days total.

Controversy exists over the force feeding, with some believing the duck must be in pain during feeding but studies show the ducks' esophagus is like an extension of its beak and has no sensory. The duck in the wild can handle very large amounts of feed when preparing for migration. Even though Moulard ducks are not migratory they possess some of the same traits. Contrary to some viewpoints the process of gavage is reversible, in other word, the liver once engorged will return to normal size if the heavy feeding is halted.

The livers are graded like other poultry using A, B, C for quality. The A liver is the highest quality and is firm without blemishes and bruises. It has fewer veins than a B grade. The B is good quality but may have some defects. The C may not be graded but simply sold as a processed item such as a mousse or pate.

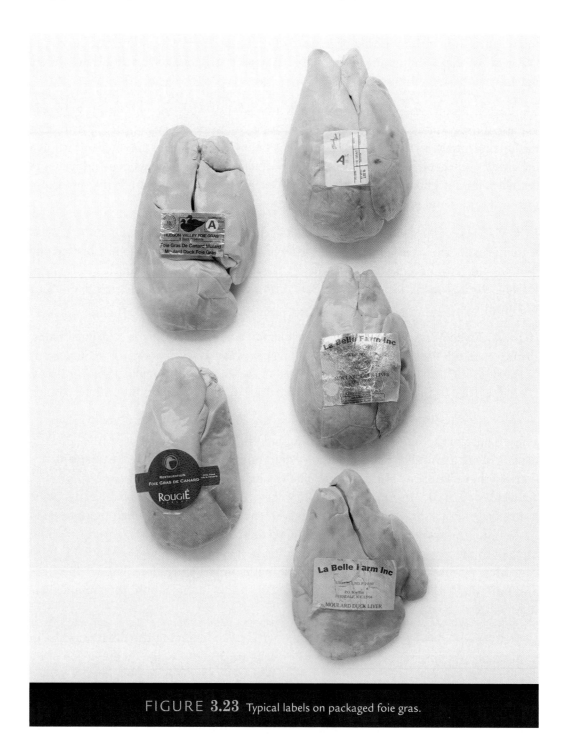

FIGURE **3.23** Typical labels on packaged foie gras.

There are some differences in size and flavor between the New York and French styles of liver. The New York tends to be solid and larger, which is better for searing whole pieces whereas the French is softer and a little richer making it a better formed liver. Many chefs dispute which is better but it should be sampled to truly understand the difference.

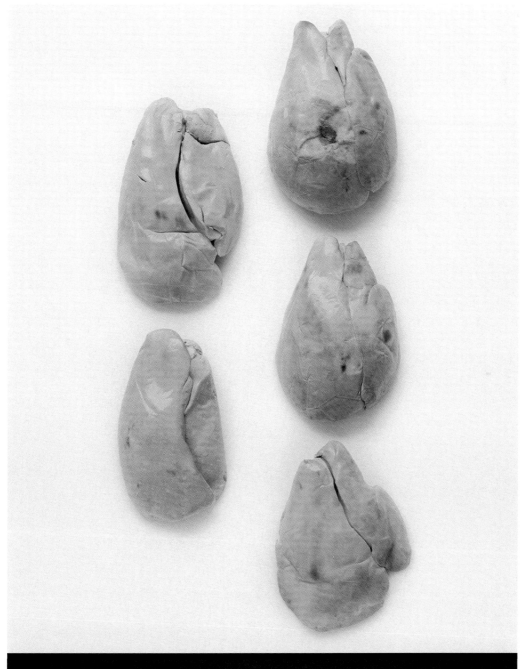

FIGURE **3.24** French foie gras (bottom left) compared to New York foie gras.

4

GOOSE

In nature the goose is a migratory bird able to fly thousands of miles at high altitude. Geese have been known to fly over the Himalayan Mountains in migration. This feat requires huge amounts of energy and the goose's physiological makeup enables this. The goose has the ability to store large amounts of fat, which is one of the reasons it is a culinary favorite. Its meat is dark red and rich in flavor because of its ability as a flier. It is high in iron and therefore high in taste. The goose is often slow roasted, similar to duck, for a festive entrée served as a holiday traditional treat. The meat, being dark red, can be cured as *charcuterie* or *salumi* items such as smoked breast "ham" or stuffed, dry cured slicing salamis. The fat rendered from it is revered as a frying fat or for shortening used in pastries. The Jewish community substituted goose in place of pork fat and meat to create similar flavors without compromising religious laws. Fattening the goose was done to create this quality fat and a fattened liver was the resulting by-product. This fattened liver known as *foie gras* in French is a prized delicacy.

Today goose is available as the traditional whole raw bird, fabricated into parts, or processed into precooked or cured products. The goose is found on menus throughout Europe and dishes such as the *Alsatian Roast Goose with Apples* are a mainstay in that French region. The famous French dish Cassoulet is a rich combination of meats and beans typically calling for duck or goose. Making a preserved *confit* from the goose is done similar to duck in that the legs are cooked slowly in fat to tenderize the meat.

Italian salami made from goose can be found in the Fuila and Lomellina regions. These sausages are seasoned and stuffed similar to pork salami. In traditional style the skin from the neck can be used as the casing.

In China the goose is cooked similar to duck, being that its meat and fat are similar. It is found on ethnic Chinese menus around the world. There are many Chinese roast goose recipes that require glazes and spicing similar to what is used on duck.

The goose is larger than duck and therefore it is not as versatile and can be difficult to serve as a single portion breast or leg, but with a little inventiveness the goose becomes a specialty that can differentiate a menu from the norm. Chefs who seek out the goose will not be disappointed.

Traditionally the goose shows up on menus around winter holiday times. The goose being harvested in late fall is the perfect meat for harvest festivals. All throughout Europe early tribes celebrated feasts with the goose. Early Germanic and Norse peoples feasted on goose to celebrate harvest and the change of seasons. The Celts of Britain harvested the goose twice in a year's time, once in the early summer when the goose is very young and also in the late fall when they are mature and fattened for the cold winter months. As Christianity spread, the goose became part of the Christmas holiday. The Traditional English roast Christmas goose conjures up visions of finery and splendor. The goose slow roasted with its cracklin' skin and rich dark sauce, presented on a large platter is a mouthwatering sight!

HISTORY OF THE GOOSE

Many stories and fables center on the goose. "The goose that laid the golden egg" is a fable by Aesop telling a story of greed. Aesop, the Greek slave and storyteller who lived from 620 to 560 B.C., is famous for his tales about human nature. Much of the population was subsistence farmers. This implies the goose was an established farm animal at that time.

The Egyptians have the goose carved in depictions of the god Geb. Geb, the god of earth also known as the "great cackler," would sometimes take the form of a goose when on earth. The Nile goose was native to Egypt and was domesticated and allowed freedom through many gardens. During harvest times geese were fed heavily to fatten them and their livers creating an early version of foie gras.

It is thought that Jewish slaves raised and fattened geese for the pharaoh in Egypt and when they left for the Promised Land they took the farming knowledge for geese with them. The goose complies with kosher laws and was and is a traditional Jewish food.

Aristotle and Homer, the Greek authors, include the goose in their writings, praising the animal's incredible flavor when roasted.

BEYOND FOOD

The goose is loud and aggressive. It acts as a guard of the farmyard and will alert other animals of impending danger. This ability assured the goose a place in Roman history. In the year 390 B.C., a Gaul tribe, the Senones, attacked Rome and surrounded and besieged Capitol Hill. During the night the Gauls attempted to climb the hill in a surprise attack. They avoided guard dogs posted but the effort was thwarted by the alarm raised by the honking of a flock of geese. The goose was held in high regard in Rome and was seen as a valuable asset as a guard animal.

The Romans also raised the goose for its fat, which was used as an emollient and lotion for the skin. Ancient Egyptians used goose fat to bind minerals to form cosmetic blushes and colorations for ceremonies.

The conquering barbaric tribes, which were the eventual downfall of Rome, also raised and fattened geese. The nomadic tribes of northern Europe kept the goose and due to its herding ability took it along as they moved. In Medieval times the goose was part of pagan sacrifice which gave way to Christian traditions that called for the goose for feasts in the fall. These feasts would take place during the goose migrations south. The seasonality of the goose fattened on the year's harvest continues into modern times.

Many of the royal courts around the world had breeds of geese that were kept as pure-breds. Often the geese outlived the monarchs of many of the royal families in Europe and Asia who kept them.

The tradition of French geese raising and fattening was fortified in 1509 when King Louis the XII signed patents granted to goose farmers which gave them rights over other poulterers. Ensuing monarchs continued to support goose farming and it became a French mainstay food. By the eighteenth century goose fat was used for pastries and baking and its liver was being fattened for foie gras. This tradition of fattening the goose for its liver was done by Jewish communities in Hungary primarily

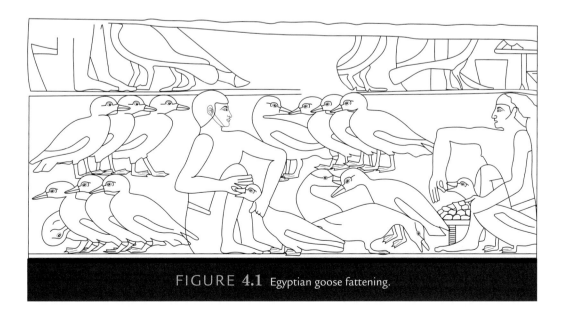

FIGURE **4.1** Egyptian goose fattening.

as a by-product from overfeeding geese to create fat which was used in place of pork lard. Hungary and France continue the tradition of foie gras production today.

Geese were often kept on farms to act as an alarm against predators. Geese are very intelligent and develop a strong bond with their owners and other farm animals. They are very territorial and will attack strangers. They remember people and situations and will alert a farmer of thieves and poachers. Trained, domestic geese are often left to roam the barnyard and do not require confinement. A goose enraged by a predator or stranger will honk loudly, signaling a warning, then lower its head and spread its wings, hiss and attack. Its beak is extremely strong and a goose will attach to a foe and not release easily causing extreme pain. Geese will attack in pairs if there are young around, the male becoming extremely aggressive. They have a keen sense of fear in their opponent and will attack a fleeing predator from behind. Numerous attacks by wild geese are reported each year in the media. House cats, large dogs, and many people have paid the price of getting too close and not heeding the warning geese produce. Often at displays of geese at fairs or poultry shows signs are posted on goose cages not to poke fingers into them for fear of losing one.

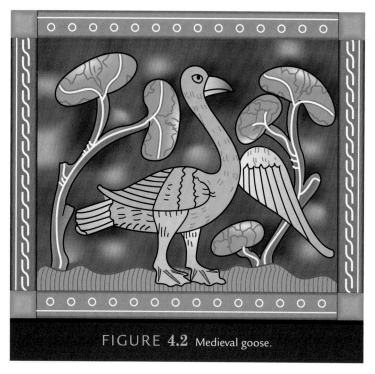

FIGURE **4.2** Medieval goose.

Another task performed by geese for early crop farmers was as a weeder. Geese will readily eat grass and small plants but leave large leafy plants alone. This makes them good for weeding field crops such as cotton, tobacco, potatoes, strawberries, fruit trees, and berry bushes. Geese will eat a large variety of water plants so they will keep irrigation and drainage ditches clear. They also eat bugs and snails that may be harmful to crops. Geese were used in the cotton fields as weeders in the 1950s but the advent of herbicides eliminated their need. Recent experiments and cost evaluations have concluded that geese can feasibly be used in place of herbicides

FIGURE **4.3** Goose flock.

on a large scale. The practice may not be as animal friendly as most think though. When the goose was used for weeding it was often kept from drinking water to force it down rows between plants. A goose is highly effective and sustainable as opposed to chemicals, but it is stressful if done incorrectly. Some organic farmers are now reconsidering the use of geese as weeders. The meat from weeders is extremely tough and not considered marketable.

Geese are naturally flocking birds. As young goslings they will follow their mother along grassy banks along lakes and streams. They will swim in a group and follow each other in flight. Migrating geese are often seen in an aerodynamic V-shape with the leader changing off every so often to maintain speed. All of these instincts make the goose a good candidate for domestication. It will follow the flock into pens and yards without much prompting as long as the geese trust the farmer.

The goose is a hardy animal that will live a long life if allowed. The typical goose can live 40 to 50 years. The oldest goose in the United States reached 82 years old.

MODERN GOOSE PRODUCTION

Modern farming of geese is done in a way that cannot be rushed. The goose is raised slowly according to the calendar. Most processors harvest only during the fall. Most geese are sold frozen but can be found fresh during late fall months.

The goose is raised naturally in that it makes a nest, lays eggs, and guards and incubates them. Eggs are hatched and the goose spends some time indoors to protect it while very young. Then geese are placed outside in large grazing pens. They graze similar to cattle and need quality greens such as alfalfa for food. They cannot be fed entirely grain. Most are fed pasture throughout the summer and are only fattened on grain in the fall. Geese are hardy and do not require a pre-emptive antibiotic to thrive. Geese are raised free range and have more than eight square feet per animal in their outdoor pens.

BY-PRODUCT OF GEESE

Similar to its duck cousin, the goose is grown as a dual-purpose animal. It is used for meat but also possesses a valuable down which is considered the highest quality. Geese have been raised strictly for their down which can be harvested without slaughtering the animal. The down on a goose is used in pillows, coats, blankets, and many other items. The down of geese can be measured and graded to establish its "fill power" or fluffiness. Certain feathers have a higher fill power and therefore warrant a higher price. Sorting and processing feathers has become a mechanized industry whereas years ago it was done entirely by hand.

A point of controversy over goose down feathers is the brand naming of "Siberian Goose" down products. Pillows containing the so-called Siberian Goose down sell for over $200 but in reality the down is simply a refined feather from any commercial goose and the true Siberian Goose is protected. More than likely the down sold as Siberian is from Hungary or other European manufacturers. The use of the name Siberian Goose down appears to be purely for marketing purposes.

Eggs are another by-product and are sold for their decorative value. Goose eggs are very hard and are fairly durable. They are typically eight to ten times larger than a chicken egg.

BREEDS OF GEESE

All geese are in the *Anatidae* family. There are many genuses of geese and breeds that have been created by crossbreeding and modern farming techniques. Wild geese such as the Canadian goose, which are in the *Branta* genus, were almost eliminated by overhunting but now populations have rebounded due to protections. Most domestic breeds used for meat production are related to the Greylag goose, genus *Anser*, which is found wild in Europe, the Middle East, and eastern Asia. This "grey" goose was domesticated and selections were made to create larger geese that produced better meat yields. Another wild breed in the *Anser* genus is the Swan goose which is found in Central Asia. This breed was also domesticated to form important breeds that are commercially available in China and Russia today. The wild Swan goose is now considered endangered due to overhunting. This publication will focus primarily on meat breeds excluding the wild breeds that are not commercially available.

The largest producer of geese for meat production in the United States, Schiltz Foods has its own patented breed. Specific breeds are developed for demeanor, maximum gain, yield, and feathers.

A male goose is called a *gander* and the female is the actual goose. Male and female differ in size and sometimes in coloration. The male tends to be a few pounds larger.

AFRICAN GOOSE

This goose is related to the wild Swan goose and is large with good meat flavor. It averages around 15 to 20 pounds live and has been crossbred with others for commercial use.

African geese can be found worldwide as a commercial or hobby farmed breed.

CHINESE GOOSE

Related to the Swan goose and is found as either White or Brown Chinese. It is a smaller cousin of the African goose and is not typically raised for meat in the United States. It is raised for egg production and as an exhibition bird.

EMBDEN GOOSE

The most typical meat breed, the Embden has a good yield and grows rapidly. A typical weight is anywhere from 16 to 25 pounds live and its color is pure white. It originates from German and English breeds and has become the dominant breed for meat production in Europe and the United States. It is also crossbred with the large Toulouse goose to create specialty breeds used entirely for meat and eggs.

TOULOUSE GOOSE

Related to the wild Greylag goose, the Toulouse originated in southern France and is named for the city of Toulouse. This goose was used for foie gras production and its large size and rapid gain made it a good meat producer as well. It can be very aggressive therefore it is used primarily for mixed breeding with other species or as a niche market bird.

FRANKONIAN GOOSE

The Frankonian goose is an old breed from Bavaria, Germany. It is small and therefore not considered commercially viable for meat production although they are prolific breeders.

HEIRLOOM VARIETIES

Some breeds are not as significant as meat breeds and are typically raised as show birds. Some can be considered heirloom breeds and may be in danger of extinction due to the fact that they are not commercially as viable. Below are some breeds found worldwide that are not typically raised for meat. Geese such as the Cotton Patch were raised to weed fields and can deal with very hot climates. Because we now use herbicides, these geese are no longer popular.

- American Buff
- Bavent or Normandy
- Brecon Buff
- Cotton Patch
- Leinegeese
- Lippegänse
- Norwegian Spotted or White
- Pilgrim
- Pomeranian
- Roman
- Scania
- Sebastopol
- Shetland
- Steinbacher

CLASSES OF GEESE

The classes of geese are very basic, either *young* or *mature*. Young geese are raised similar to ducks and growers get them to market weight as soon as possible. An older or mature goose can be very tough and have large sinews and connective tissues. Most mature geese are exported.

GOOSE CLASSIFICATIONS			
NAME	DESCRIPTION	SIZE	AGE
Young goose	Typical commercial goose	8–16 lbs	10–16 weeks (can be slightly older for larger birds)
Mature goose	Larger goose, used for breeding, tougher	14–20 lbs	25 weeks or older

PURCHASING SPECIFICATIONS

Goose is typically sold frozen. They are flash frozen giving the skin a whitish color. A fresh goose will have a somewhat tan color. Once thawed a goose will last about three or four days.

GOOSE PURCHASING AND USAGE SPECIFICATIONS				
ITEM AND NAMP NUMBER	DESCRIPTION/ FABRICATION	SUGGESTED COOKING METHOD/ APPLICATION	AVERAGE SUGGESTED WEIGHT LBS.	TYPICAL PACKAGE SPECS
P4000 Young goose P4001 w/giblets P4100 Mature Goose	Whole bird, usually sold w/giblets	Dry cook, roast whole or half, cut for parts	8–16 lbs	4 per case individually packaged, typically frozen
Young goose, Confucius style	Whole bird, w/head and feet attached	Cooked whole for Asian style	10–17 lbs	4 per case
P4012 Goose breast, bone-in	Whole unsplit breast	Roasted whole, carved	5–8 lbs	8 per case
P4013 Goose breast, boneless, skin-on or skin-off	Whole unsplit breast	Grill, broil, roast	1.5–3.5 lbs each pack	12 packs per case
Smoked goose breast	Whole or half	Ready to eat, slice like ham, served warm or cold	½ lb each	12 per case
P4030 Goose leg quarters	Includes thigh and drumstick	Roast, confit, slow cook, braise, stew	¾–1 lb each leg	4 legs per pack, 8 packs per case
P4036 Goose wing	Consists of two sections excluding the tip	Slow cook, slow roast	¼ lb each	4 lb packs, 10 packs per case

(Continues)

The goose is larger than duck or chicken implying the parts will create multiple portions. A whole goose breast will serve four to six people depending on its size. Much of the goose is covered with fat which can make portioning deceptive.

(*Continued*)

ITEM AND NAMP NUMBER	DESCRIPTION/ FABRICATION	SUGGESTED COOKING METHOD/ APPLICATION	AVERAGE SUGGESTED WEIGHT LBS.	TYPICAL PACKAGE SPECS
P4043 Giblets	Includes neck, heart, gizzard, liver	Sauces, stock	Varies	Varies
Goose chitterlings	Defatted, split, and cleaned	Slow cook, Asian recipes	Varies	5-lb packs
Goose livers	Dark purplish-red color, sold in bulk, may require some cleaning and deveining	Pate, terrines, sausages, sauces	Sold in bulk	2-lb, 5-lb, 10-lb packs
Goose liver, naturally fattened	Light brownish, purple, grade 1 or 2	Used as natural foie gras, pate, terrines, seared	½ lb each	1 per bag
Goose liver, foie gras	Light beige, firm, fatty	Pate, terrines, seared	1–2 lbs each	1 per bag
Goose feet	Reddish, large	Steamed or simmered, Asian recipes for soup	1–2 oz each	5 lbs per bag

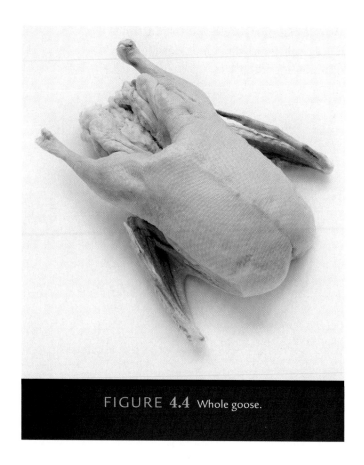

FIGURE 4.4 Whole goose.

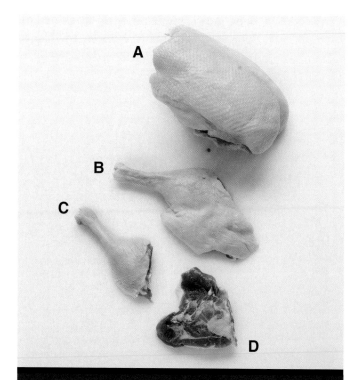

FIGURE 4.5 A: Bone-in goose breast; B: Goose leg; C: Goose drumstick; D: Goose thigh, bone-in.

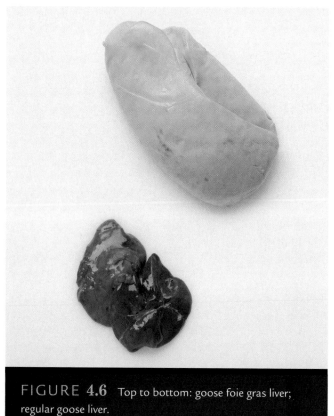

FIGURE 4.6 Top to bottom: goose foie gras liver; regular goose liver.

FIGURE 4.7 Top to bottom: raw goose fat; rendered goose fat.

FIGURE **4.8** Smoked goose breast.

GOOSE FABRICATION

The goose is typically larger than the duck or chicken but the bone structure is similar. The difficulty in fabrication lies in the fact that the goose is very fatty making the definition of where to cut a little challenging. Geese are typically sold with the offals in a bag on the inside. Be sure to remove them.

TRUSSING A GOOSE FOR STUFFING

Like the duck, the goose has squat legs and a large breast. It may require trussing to cook evenly. A more typical reason would be to truss the goose for stuffing. One technique would be to use the skin flaps at the back of the bird by sewing the opening closed using a trussing needle.

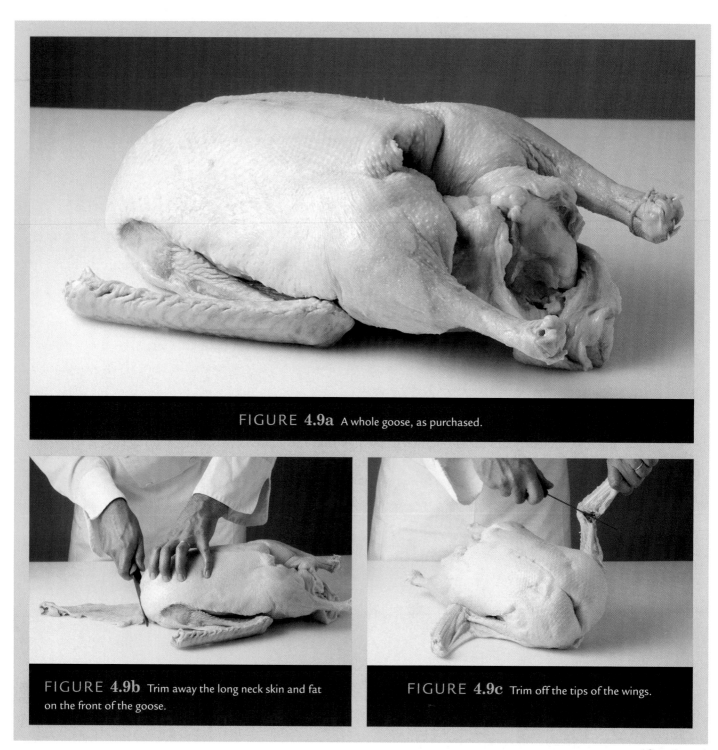

FIGURE **4.9a** A whole goose, as purchased.

FIGURE **4.9b** Trim away the long neck skin and fat on the front of the goose.

FIGURE **4.9c** Trim off the tips of the wings.

(Continues)

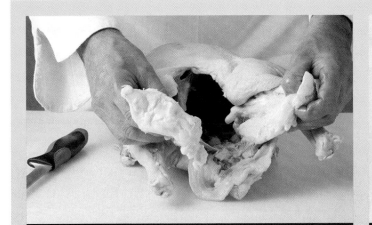

FIGURE **4.9d** Remove the heavy fat along the back, leaving most of the skin. Reserve the fat for rendering.

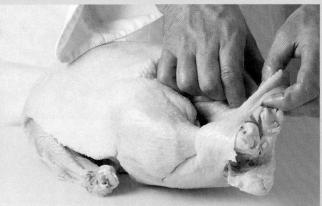

FIGURE **4.9e** The goose can be trussed by poking holes in the back skin and tucking in the legs.

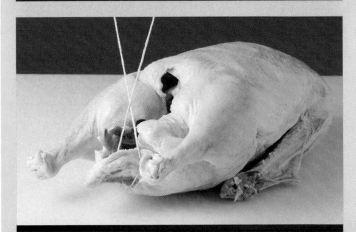

FIGURE **4.9f** Alternatively, the goose can be trussed using butcher's string. Place the string under the rear end, drawing it upward to create an "X."

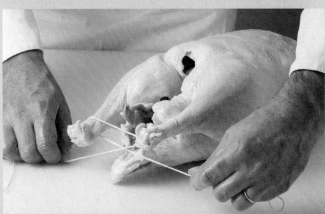

FIGURE **4.9g** Encircle the legs and cross the string again to draw the legs together and close off the back end.

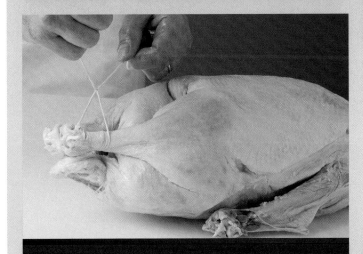

FIGURE **4.9h** Tie the string to complete the truss.

FIGURE **4.9i** A properly trussed goose ready for roasting.

DISJOINTING A GOOSE

Dividing a goose into sections is very similar to duck. Both are heavily fatted and divisions are not easily seen. Trimming some of the fat before starting may help in determining where to cut.

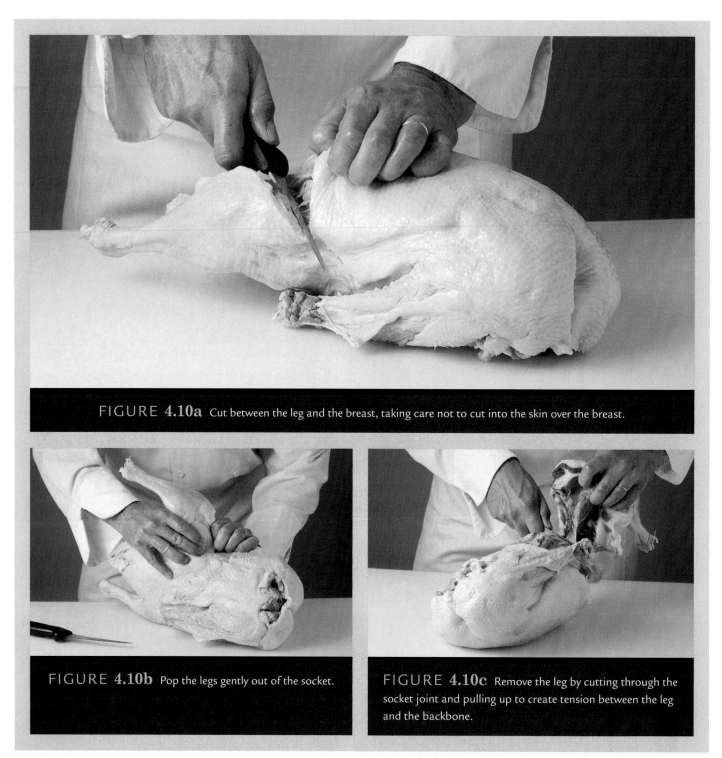

FIGURE **4.10a** Cut between the leg and the breast, taking care not to cut into the skin over the breast.

FIGURE **4.10b** Pop the legs gently out of the socket.

FIGURE **4.10c** Remove the leg by cutting through the socket joint and pulling up to create tension between the leg and the backbone.

(Continues)

(Continued)

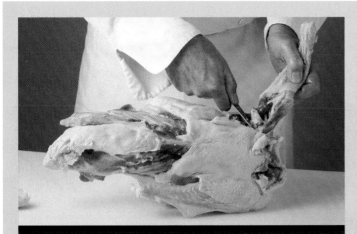

FIGURE **4.10d** Cut the wing off the back, careful not to cut into the breast meat.

FIGURE **4.10e** Bone out the breast by running the knife along the back and scraping the rib cage toward the keel bone.

FIGURE **4.10f** The components of the goose, divided.

TYING THE GOOSE BREAST FOR ROASTING

Tying a goose breast for roasting ensures an even cooking and quality plate presentation. It also can be helpful when smoking the product like ham. The technique used here is the continuous knot.

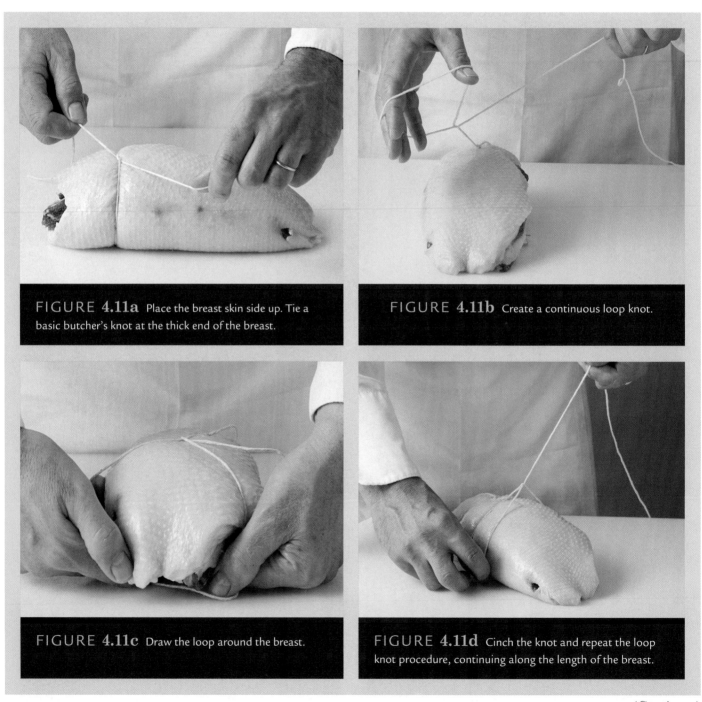

FIGURE **4.11a** Place the breast skin side up. Tie a basic butcher's knot at the thick end of the breast.

FIGURE **4.11b** Create a continuous loop knot.

FIGURE **4.11c** Draw the loop around the breast.

FIGURE **4.11d** Cinch the knot and repeat the loop knot procedure, continuing along the length of the breast.

(Continues)

BONING A GOOSE FOR PATE OR SAUSAGE

Some styles of pate or sausage require the goose to be boned and roasted partially for flavor. Boning the entire goose can be useful for stuffing and roasting as well.

(Continued)

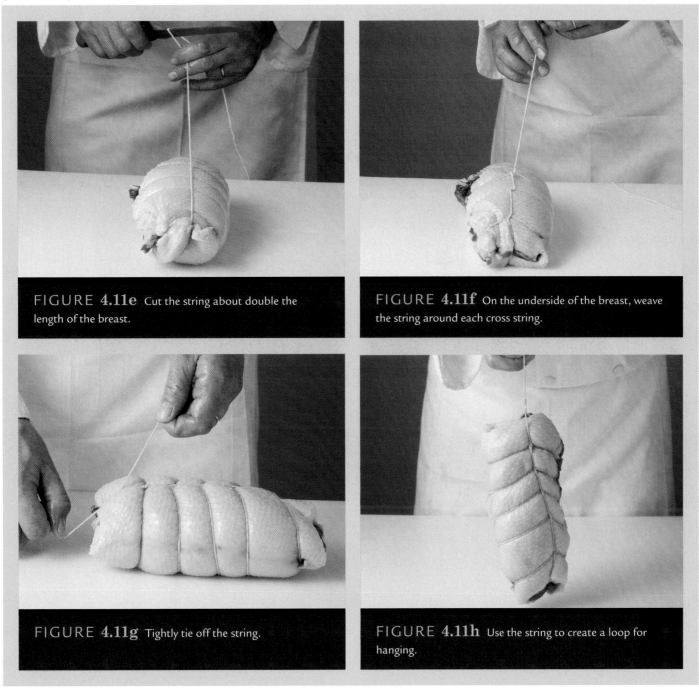

FIGURE **4.11e** Cut the string about double the length of the breast.

FIGURE **4.11f** On the underside of the breast, weave the string around each cross string.

FIGURE **4.11g** Tightly tie off the string.

FIGURE **4.11h** Use the string to create a loop for hanging.

BRINING GOOSE BREAST FOR SMOKING

Preparing the goose breast for smoking requires a simple brine mixture. The breast is soaked in the brine for about two days to ensure a proper cure.

FIGURE **4.12** Ingredients used for brining: boneless goose breast, spice, sugar, and salt. Mix ingredients, being sure to dissolve all the salt. Submerge the breast in the brine, and after brining, tie as for roasting.

5

TURKEY

When Dickens' character Scrooge shouts down to a boy in the street ". . . Do you know whether they've sold the prize turkey was hanging up there . . .?" And the boy replies "What, the one that's big as me?" you get an idea of how large a turkey can be. That question presented by Scrooge on Christmas morning was set in 1843 in England. By that point the turkey had long been established as a domesticated poultry item.

HISTORY OF THE TURKEY

The turkey, like the chicken, is primarily a ground bird. It is not migratory and forages through leaves for acorns, grubs, insects, and even small lizards or snakes. Wild turkeys will forage in groups and the forest floor will look as though someone has raked the area after they pass by. The wild turkey is elusive and has a keen sense of smell and hearing. It is not sluggish like its domestic cousin. A wild turkey can fly up to 55 MPH for short distances and can run up to 30 MPH. Unfortunately, it also has a weakness for grains which enabled hunters to bait and trap or shoot it. The call of the male during mating season, the familiar "gobble gobble," is often recreated by hunters to lure the unsuspecting bird.

The turkey is native to the Americas. Archeologists suggest the wild turkey had been domesticated by the Mayan Indians around 100 B.C. to 100 A.D. Many of the eastern tribes of North America had harvested wild turkey long before Europeans arrived. By the time the Spanish arrived in Mexico, the Aztecs had domesticated turkeys and kept them in pens. They were used for meat and their ornamental feathers adorned ceremonial costumes.

The Pueblo Indians of the Southwest also showed signs of early turkey domestication. Early Navajo people struggled with turkeys raiding crops and eventually decided to fence in the fields with the bird still intact creating quasi-domestication. The wild turkey's range extends from Mexico to as far north as Maine and southern Canada. There are two separate breeds of turkey found in the Americas with many sub-breeds creating variations in size and color. The first, *Meleagris gallopavo,* is the breed found in North American eastern woodlands originating from northern Mexico. There are six accepted wild sub-breeds of this bird, each varying somewhat in size and color. The other breed category is the *Meleagris ocellata* found further south on the Yucatan in Mexico into Guatemala.

Early Spanish explorers brought the turkey back to Europe. The famous explorer Cortez returned with the new poultry from what was then thought to be part of Asia. At the time many believed it was a relative to the Asian Indian Peacock or the Guinea Fowl which was also known as turkey at the time. In Europe the turkey rapidly gained popularity as a poultry item due to its good yield compared to chicken, duck, or goose. It was also similar to those birds in that it was naturally flocking and could be penned and bred easily. By 1550 the turkey was already found in England. William Strickland, a lieutenant and navigator with the explorer Sebastian Cabot, returned with the turkey from the New World. Later Strickland became a member of Parliament and granted arms or a royal family crest that included the image of the tom turkey.

The farming of turkeys grew so rapidly that by the early 1600s turkey was grown in many parts of Europe and England. By the time the Pilgrims landed at Plymouth Rock, turkey was an established European fare and in fact the Pilgrims brought turkey with them on the Mayflower. The newcomers were surprised to find wild turkeys already living near their settlement. The turkeys raised in Europe were already changing from the wild birds found in the Americas. Birds were selected for breast size and over time the turkey developed into the large white meat bird we know today.

In 1776 Benjamin Franklin was on a committee formed by the Continental Congress to create an official seal for the new nation. John Adams suggested the regal eagle to represent but Franklin suggested the turkey. His reasoning read as follows: "*I am on this account not displeased that the Figure is not known as a Bald Eagle, but looks more like a Turkey. For the Truth the Turkey is in Comparison a much more respectable Bird, and withal a true original Native of America . . . He is besides, though a little vain & silly, a Bird of Courage, and would not hesitate to attack a Grenadier of the British Guards who should presume to invade his Farm Yard with a Red Coat on.*" Franklin's bid was voted down but the turkey remains an icon for American culture.

By the mid-1800s the turkey had been hunted to the point where it inhabited only half of its original range. It was considered an inexpensive meat suitable for the poorer peoples. By 1900 only 30,000 wild turkeys were thought to be left in the wilds.

In the late 1700s and early 1800s domestic, farm-raised turkeys were often brought to market like cattle, driven in bunches. These "turkey trots" brought birds from rural farms into large cities like Boston, Philadelphia, or New York. Turkey drovers would bring birds to market twice a year, in spring and fall. Pens were set up near taverns so drovers could sleep and their birds kept safe for a small fee. With the invention of the steamboat and railroad, turkey driving was phased out by the mid-1800s.

MODERN TURKEY PRODUCTION

The domestic turkey poultry industry grew steadily throughout the nineteenth and twentieth centuries but was consistently focused on seasonal sales. Turkey sold primarily for the Thanksgiving and Christmas holidays. Many children in the United States grow up recognizing the turkey as a symbol of the Thanksgiving holiday. The turkey was bred to an ever larger size, especially for its breast meat. In the 1950s breeds were developed that made such a large breast that the bird could no longer fly or even breed without artificial insemination.

In the 1980s and 1990s turkey marketing became more aggressive. Turkey was sold as another red meat alternative and many products were developed to increase its marketability beyond its traditional holiday acceptance. By 2007 turkey developed a firm market share and was no longer a seasonal food. Production reached 7.87 billion pounds with the export market growing and each person consuming over 17 pounds annually in the United States. Turkey production and popularity continues to rise worldwide. Turkey consumption per capita is highest in Israel at about 35 pounds per person annually followed by Slovakia, the United States, France, and Hungary.

TURKEY FEED

In the wild turkeys are omnivores. They can graze on certain vegetation but prefer grains and nuts. They will forage for insects, grubs, and worms. If allowed to forage their meat has a distinctly more pronounced flavor.

Modern turkey farms feed a mixture similar to chicken feed containing corn, soy, and added vitamins to ensure health. As with other birds, there are no steroids approved for turkey growth promotion but turkeys may be fed a pre-emptive antibiotic. Turkeys take longer to mature than chickens and are harvested typically from 10 to 18 weeks but larger birds go beyond 28 weeks.

FIGURE **5.1** Turkeys grazing in the wild.

FIGURE **5.2** Turkeys grazing on modern farm.

BREEDS OF TURKEY

AUBURN

A heritage breed that was once considered valuable due to its ability to withstand the rigors of the old turkey drives to market. The Auburn is related to the Bronze turkey. They are no longer raised commercially but found as a heritage breed.

BELTSVILLE SMALL WHITE

A breed introduced into the United States in the 1940s and 1950s. It was a hybrid bird developed by the University of Wisconsin as a meat bird. It was small but possessed a larger, wider breast. Very few purebred birds are left but its influence is found in other breeds today.

FIGURE **5.3** Auburn.

FIGURE **5.4** Beltsville Small White.

BLACK TURKEY

The Black Turkey was developed in Europe after the first wild breeds were brought back from the New World. Found earliest in Spain and then soon after in England, the Black was the most popular turkey raised in Europe. The Spanish Black and the Black Norfolk are their official breed names. Due to the introduction of oversized hybridized white breeds, the Blacks are now a rare heritage breed.

FIGURE **5.5** Black Turkey.

FIGURE **5.6** Bourbon Red.

FIGURE **5.7** Broad Breasted Bronze.

BOURBON RED

The Bourbon Red is a heritage breed originally brought to Kentucky and southern Ohio by settlers. Also known as the Kentucky Red. Quality breed often raised today as a niche market item. It is typically found as a foraged bird where it is allowed freedom to scratch and find natural feedstuffs creating a unique flavor.

BROAD BREASTED BRONZE

Bred specifically for size and gain from its original breed the standard Bronze. The original was developed in Rhode Island in the 1830s. These birds are rapid growers and can reach 25 pounds in 28 weeks. They are found on commercial farms and are still very popular. They cannot reproduce on their own and must be artificially inseminated.

FIGURE **5.8** Buff or New Jersey Buff.

FIGURE **5.9** Narrangansett.

BUFF OR NEW JERSEY BUFF

It is a heritage breed dating back to the 1880s. The Buff was originally bred due to the fact that its feathers pluck out clean. Other bird's pinfeathers would be visible after plucking. This made it a more marketable bird. Today it is seen as a heritage breed and is raised as a popular niche market item.

NARRAGANSETT

A popular heritage breed originating in Rhode Island from the crossing of then-established European breeds (most likely Blacks) with the local wild turkey. It has an excellent meat quality and is considered the finest tasting of all turkeys. Today many are raised as forage birds which may contribute to its flavor.

OCELLATED

Original wild breed *Meleagris ocellata* from Central America. Not related to the North American wild turkey breeds. It is small and peacock-like and not commercially raised on a large scale.

FIGURE **5.10** Ocellated.

FIGURE **5.11** Royal Palm.

FIGURE **5.12** Porcelain.

ROYAL PALM

The Royal Palm is the only bird not raised specifically as a meat item. Its unique feathers were harvested for decoration and ornamental reasons. They are not popular today but can still be found as a hobby bird.

PORCELAIN

This bird was developed in France and is considered a very high-quality eating bird. Porcelain is not typically found in United States.

WHITE HOLLAND OR BROAD BREASTED WHITE

The most popular commercial breed used for meat today. They are all white, very fast growing, large breasted with an ideal skin that doesn't show pinfeathers. Most modern commercial breeds are developed from the original White Holland. As with the Broad Breasted Bronze, the White cannot breed naturally and requires human intervention.

NORTH AMERICAN WILD TURKEY

A number of wild breeds of *Meleagris gallopavo* are found in the woodlands throughout the United States. There are some crossbred birds that resemble pure wild breeds available as a niche market item. The closest domestic bird relative is the Narragansett. Wild turkeys are protected and have a specific season for hunting. True wild birds cannot be sold in any foodservice establishment.

FIGURE **5.13** White Holland or Broad Breasted White.

FIGURE **5.14** North American Wild Turkey.

CLASSES OF TURKEY

Turkey is divided into two separate basic categories, by age and sex. The age will determine the basic size of the bird. The term *young* refers to a turkey that is less than 24 weeks old. Most turkeys sold for foodservice will be within this age group. The sex can be part of the marketability. The females or *hens* are smaller with the males or *toms* larger. There can be some overlap and the mid range of turkey may be either sex. Mature birds can be sold as oversized toms but these are not always available. The drumsticks will develop strong bone sinews that make them almost inedible.

CLASSIFICATION OF TURKEY			
NAME	DESCRIPTION	SIZE	AGE
Young	Full breasted, plump	8–24 lbs Hen 8–16 lbs Tom 16–24 lbs	10–24 weeks
Mature	Very large, ossification in drumstick	26–36 lbs	over 24 weeks

PURCHASING SPECIFICS

RAW PRODUCT

Turkey is sold typically around holiday seasons as a whole bird. It is sold in increments of two pounds. Turkey is also sold as many parts and configurations and as many processed items. By processing the turkey it can be marketed as numerous products that are sold year-round. Cold cuts, sausages, turkey bacon, and ham are all available today.

Raw turkey is sold fresh or frozen. Fresh turkey can be slightly frozen, chilled rapidly to 25°F/−4°C and but are not frozen all the way through. Frozen turkey is brought down below 0°F/−18°C very quickly in large blast freezers. This procedure ensures small ice crystals and minimizes damage caused by freezing. There is a slight quality difference between fresh and frozen. Fresh is considered a higher quality but if the frozen is thawed correctly, slowly at 35° to 40°F/2°C to 4°C, there is little difference between the two.

There are a variety of enhanced turkey products available. Enhanced products are pumped with a moisture-increasing agent or agents. The two basic categories of enhanced products are "basted" and "marinated." Basted products are primarily moisture-enhanced without flavorings added. Marinated products have a variety of flavorings added as well as moisture. Salt and water are typically part of the mix but

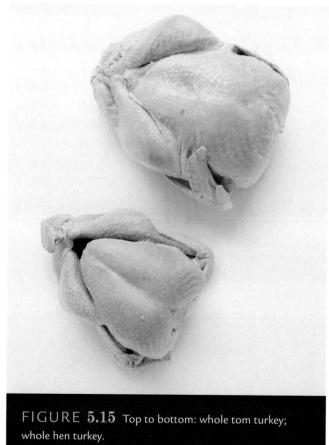

FIGURE **5.15** Top to bottom: whole tom turkey; whole hen turkey.

many other ingredients are often added. Natural ingredients such as turkey stock or broth may be added to keep the term "natural" on the label. Sodium phosphate is often added to force moisture retention. Other ingredients include sugar, hydrolyzed vegetable protein, isolated soy proteins, sodium lactate, lactic acid, artificial and natural flavorings, a large variety of spices, and smoke or smoke flavorings. Enhanced products will be moister and more tender but the buyer will be paying for added water weight. Typically enhanced products will add an extra 10 to 15 percent water. Some products are enhanced with up to 25 percent added product. Be sure to ask the purveyor if the product is enhanced and by how much.

Commercially raised turkey, like chicken, has a high incidence of bacterial contamination especially Salmonella. Be sure turkey is fresh or used within a day of thawing. Listeria is another contaminant that is associated with cooked and processed meat items. Again use caution and be sure to use only fresh products.

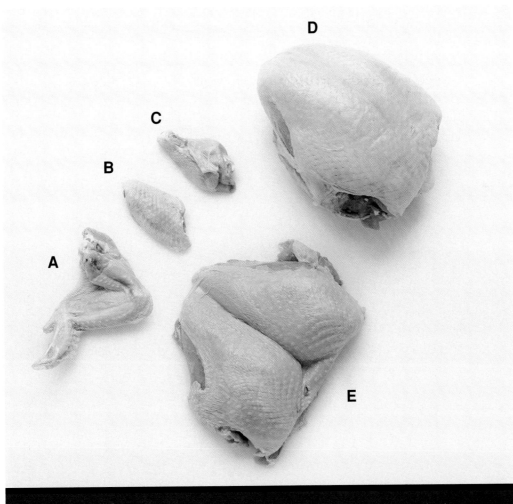

FIGURE **5.16** A: Whole turkey wing; B: Wing flap; C: Drumette; D: Whole turkey breast, bone-in with rib meat; E: Boneless turkey breast.

TURKEY PURCHASING AND USAGE SPECIFICATIONS				
ITEM AND NAMP NUMBER	DESCRIPTION/FABRICATION	SUGGESTED COOKING METHOD/ APPLICATION	AVG. SUGGESTED WEIGHT LBS	TYPICAL PACKAGE SPECS
Whole young turkey, sold fresh or frozen NAMP P2001	Whole bird, usually sold with giblets. Sold with or without enhancement ingredients	Roast whole	8–24 lbs	Individually packaged, sold 2 or 4 per box
Young hen turkey	Whole bird, sold with giblets	Roast whole	8–16 lbs	Individually packaged, sold 2 or 4 per box
Young tom turkey	Whole bird, sold with giblets	Roast whole	16–24 lbs	Individually packaged, sold 2 per box
Mature tom turkey	Whole bird, sold with giblets	Roast whole	24–35 lbs	Individually packaged, sold 1 per box
Young turkey, front half NAMP P2003	Full breast with back and wings attached, also known as "Hotel Breast"	Roast whole	6–20 lbs	Individually packaged, 4 or 6 per bag
Whole turkey breast with ribs NAMP P2012, P2014	Full breast, unsplit or split	Roast whole, bone out and carve	4–18 lbs	Individually packaged, sold 4 or 6 per box
Boneless turkey breast	Full breast with skin-on or skin-off, with or without extra rib meat, whole or half	Roast whole, slicing meat, cutlets	2–8 lbs	Varies, 4–6 per case

(Continues)

ITEM AND NAMP NUMBER	DESCRIPTION/FABRICATION	SUGGESTED COOKING METHOD/ APPLICATION	AVG. SUGGESTED WEIGHT LBS	TYPICAL PACKAGE SPECS
Breast cutlets, slices, tenderloins, cubes	A variety of precut portions, cut from the breast	Sauté, grill, breaded	Varies	Varies
Young turkey leg NAMP 2031 or 2030	Full leg sold with or without back bone attached	Roast, stew, soup	2–6 lbs per pair	Varies, can be sold in small packs or large bulk
Young turkey drumstick NAMP 2035	Bottom half of leg cut a stifle joint	Roast, stew, osso buco	1–2 lbs each	Varies, sold in small packs or bulk
Young turkey thigh NAMP 2033	Thigh sold bone-in or boneless	Roast, stew, grind for forcemeats, turkey "ham"	1–2 lbs each	Varies, sold in small packs or bulk
Ground turkey	Sold as bulk, patties, sausage, seasoned with other ingredients added	Meat sauces, sausages, meat balls, forcemeats	Bulk	Varied packaging bulk
Young turkey wings NAMP 2036	Sold as whole wing or sectioned into flap or drumette	Roast whole, BBQ, hot wings, braise, stew	¼ to ½ lb each	Varies, sold in small packs or bulk
Turkey giblets	Gizzard, liver, heart	Sauces, gravy	Bulk, varies	Bulk, varies
Turkey neck	Typically frozen, 5–6 inches long	Sauces, gravy, stock	Bulk, varies	Bulk, varies, 20-lb box

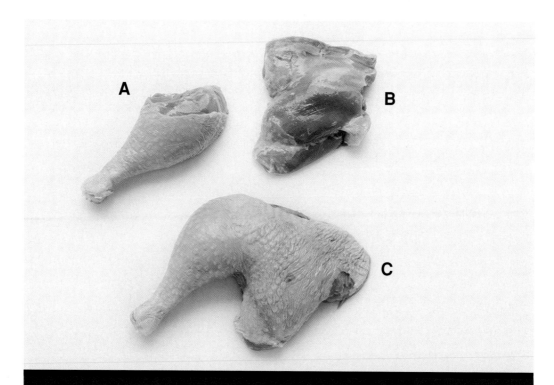

FIGURE **5.17** A: Drumstick; B: Boneless, skinless thigh; C: Whole turkey leg.

FIGURE **5.18** Ground turkey.

PROCESSED COOKED TURKEY PRODUCTS

There are numerous processed turkey products that vary greatly in flavor and quality. The breast can be sold as a whole muscle precooked, seasoned, and ready to eat. There are also many turkey products made by tumbling the meat in a vacuum to loosen proteins enabling the meat to be seasoned, formed, shaped, and then cooked. Many of these items are used as cold cuts for slicing. Turkey breast, turkey roll, and chopped and formed turkey are slicing items that vary greatly in quality.

There are many ground or emulsified turkey products such as hot dogs, bologna, salami, and seasoned patties.

Turkey is often found cured and smoked. The entire bird, breast, legs, drumsticks, thighs, and wings are all found brined and smoked to give the meat a ham-like flavor. Turkey bacon has a flavor similar to pork and can be used as a substitute.

Lower-quality turkey products are made from mechanically separated meat which is extracted from bones and then formed. These can be made from light or dark meat or a combination of both.

TURKEY FABRICATION
TRUSSING A STUFFED TURKEY

For holidays, many turkeys are stuffed with bread stuffing. Keeping stuffing intact may require the rear cavity to be sewn shut.

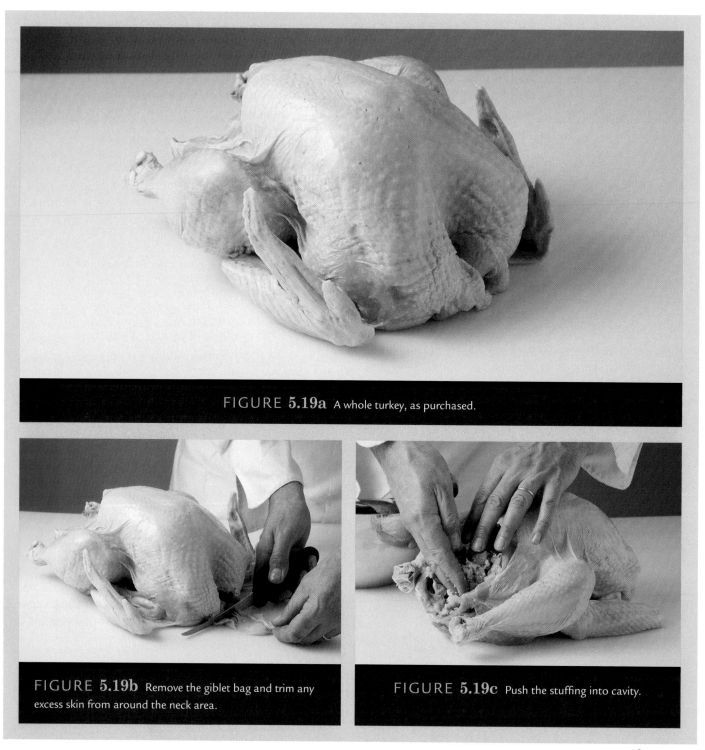

FIGURE **5.19a** A whole turkey, as purchased.

FIGURE **5.19b** Remove the giblet bag and trim any excess skin from around the neck area.

FIGURE **5.19c** Push the stuffing into cavity.

(Continues)

(Continued)

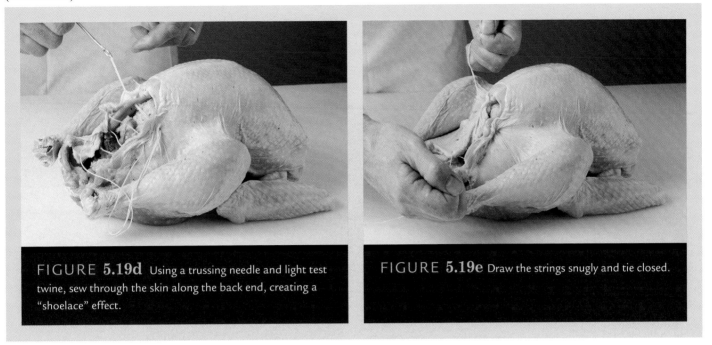

FIGURE **5.19d** Using a trussing needle and light test twine, sew through the skin along the back end, creating a "shoelace" effect.

FIGURE **5.19e** Draw the strings snugly and tie closed.

BASIC TRUSS

The turkey may be trussed for roasting, rotisserie cooking, or deep fat frying.

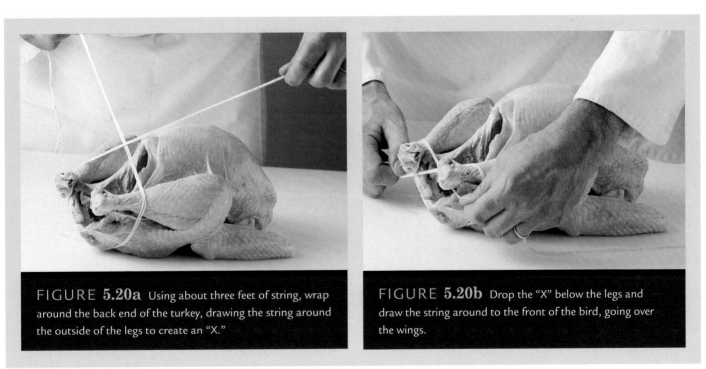

FIGURE **5.20a** Using about three feet of string, wrap around the back end of the turkey, drawing the string around the outside of the legs to create an "X."

FIGURE **5.20b** Drop the "X" below the legs and draw the string around to the front of the bird, going over the wings.

(Continues)

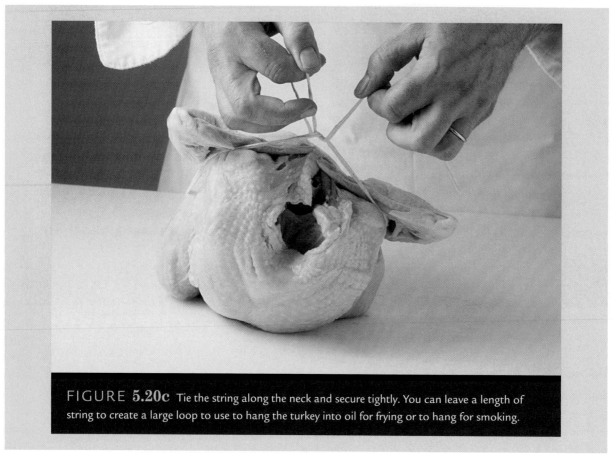

FIGURE **5.20c** Tie the string along the neck and secure tightly. You can leave a length of string to create a large loop to use to hang the turkey into oil for frying or to hang for smoking.

REMOVING LEGS

Buying a whole turkey and cutting into parts enables each to be utilized separately. The legs can be used for braising, sausage, soups, or stock while the breast can be carved for roast turkey or sandwiches.

BONING A TURKEY BREAST, WHOLE

The breast can be boned whole, tied, and roasted to be used as a carving item.

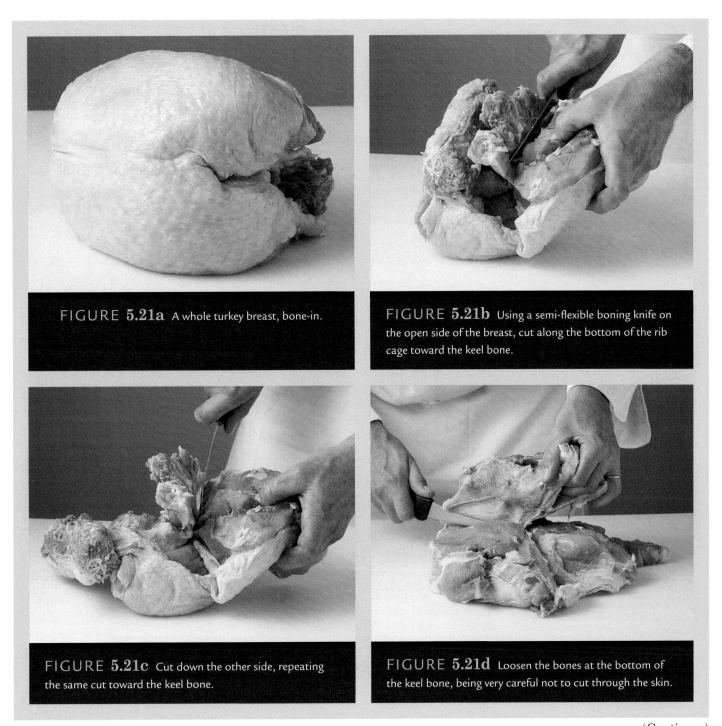

FIGURE **5.21a** A whole turkey breast, bone-in.

FIGURE **5.21b** Using a semi-flexible boning knife on the open side of the breast, cut along the bottom of the rib cage toward the keel bone.

FIGURE **5.21c** Cut down the other side, repeating the same cut toward the keel bone.

FIGURE **5.21d** Loosen the bones at the bottom of the keel bone, being very careful not to cut through the skin.

(Continues)

FIGURE **5.21e** Breasts can be tied whole or split. To split, simply cut directly between the lobes, being sure that the skin is cut evenly along with the breast meat.

FIGURE **5.21f** Tie the breast using a continuous knot starting on the thicker end.

FIGURE **5.21g** A finished, tied breast.

CUTTING TURKEY CUTLETS

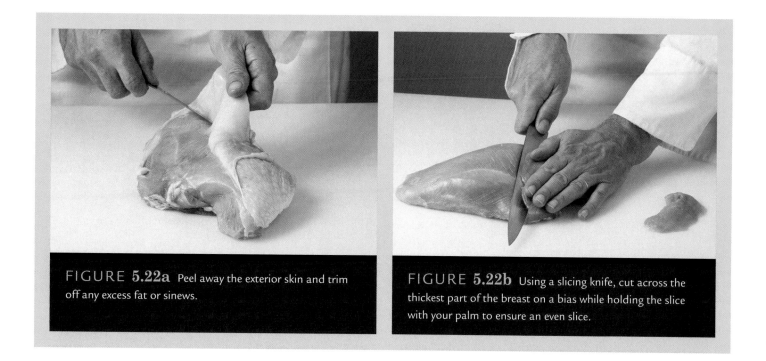

FIGURE **5.22a** Peel away the exterior skin and trim off any excess fat or sinews.

FIGURE **5.22b** Using a slicing knife, cut across the thickest part of the breast on a bias while holding the slice with your palm to ensure an even slice.

BONING A WHOLE EASY-CARVE TURKEY FOR ROASTING

The entire turkey can be boned to produce a roast that has both light and dark meat.

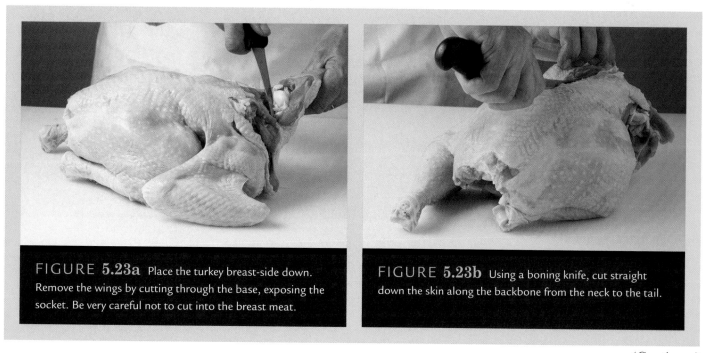

FIGURE **5.23a** Place the turkey breast-side down. Remove the wings by cutting through the base, exposing the socket. Be very careful not to cut into the breast meat.

FIGURE **5.23b** Using a boning knife, cut straight down the skin along the backbone from the neck to the tail.

(Continues)

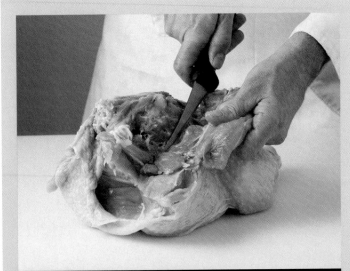

FIGURE **5.23c** Open the meat along the rib cage and through the leg socket joint.

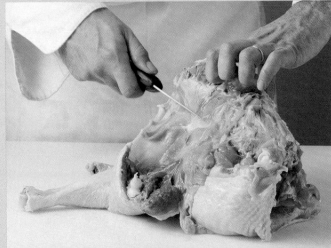

FIGURE **5.23d** Cut downward, staying close to the rib bones and finishing at the base of the keel bone and making sure not to cut through any skin.

FIGURE **5.23e** Repeat the previous cuts on the other side of the bird and free the bone structure from the main carcass—but the legs will still be intact.

FIGURE **5.23f** Remove the drumsticks from the thigh by cutting directly through the joint.

(Continues)

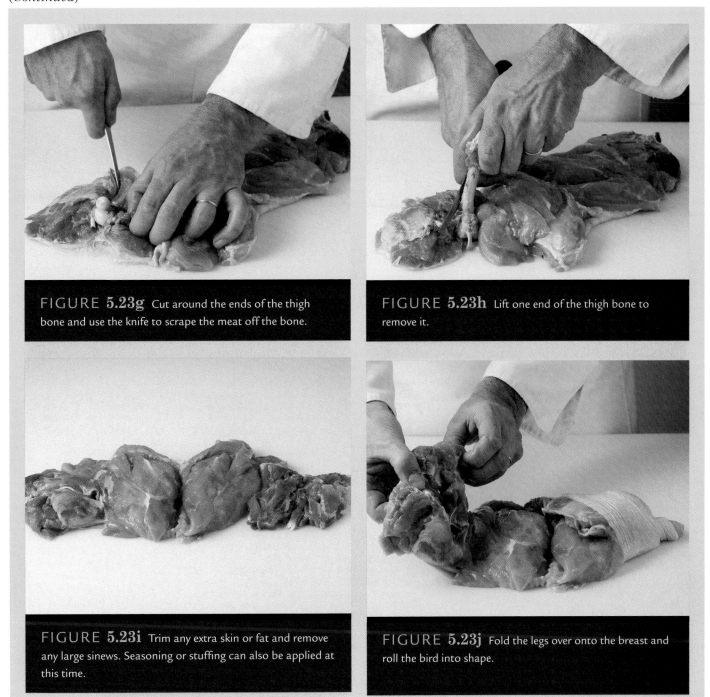

FIGURE **5.23g** Cut around the ends of the thigh bone and use the knife to scrape the meat off the bone.

FIGURE **5.23h** Lift one end of the thigh bone to remove it.

FIGURE **5.23i** Trim any extra skin or fat and remove any large sinews. Seasoning or stuffing can also be applied at this time.

FIGURE **5.23j** Fold the legs over onto the breast and roll the bird into shape.

(Continues)

FIGURE **5.23k** Using a trussing needle, sew the ends of the roast closed, securing the legs through the skin.

FIGURE **5.23l** Tie the roast, being sure to apply a securing string the entire length of the roast. Knots should be snug but not overly tight.

FIGURE **5.23m** The completed roast will be easy to carve and each slice will have a both light and dark meat.

FABRICATING OSSO BUCO FROM A DRUMSTICK

The turkey drumstick can be cooked as an osso buco style braise. First the leg must be divided into thigh and drumstick.

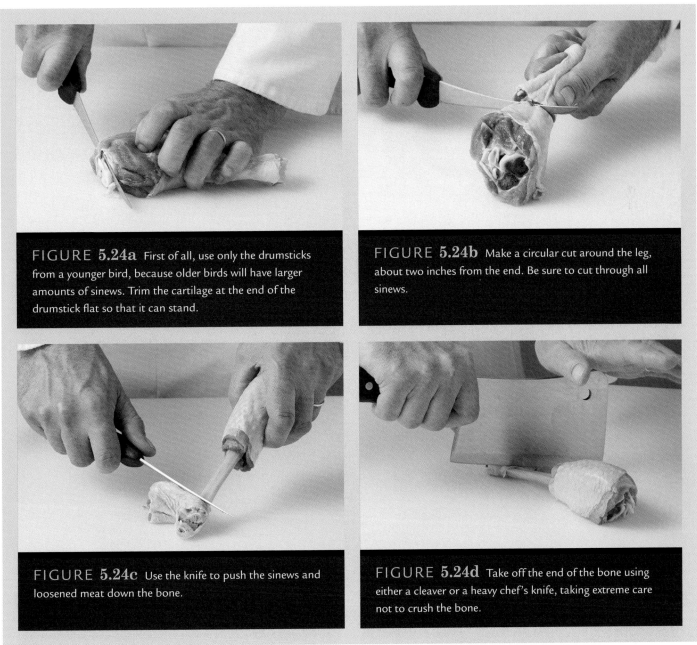

FIGURE **5.24a** First of all, use only the drumsticks from a younger bird, because older birds will have larger amounts of sinews. Trim the cartilage at the end of the drumstick flat so that it can stand.

FIGURE **5.24b** Make a circular cut around the leg, about two inches from the end. Be sure to cut through all sinews.

FIGURE **5.24c** Use the knife to push the sinews and loosened meat down the bone.

FIGURE **5.24d** Take off the end of the bone using either a cleaver or a heavy chef's knife, taking extreme care not to crush the bone.

(Continues)

FIGURE **5.24e** The completed drumstick can be either braised or roasted.

BRINING A TURKEY

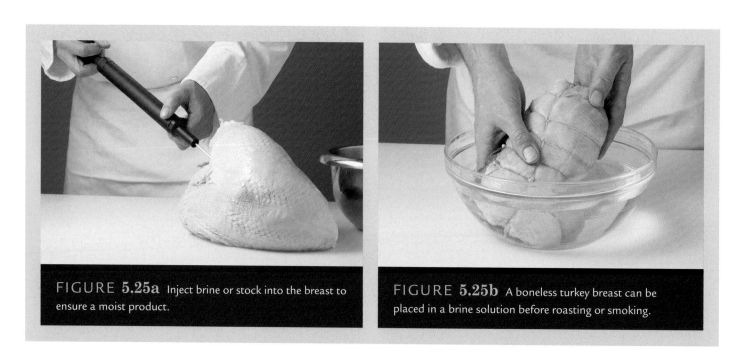

FIGURE **5.25a** Inject brine or stock into the breast to ensure a moist product.

FIGURE **5.25b** A boneless turkey breast can be placed in a brine solution before roasting or smoking.

CARVING A COOKED TURKEY

Carving a turkey off the bone is a classic fabrication. Understanding the grain of the meat is important.

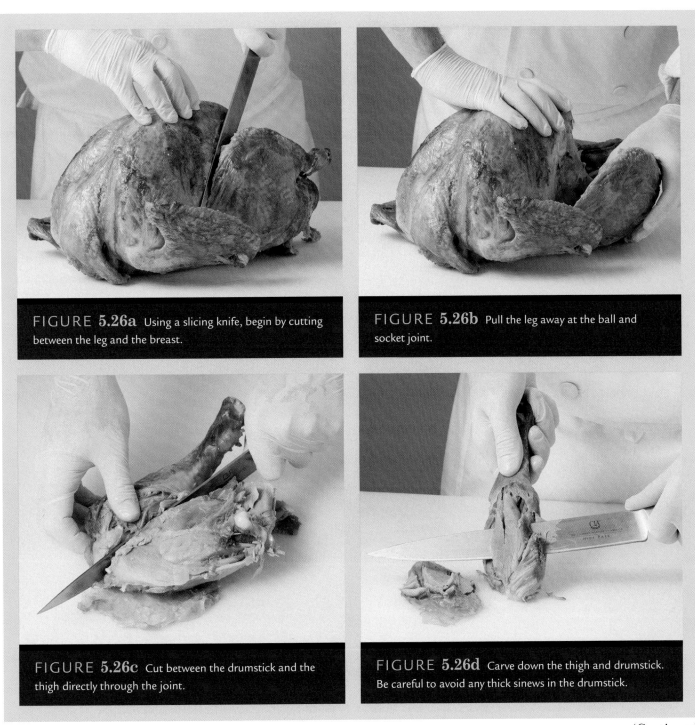

FIGURE **5.26a** Using a slicing knife, begin by cutting between the leg and the breast.

FIGURE **5.26b** Pull the leg away at the ball and socket joint.

FIGURE **5.26c** Cut between the drumstick and the thigh directly through the joint.

FIGURE **5.26d** Carve down the thigh and drumstick. Be careful to avoid any thick sinews in the drumstick.

(Continues)

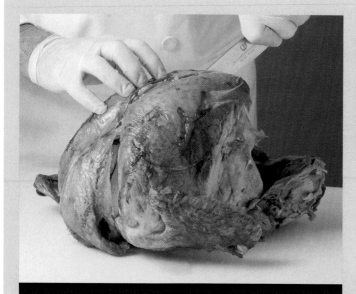

FIGURE **5.26e** Make a cut directly down the keel bone, loosening the meat as you go. Be sure to cut around the wishbone.

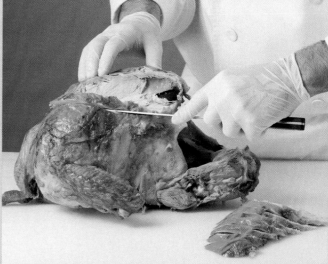

FIGURE **5.26f** Working parallel to the table, carve across the breast into the bone.

FIGURE **5.26g** Lay the meat out in layers to maintain moisture.

(Continues)

(Continued)

FIGURE **5.26h** The yield from a 12-pound turkey.

GAME BIRDS

All modern farm-raised poultry is related to wild game but has been bred to possess traits that improve the meat quality. Game birds that are commercially sold have not been altered and are closely related to their wild cousins. Typically game birds are raised similarly to domestic fowl in that they may be raised in large pens or barns and fed a controlled diet. But the game bird industry is not as standardized as the larger volume meat bird industry. There are many small and unique producers that try to mimic the flavor of a true wild bird by allowing their game birds to forage and roam freely. The idea of a game menu item is that it will possess some of the wild attributes that make it unique from domestic fowl. Game birds should have a more robust flavor. They tend to be leaner and smaller than their domestic counterparts. Traditionally cooking game birds presented challenges in that they can be slightly dry and somewhat tougher. Today the quality of the raw bird will dictate how the bird is cooked. If it is raised similar to most modern poultry and fed a grain diet it will be more tender and moist. If it is raised as a foraged bird and allowed a lot of freedom it can be tougher and drier but have a much more intense flavor. When choosing game birds it is important to have some knowledge of the farming technique and also how to identify quality features.

HISTORY OF GAME BIRDS

The term *game* is defined as traditionally hunted. Bird hunting has a long history dating back to prehistoric times. It is thought that the earliest humans sought out eggs from birds as an easy source of protein. Hunting and trapping birds was done by using baited snares and nets to capture wild birds. As humans moved around the globe they encountered some species of bird that were isolated and had no real predators. Often these flightless birds were hunted into extinction. Humans arriving on isolated islands in the South Pacific discovered birds that had previously known no enemies and were easy prey.

Ancient cave dwellings in Europe dating back thousands of years have pictures depicting waterfowl. These cave people hunted for meat as well as the by-products such as feathers.

Some Egyptian tombs have images of waterfowl being lured and captured using traps and blinds or camouflaged boats.

As humans progressed, their hunting skills increased. Soon birds were targeted on a large scale globally. Methods included beating the bush with noisemakers and dogs to scare birds in the direction of the hunters. The invention of guns and cannons further led to decline in certain populations. Placing *shot* in a gun or cannon meant a large amount of lead BBs could be fired in the general direction of a flock of birds disabling a large number. Small scatter or *punt* shot gun cannons were placed on the front of boats and sent out into seaside bays to shoot resting migratory waterfowl. This highly effective hunting method nearly destroyed entire populations of ducks, geese, and swans.

In the United States the Passenger Pigeon numbered in the billions in the 1700s. The birds were so numerous they would literally block out the sun for two days as they flew over in migration. The Passenger Pigeon was a very social bird and needed large numbers to mate and survive. They roosted in trees and shrubs in large groups making them easy prey for hunters. During the 1800s the pigeon was hunted mercilessly for inexpensive meat. By the 1900s it was no longer abundant in the wild and by 1914 it was extinct. This and the fact that many other species were on verge of extinction led to legislation that began protecting species and created seasons in which birds could be hunted.

FIGURE **6.1** Passenger pigeon.

In Europe and England hunting game birds for sport is a tradition that dates back to the Middle Ages. Depending on wild game as a viable food source became less important as farming of domestic animals increased. Game bird hunting became the sport of nobles and the aristocracy. Game refuges were set up on large forested lots and game-keepers were assigned the duties of catching poachers and maintaining healthy bird populations. Dogs were introduced to scare up fowl for easier capture. By the 1600s an established hunting protocol existed whereby dogs became the primary hunting aid for game birds. The shotgun was invented allowing dogs to flush game birds into the air and the hunter to showcase their skill in hitting a moving target before it flew out of range. Many game birds will wait until the last possible moment before launching into the air in a flurry. Game birds were sought for this reason and the fact that they were considered delicacies on the dinner table.

The act of hunting with a bird of prey was practiced in many cultures. Falcons were trained for hunting due to their extreme speeds and ability to change direction. *Falconry* bird hunting began as early as 700 B.C. in Mesopotamia. Feudal Japanese lords used falcons and hawks for hunting. The act of *takagari* or training birds of prey for hunting was reserved for wealthy nobles.

FIGURE **6.2** Hunter with dog, bird flying.

Medieval lords in Europe and Russia used falcons for hunting game birds. By the 1600s falconry was well established as a hunting method.

Today thousands of game associations maintain open spaces and stock their wild lands with game birds to be hunted later. Often hunters pay a membership fee and are allowed a quota of birds. Many of these released birds escape the preserves and increase local wild populations. The growing of release birds has led to the game bird also being raised for meat.

GAME BIRDS

Birds sold as game today vary in definition. Typically available would be birds that are hunted on preserves or game association properties. Some birds have been domesticated for many years but are unique in the marketplace and therefore are grouped and sold as game birds. There are also breeds of long-domesticated birds such as turkey and duck that are sold as game because they are raised as wild birds, having typically a smaller breast and a somewhat wild or foraged diet giving the meat a wild flavor.

Due to their uniqueness, ratites such as ostrich and emu are often included with game birds.

PHEASANT

The pheasant, or species *Phasianadae*, is related to chicken and turkey. Pheasants originate in Asia and have a range from snowy high mountains to humid jungle. The pheasant is a ground bird that can fly short distances very rapidly, making it an attractive game bird. There is a long tradition of hunting pheasants in open fields and scrub lands using dogs to flush the bird and have it rapidly fly up and out of range of the hunter. The quick flight ability indicates fast twitch muscles which translates to a light breast meat and dark legs. Its diet is primarily foraged grains, seeds, and insects. It will fatten in the wild in the fall to put on layers to get through the cold winter months. It is not a long-distance migratory bird. In the wild, there are many breeds worldwide. In the United States we find four main breeds, the Chinese Ringneck, the Kansas Ringneck, the Manchurian cross, and the Melanistic mutant. These are the breeds most typically raised for either game bird live release or as meat birds. The males have a bright plumage and are larger than the females. The females are brown and blend in very well with natural surroundings.

Commercially raised pheasants are hatched in incubators, placed in temperature-controlled barns until about 3 weeks old, and then placed in large outdoor pens covered with netting. They are fed primarily a corn-based diet but will forage for other feedstuffs if allowed.

Pheasants are harvested at 16 to 20 weeks on average.

Cooking pheasants is similar to cooking chicken but can present more challenges. The pheasant is an active bird and can develop a more robust hardy flavor. This is one reason it is desired by many chefs. If cooked incorrectly, pheasant can result in a dry meat. This is avoided often by cooking to the correct temperature or moist cooking to break down fibers. The breast is often sautéed. The skin should remain intact to maintain moisture.

Due to its age the pheasant legs can develop some sinews and may be braised to break down these fibers.

Commercially raised products can vary so the bird should be examined for quality. A high-quality name brand can ensure consistency. Its size is similar to that of a broiler chicken at about 3 pounds on average. Commercially available meat is not USDA graded and does not require USDA inspection but most birds are state inspected and the food safety of game birds tends to be very good. Check the back of the bird to see how much fat is accumulated there. If there is a covering of white or yellow fat under the skin it will indicate a bird that is well fed and high quality.

Pheasant is available both fresh and frozen depending on the purveyor. Ensure frozen birds are not damaged or freezer burned.

PURCHASING SPECIFICS

The following items are available in wholesale markets. These are only basic guidelines. Individual processors may have different specifications available. Be sure to ask your purveyor about size and availability of products.

PHEASANT PURCHASING AND USAGE SPECIFICATIONS				
ITEM AND NAMP NUMBER	DESCRIPTION/ FABRICATION	SUGGESTED COOKING METHOD/ APPLICATION	AVERAGE SUGGESTED WEIGHT LBS	TYPICAL PACKAGE SPECS
Pheasant NAMP 7200	Whole bird, usually sold with giblets	Dry or moist cook, roast whole or half, cut for parts	2–4 lbs	Individual bags 5–12 birds per case depending on size
Pheasant breast, airline, skin-on NAMP P7316	Double lobes of breast sold attached with first wing portion	Sauté, pan sear, served with sauce	6–8 oz each lobe	2 breast (4 portions) per tray pack, 11–16 trays per case depending on size
Pheasant breast boneless, skin-on	Double lobes of breast	Sauté, pan sear with sauce	4–6 oz each lobe	2 breast (4 portions) per tray pack, 12–16 trays per case depending on size
Pheasant legs	Whole with skin-on	Slow cook, braise	4–6 oz each	4 legs per tray
Pheasant backs	NA	Used for stock		Bagged, varied weights
Smoked pheasant, whole	Whole bird smoked, ready to eat	Serve as is or heat	2–3 lbs each	1 per bag 10–12 per case
Smoked pheasant breast	Whole breast folded into "football" shape	Serve as is or heat	½–¾ lb each	1 per bag

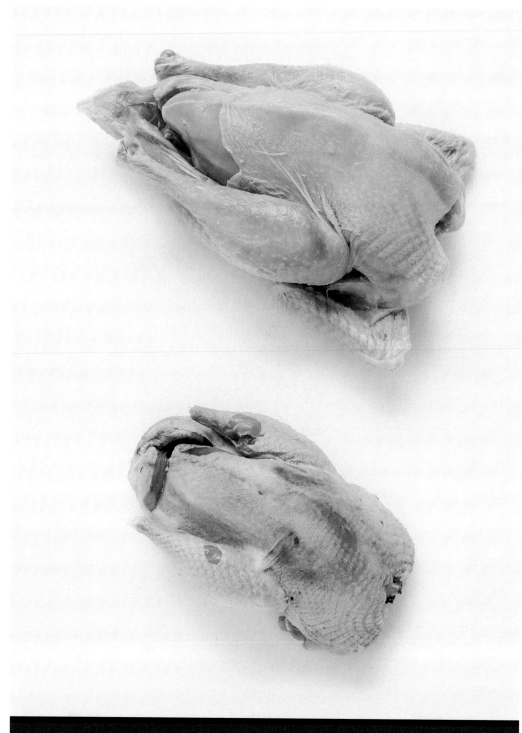

FIGURE **6.3** Top to bottom: farm-raised pheasant; wild Scottish pheasant.

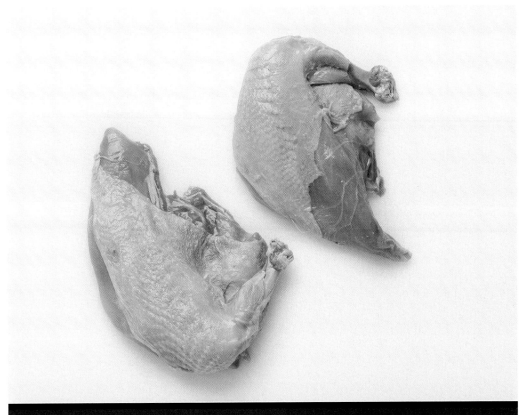

FIGURE **6.4** Pheasant breast.

WILD TURKEY

Wild turkey is basically the breed found in forests throughout the United States. They are typically sold as heritage breeds and are often allowed to forage as opposed to the more intensive farming for large-scale turkey production. Wild turkey has a much smaller breast and lower yield. It is often no larger than 14 pounds and can be slightly tougher and drier than regular turkey. This can vary with the producer, feed style, and seasonality. The reward of serving the wild foraged turkey is its hearty, robust flavor profile. Wild turkey is richer and higher in Omega-3 fatty acids if fed a wild acorn diet. Most wild turkeys are sold whole.

GUINEA FOWL

Guinea fowl is also known as guinea hen, pintade, or faraona and resembles chicken in size. It is in the *Numididae* family, which is related to pheasants, chicken, and turkey. Like those species, the guinea fowl is not a migratory bird and is primarily a ground forager. It eats a variety of seeds, insects, worms, and plant life. Often kept as pets, the guinea fowl is excellent as a natural insecticide and effectively controls tick and ant populations. Like the goose, the guinea fowl is an unbelievable guard animal. It has the ability to sense predators and strangers lurking around a farm and will sound a loud screeching that intimidates even hawks. Beyond eating ticks

GUINEA FOWL PURCHASING AND USAGE SPECIFICATIONS				
ITEM AND NAMP NUMBER	DESCRIPTION/ FABRICATION	SUGGESTED COOKING METHOD/APPLICATION	AVERAGE SUGGESTED WEIGHT LBS	TYPICAL PACKAGE SPECS
Guinea fowl NAMP P5000	Whole bird	Roast whole or disjoint into parts	2½–4 lbs each	1 per bag 12 per case, varies
Guinea fowl airline breast NAMP P5016	Single or double lobes with section of wing	Sauté or pan sear, grill	7–10 oz each breast	2 per pack varies
Guinea fowl, boneless breast	Single or double lobe, sold skin-on	Sauté, pan sear, grill	6–7 oz each	2 per pack, varies
Guinea fowl leg quarters NAMP P5030	Whole legs	Broil, grill, braise, stuff	4–6 oz each leg	4 per pack

FIGURE **6.5** Guinea fowl.

and bugs, it also attacks small rodents such as mice or moles and it is known to attack snakes.

The guinea fowl is native to West Africa where it is believed to have been first domesticated. Today we find a number of varieties and colors available but most are the same size.

Guinea fowl are raised similar to pheasants and are ready at about 10 to 16 weeks. Young guinea fowl are known as *keets*.

As a meat animal the guinea fowl is somewhat similar to chicken but with a richer non-gamey taste. It has a pleasant robust flavor that is popular in many upscale restaurants. The yield of a fowl is very good at over 50 percent of the carcass being usable meat. It is readily available from specialty purveyors and is found fresh or frozen. It can be purchased as parts.

QUAIL/PARTRIDGE/CHUKAR/GROUSE

Quail are in the same family as pheasants. There are many breeds including the Bob-white, Brown Pharaoh, Texas A M White, Manchurian, Tuxedo, and Chinese Painted, all of which are raised for either meat or release for hunters. The Pharaoh or Cortunix is typically raised for meat due to its fast growing capability and disease resistance. This is the common quail found in Europe.

Quail are found in the wild and are experts at hiding and then rapidly fleeing their predators. Often hunted by using dogs to flush out the birds, quail will hide in scrub brush, which they blend into very well. The quail will fly with startling speed and only a quick reaction will enable the hunter to hit the moving target with a blast from a shotgun. This ability to fly rapidly gives the quail a darker meat color than pheasant. Farm-raised quail, especially Pharaoh quail, which are not allowed to fly, tend to have a somewhat lighter color breast meat and milder flavor. They are grain fed and do not have all the "gamey" flavor but are often more acceptable by diners. True game birds vary depending on age, diet, and seasonality.

Quail are very small, only about 4 to 5 ounces each. They are often sold as individual appetizers or small course entrees. Quail are purchased either whole, semi-boneless or glove boned, or cut into legs and breast. Glove boned quail are boned by eliminating the backbone, rib cage, and keel bone but leaving the legs and wings attached. This enables the chef to stuff the quail. These are sometimes known as "Euro-quail." There are some marinated or smoked products available as well.

Partridge are very similar to quail in size and flavor. They are often sold similarly on menus. There are red-legged partridge, common grey partridge, Hungarian partridge, rock partridge or chukar. All partridge and chukar originate in Asia but breeds such as the red-legged partridge were circulated throughout Europe and England many hundreds of years ago. Many varieties have been released for hunting in the United States and are now a fixture in many open scrub lands and prairies.

The Grouse is a wild bird not typically commercially raised. It is also known as a "partridge." They are a protected species. There are some Scottish imported grouse available from specialty purveyors.

All of these are small birds, only a few ounces each. Partridge tend to take longer to mature than quail and have a more robust flavor. Most are raised outdoors in flying pens but there are quail being raised indoors similar to chicken.

SMALL GAME BIRD PURCHASING AND USAGE SPECIFICATIONS				
ITEM AND NAMP NUMBER	DESCRIPTION/ FABRICATION	SUGGESTED COOKING METHOD/ APPLICATION	AVERAGE SUGGESTED WEIGHT LBS	TYPICAL PACKAGE SPECS
Quail NAMP P7000	Whole bird, can be purchased split, typically without giblets	Roast whole, grill, broil	4–5 oz each Jumbo 5–7 oz	4 or 6 per pack depending on producer
Semi-boneless quail "Euro-quail"	Whole bird glove boned with legs and wings still intact	Roast whole, stuff, grill, broil	3 oz	4 or 6 per pack
Boneless breast	Very small, used for stuffing	Grill, broil, pan sear	1½–2 oz	Varies
Semi-boneless legs	Small, femur bone removed	Grill, roast, pan sear, braise	1½–2 oz each	Varies, bulk pack
Partridge, whole NAMP P7400	Whole bird, typically without giblets	Roast, grill whole, split	3–5 oz each	Individual pack, 12 per case
Scottish grouse	Whole bird	Roast whole	4–5 oz each	Individual pack

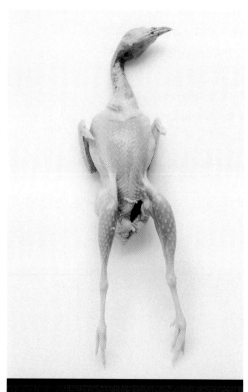

FIGURE **6.6** Partridge.

FIGURE **6.7** Left to right: semi-boneless Euro-quail; whole quail, head-on, feet-on.

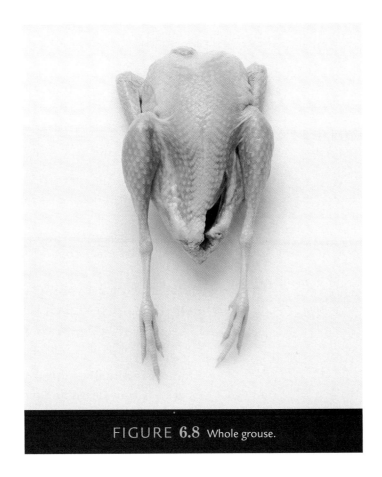

FIGURE **6.8** Whole grouse.

Other items can be special ordered. Realize these items are very small and may require multiples for portions. Be sure to check all game birds for freshness. Some game birds will have small pinfeathers stuck in the skin that may require extra time to remove.

SQUAB/PIGEON/DOVE

Many people have a vision of pigeon wandering through city parks or perched on statues. These birds have the undistinguished reputation of being dirty. In the wild the pigeon is as any other game bird. They forage seeds, grains, bugs, etc. Although farm-raised pigeons do not fly for any distance they do fly in the wild. Pigeons do not migrate the distances that ducks or geese travel but they can travel long distances. Pigeons are often kept as pets and used as *homing* pigeons where they are released many miles from their home and miraculously find their way back. Pigeons were used in war times as a messenger service and there are many stories of heroic pigeons carrying important messages while injured. The Croix de guerre or French medal for distinguished service was given to a pigeon named Cher Ami who saved an entire battalion after being shot by enemy forces and flew on and delivering its message. Pigeons are strong flyers and can reach up to 40+ MPH.

Pigeon originate from the Middle East and eastern Asia. The species is actually millions of years old and there are many sub-species. They have been captured and raised

PIGEON/SQUAB PURCHASING AND USAGE SPECIFICATIONS				
ITEM AND NAMP NUMBER	DESCRIPTION/ FABRICATION	SUGGESTED COOKING METHOD/APPLICATION	AVERAGE SUGGESTED WEIGHT LBS	TYPICAL PACKAGE SPECS
Pigeon/squab NAMP P6000	Whole bird, can be sold with head and feet on	Roast whole	1 lb each	1 per bag 12–24 per case, varies

FIGURE **6.9** Squab.

for over 10,000 years but are still considered a game animal. They cannot be raised as chickens and must pair up and mate naturally. They will feed their young much longer than most birds. Some young actually surpass the weight of their parents.

The dove is actually a breed of white pigeon. Doves are considered an international sign of peace. They have been released at special events such as weddings. Wild dove are protected in many states and may only be hunted in season if at all.

There are a few commercially available dove products, typically Rock Dove which is basically pigeon.

The domestic pigeon, *Columba livia*, has been bred for many years as a food item. Its offspring will remain on the roost for a longer time than most game birds. The young *squeakers* will grow to what is known as *squab*. Squab is a pigeon that has just lost its down and has left the roost. They are 28 to 30 days old and are about the size of a Cornish game hen or about 1 pound. Squab has a good yield and is tender. It is considered a delicacy and is popular in many fine restaurants. Squab is hearty and a darker red meat color but fairly lean. It can be purchased both fresh and frozen. Due to its size it is primarily sold whole.

OSTRICH/EMU

Ostrich and emu are ratites in the family *Struthionidae,* which defines a group of large flightless birds. Ostrich are native to the grasslands of Africa. They are the fastest of all birds on land, reaching speeds of over 40 MPH. It is large, weighing over

200 pounds fully grown. Large males have reached weights over 340 pounds. This indicates that it has a much larger leg structure and is a very meaty bird compared to smaller species. A leg of ostrich is similar to the size of a small veal leg. The emu is smaller and native to Australia. It is still quite large and a very fast runner as well. Both species are social birds and will travel in herds of five to fifty.

The Rhea is another ratite native to South America that is gaining some popularity as a meat bird.

The primary reason for farm raising ostrich was to harvest its leather. Ostrich leather is considered some of the highest quality and is valuable. Other by-products are feathers which are sold for decoration. In the late 1800s and early 1900s ostrich feathers adorned many women's hats. Emu are also harvested for their leather and the oil that is derived from its fat. Emu oil is used as a skin moisturizer and healing agent. It has the quality to be easily absorbed into the skin.

All of the large ratites produce very large eggs. The eggs are harvested for food as well as decorative value. A large ostrich egg can feed as many as 12 people! It tastes very similar to a chicken egg.

Ostrich and emu meat is similar to the red meat of game mammals. It can be tender but does not have much fat. It is also very low in cholesterol and high in iron. The fact that it is very lean indicates it can cook very dry if not prepared properly. Ostrich steaks should not be cooked to well done unless braised. Certain cuts such as the *fan* and the *back filet* can be cooked similar to beef. Steaks can be grilled from some of the better cuts. Braising and stew is best for the tougher cuts. Often it is ground for burger.

The World Ostrich Association has a grading system designed for the industry. Grades are Prime, Choice, Select, Utility, and non-food grade. Grades are determined by age, lean muscle color, fat color and amount, and lack of disease to name a few.

The ostrich carcass is fabricated differently than any other meat. It is large, 50 to 90 pounds including both legs, and has its own nomenclature and muscle system. It has a number of meat cuts that are seamed out and sectioned into what are considered very tender, moderately tender, and tougher cuts. The cuts vary due to activity level. Subprimal cuts include the oyster, fan, top strip, inside strip, back strip, wing, and neck. Typically only the very tender cuts are sold for steaks, medallions, or roasts and the rest is often used for grind. There are a number of value-added cuts and processed products produced from ostrich such as sausages, jerky, bacon, and more.

OSTRICH PURCHASING AND USAGE SPECIFICATIONS				
ITEM AND NAMP NUMBER	DESCRIPTION/ FABRICATION	SUGGESTED COOKING METHOD/APPLICATION	AVERAGE SUGGESTED WEIGHT LBS	TYPICAL PACKAGE SPECS
Ostrich fan filet	2- to 3-inch thick, denuded section free of fat	Very tender, best cut for steaks, cutlets, roast	2½–3½ lbs	1 per pack, sold as an individual piece
Back tenderloin	Oval, very tender, denuded	Very tender piece similar to beef tenderloin	1–3 lbs	1 per pack, sold as an individual piece
Inside strip	Small, tender cut	Tender, used for steaks, medallions	½–1 lb each	Varies, 1–2 per pack
Outside strip	Small, medallion size pieces	Moderately tender, steaks, roast	¾–1½ lb each	Varies, 1–2 per pack
Ground ostrich	Very lean	Can cook out dry if overcooked	Varies	Varies

FIGURE **6.10** A: Ground ostrich; B: Ostrich fan; C: Ostrich tenderloin.

FIGURE **6.11** Portioned ostrich steaks.

FABRICATION OF GAME BIRDS

PHEASANT

Disjointing a pheasant is very similar to that of chicken. Use the information in the Chicken chapter to create a number of fabrications for foodservice.

The pheasant can be cut into airline breast and legs.

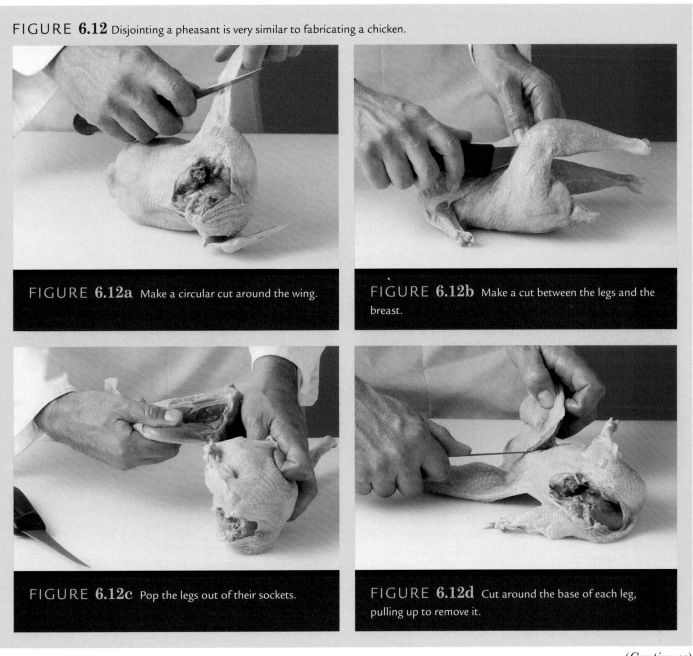

FIGURE **6.12** Disjointing a pheasant is very similar to fabricating a chicken.

FIGURE **6.12a** Make a circular cut around the wing.

FIGURE **6.12b** Make a cut between the legs and the breast.

FIGURE **6.12c** Pop the legs out of their sockets.

FIGURE **6.12d** Cut around the base of each leg, pulling up to remove it.

(Continues)

(Continued)

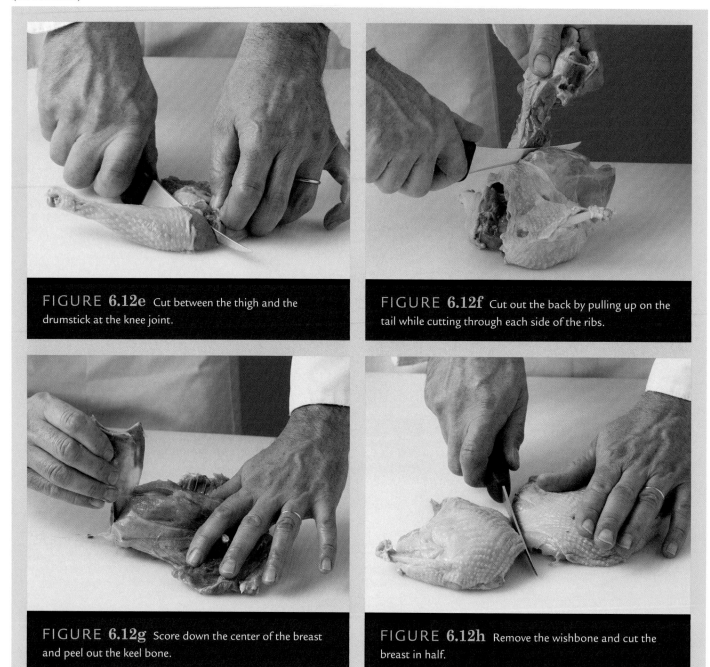

FIGURE **6.12e** Cut between the thigh and the drumstick at the knee joint.

FIGURE **6.12f** Cut out the back by pulling up on the tail while cutting through each side of the ribs.

FIGURE **6.12g** Score down the center of the breast and peel out the keel bone.

FIGURE **6.12h** Remove the wishbone and cut the breast in half.

(Continues)

(*Continued*)

FIGURE **6.12i** The yield for a disjointed pheasant.

The pheasant can sometimes cook dry. To combat this, thin slices of fat or frozen butter and seasoning can be placed under the skin for moisture.

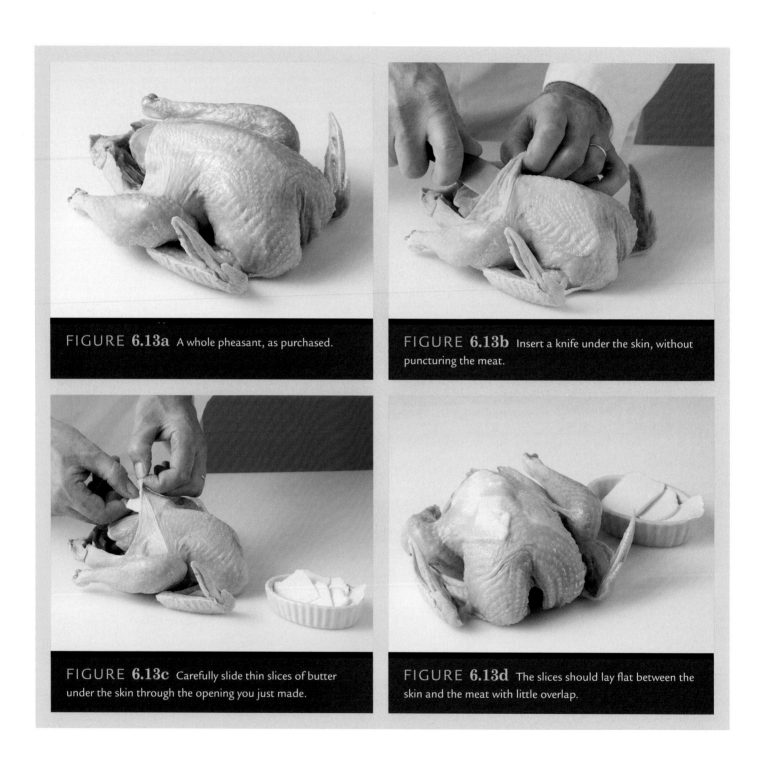

FIGURE **6.13a** A whole pheasant, as purchased.

FIGURE **6.13b** Insert a knife under the skin, without puncturing the meat.

FIGURE **6.13c** Carefully slide thin slices of butter under the skin through the opening you just made.

FIGURE **6.13d** The slices should lay flat between the skin and the meat with little overlap.

STUFFING A PHEASANT

FIGURE **6.14a** Pull the skin away from the breast and legs. Trim away the excess fat and sinews.

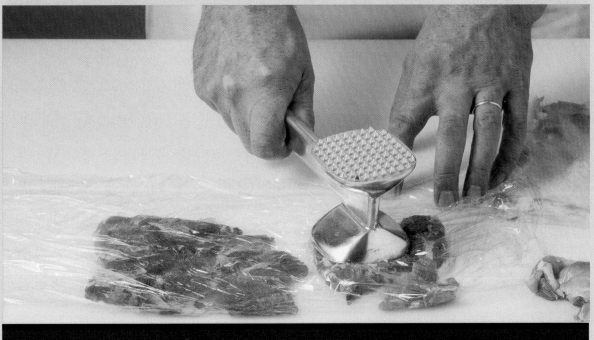

FIGURE **6.14b** Place the meat in plastic wrap and pound to an even thickness.

(Continues)

FIGURE **6.14c** Carefully trim the skin to a rectangular shape.

FIGURE **6.14d** Lay the flattened breast and legs evenly over the skin.

(Continues)

FIGURE **6.14e** Place the stuffing mixture down the center.

FIGURE **6.14f** Fold the roast into shape.

FIGURE **6.14g** Tie the ends off first to properly contain the stuffing.

FIGURE **6.14h** Finish with knots that are snug but not overly tight.

The Guinea Hen is also cut like chicken. Fabrication is identical.

QUAIL

Quail and partridge are very small. They are rarely divided into disjointed sections. Their bone structure is the same as all other poultry so if needed they can be cut the same way using a small knife.

The quail is often glove boned for stuffing. This entails removing the rib cage, backbone, and keel bone but leaving the wings and legs intact.

FIGURE **6.15** Glove boning a quail requires skill and patience.

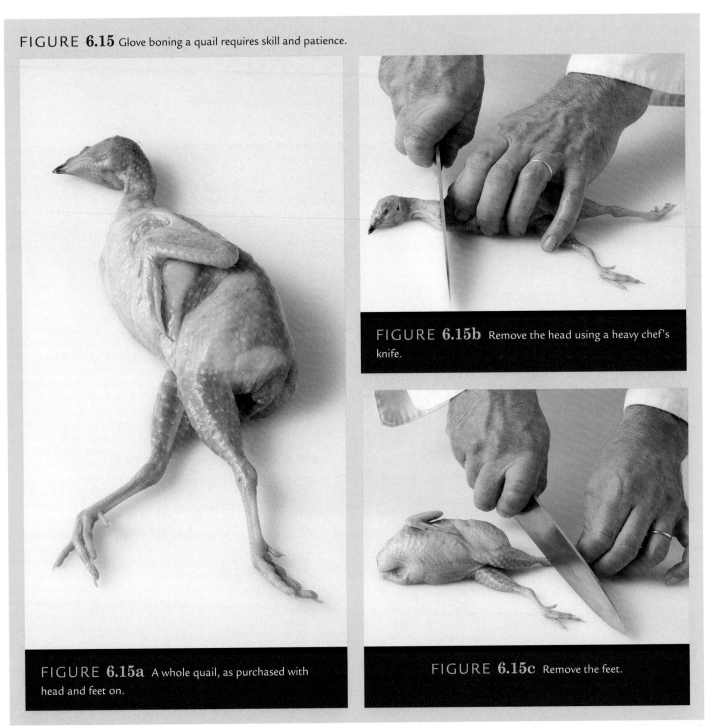

FIGURE **6.15a** A whole quail, as purchased with head and feet on.

FIGURE **6.15b** Remove the head using a heavy chef's knife.

FIGURE **6.15c** Remove the feet.

(Continues)

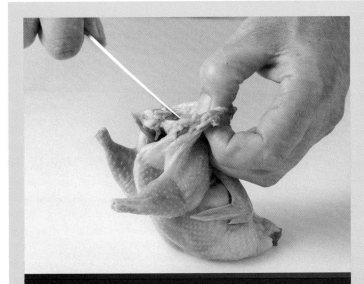

FIGURE **6.15d** Place the bird front-side down. Cut under the skin at the tail. Then cut through the leg sockets, loosening them.

FIGURE **6.15e** Cut around the wishbone to loosen it. Push the meat away from the rib cage using your fingers.

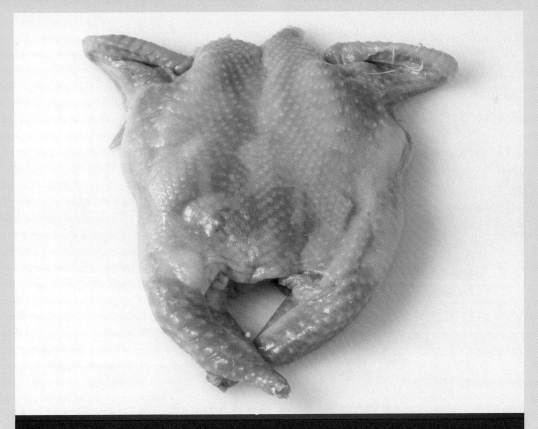

FIGURE **6.15f** Finish by pulling away the main carcass bones, taking care not to cut the skin. A glove boned quail can be stuffed and served whole.

FIGURE **6.16a** Press the squab into the pan and hold until the skin is crisped.

FIGURE **6.16b** Turn the squab and finish searing the other side. Be careful about pressing down on the seared skin, because the skin can easily crack, ruining the presentation.

OSTRICH

The cuts of ostrich are typically fabricated into sections and sold denuded. Fabrication would be similar to cutting veal or venison. It is often cut into medallions or steaks. Also small roasts can be made by dividing into sections.

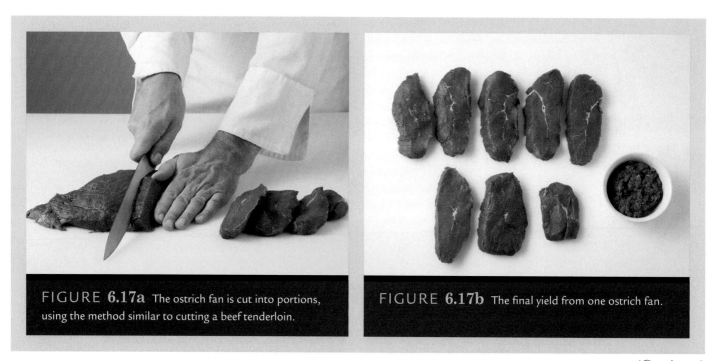

FIGURE **6.17a** The ostrich fan is cut into portions, using the method similar to cutting a beef tenderloin.

FIGURE **6.17b** The final yield from one ostrich fan.

(Continues)

(Continued)

FIGURE **6.17c** For medallions, you begin by cutting away any heavy sinews or blood vessels.

FIGURE **6.17d** The tenderloin section of the ostrich, free of sinews and ready to be rolled.

FIGURE **6.17e** Use plastic wrap to shape and roll the tenderloin.

FIGURE **6.17f** Cut the roll into even portions.

(Continues)

(*Continued*)

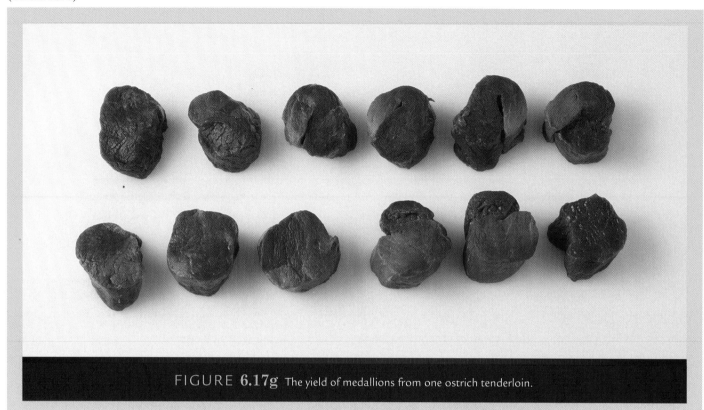

FIGURE **6.17g** The yield of medallions from one ostrich tenderloin.

POULTRY NUTRITION

Nutrition derived from poultry products varies from species to species. The most publicized poultry, chicken, makes claims that rival its red meat competitors. High protein and low fat are attributes that make it appealing for menu items. But as with all meats, overconsumption can result in high cholesterol counts and saturated fat. Fat type is often considered when evaluating poultry in many diets. Traditional commercially raised poultry has a mix of saturated, monounsaturated, and polyunsaturated fats. Trim levels and fat removal will greatly affect the amount of fat and cholesterol found in the dish. Serving a completely denuded chicken breast is appealing nutritionally but as a dining experience it could result in a bland entrée. When considering the nutritional value of poultry portions you must consider a realistic weight, skin covering, and coatings or sauces. Cooking methods such as frying will dramatically increase the amount of fat added. Many guides and labels will give a nutritional value based on an unrealistic 100-gram or a little over 3½-ounce size portions. In poultry this would be the equivalent of a single bone-in chicken thigh. Most portions are at least double this size. This publication will attempt to give a realistic portion size evaluation for various typically purchased poultry items.

Dark meat birds such as duck, goose, and squab all contain more fat than chicken but the fat is less saturated and its meat is higher in iron. Squab is leaner and has an almost red meat quality. Ground dwelling birds like chicken, turkey, and pheasant have a mix of meat types, dark meat in the legs and light and white meat in the breast. The dark meat typically contains more fat but is more flavorful.

Game birds such as quail, partridge, and guinea fowl are highly active resulting in a high-protein, relatively lean meat.

Ostrich and emu are truly red meat birds having very high iron counts and react like a lean beef or buffalo meat.

As with all meats, poultry nutritional values will reflect the diet of the bird. Birds raised on commercial feeds will have a different fat profile than those on a foraged diet. Wild bird diets will vary with the seasons and habitat. For migratory birds many plants and foodstuffs are typically available right before their flight. Grains and grasses are ripened, insects are plentiful, nuts and fruits are available. A natural fattening occurs. Droughts and habitat disruption will alter the feed available therefore each year the quality of wild birds can vary.

The commercially raised bird has a controlled diet and therefore a nutritional value that is very consistent. Feed formulations are created to grow the birds rapidly and achieve a proper meat to bone ratio. Essential fatty acids such as Omega-6 and Omega-3 are found in all poultry. A bird with a strictly corn-based diet will result in an imbalance of Omega-6 over Omega-3 as high as a 20:1 ratio. Birds allowed to forage on natural feed stuffs tend to have a higher amount of Omega-3. We find some producers trying to mimic wild foraging by allowing birds to forage for some of their feed in large fenced-in areas. Some poultry producers are adding feedstuffs that are higher in Omega-3 to create a meat that is also higher in Omega-3. These birds are raised using the same intensive feeding methods as other poultry and are not foraged.

Geese are often grazed as part of their raising and then fed corn to finish them as they get closer to harvest time. Geese and ducks have more fat than chickens but have a cholesterol count that is the same or even lower.

Turkey, like chicken, has a light and dark meat structure. The modern turkey has a huge breast structure and is relatively fatty compared to its wild ancestors. The wild turkey is leaner and much higher in Omega-3 fatty acid compared to a corn-fed bird.

OFFAL FROM POULTRY

Beyond the feed and raising style, poultry nutrition can be altered by additives injected into it. Many poultry products are basted, battered, marinated, breaded, or seasoned in some way. A variety of ingredients such as sodium phosphate, salt, sugars, nonfat dry milk, vegetable starches, and proteins can alter the nutritional value of the product. Foodservice products are not always labeled the same as retail. Often bulk packaged products will have the added ingredients on the exterior of the box but not listed on the individually packaged product.

Irradiating poultry, or exposing it to electronic beam or gamma ray radiation, can alter the vitamin content depending on the amount of exposure. Irradiated poultry is also considered "cold pasteurized" and the product has little or no bacteria left after the process. B vitamins are particularly affected by the process.

Curing a poultry product can also affect its nutrition. Adding a nitrate product will denature the proteins and protect from harmful bacteria growth. Curing can affect some nutrient values due to the ingredients that are added such as sugars, ascorbic acid, and salt. There is no significant loss of most vitamins due to curing alone. Cooking can alter vitamins but no one is suggesting a raw poultry diet!

Most poultry is high in niacin, phosphorus, and selenium. Poultry in general is a quality source of protein and the portion sizes evaluated would contain fairly significant amounts. Certain vitamins such as vitamin C are not found in significant amounts in most poultry but it is present in a few in small amounts.

The nutrition charts in this publication represent a typical 6-ounce portion of poultry unless otherwise stated. Values are for roasted poultry only. Frying can significantly alter these values depending on the type of oil or fat used. Breading can greatly increase calories, salt, and sugar amounts depending on the coatings.

NUTRITION CHARTS

CHICKEN, SKIN-ON, ROASTED	
Energy	509.4 kcal
Total Fat	34.0 g
Saturated Fat	8.5 g
Trans Fat	—
Monounsaturated Fat	13.6 g
Polyunsaturated Fat	6.8 g
Cholesterol	149.4 mg
Carbohydrate	0.0 g
Total Sugars	0.0 g
Protein	42.5 g
Dietary Fiber	0.0 g
Sodium	147.7 mg
Calcium	35.7 mg
Iron	1.7 mg
Vitamin A, RAE	178.3 mcg
Vitamin C	0.0 mg
Water	90.0 g

CHICKEN BREAST, SKIN-ON, ROASTED	
Energy	334.5 kcal
Total Fat	11.9 g
Saturated Fat	3.4 g
Trans Fat	—
Monounsaturated Fat	5.1 g
Polyunsaturated Fat	1.7 g
Cholesterol	142.6 mg
Carbohydrate	0.0 g
Total Sugars	0.0 g
Protein	49.2 g
Dietary Fiber	0.0 g
Sodium	120.6 mg
Calcium	23.8 mg
Iron	1.7 mg
Vitamin A, RAE	47.5 mcg
Vitamin C	0.0 mg
Water	105.3 g

CHICKEN BREAST, SKINLESS, ROASTED	
Energy	165.0 kcal
Total Fat	3.0 g
Saturated Fat	1.0 g
Trans Fat	—
Monounsaturated Fat	1.0 g
Polyunsaturated Fat	0.0 g
Cholesterol	85.0 mg
Carbohydrate	0.0 g
Total Sugars	0.0 g
Protein	31.0 g
Dietary Fiber	0.0 g
Sodium	74.0 mg
Calcium	15.0 mg
Iron	1.0 mg
Vitamin A, RAE	6.0 mcg
Vitamin C	0.0 mg
Water	65.0 g

CHICKEN LEGS, DARK MEAT, SKIN-ON, ROASTED	
Energy	429.6 kcal
Total Fat	25.5 g
Saturated Fat	6.8 g
Trans Fat	—
Monounsaturated Fat	10.2 g
Polyunsaturated Fat	5.1 g
Cholesterol	154.5 mg
Carbohydrate	—
Protein	42.5 g
Dietary Fiber	0.0 g
Sodium	147.7 mg
Calcium	25.5 mg
Iron	1.7 mg
Vitamin A, RAE	101.9 mcg
Vitamin C	0.0 mg
Water	98.5 g

CORNISH GAME HEN, WHOLE ROASTED		CHICKEN LIVERS, 2 OZ SERVING, SAUTÉED	
Energy	441.5 kcal	Energy	97.4 kcal
Total Fat	30.6 g	Total Fat	3.4 g
Saturated Fat	8.5 g	Saturated Fat	1.1 g
Trans Fat	—	Trans Fat	0.0 g
Monounsaturated Fat	13.6 g	Monounsaturated Fat	0.6 g
Polyunsaturated Fat	5.1 g	Polyunsaturated Fat	0.6 g
Cholesterol	222.4 mg	Cholesterol	319.2 mg
Carbohydrate	0.0 g	Carbohydrate	0.6 g
Total Sugars	0.0 g	Total Sugars	0.0 g
Protein	37.4 g	Protein	14.2 g
Dietary Fiber	0.0 g	Dietary Fiber	0.0 g
Sodium	108.7 mg	Sodium	52.1 mg
Calcium	22.1 mg	Calcium	5.7 mg
Iron	0.0 mg	Iron	6.8 mg
Vitamin A, RAE	54.3 mcg	Vitamin A, RAE	2431.5 mcg
Vitamin C	0.0 mg	Vitamin C	1.1 mg
Water	98.5 g	Water	36.8 g

DOVE, WHOLE ROASTED		DOMESTIC DUCK, WHOLE ROASTED	
Energy	371.9 kcal	Energy	572.2 kcal
Total Fat	22.1 g	Total Fat	47.5 g
Saturated Fat	5.1 g	Saturated Fat	15.3 g
Trans Fat	—	Trans Fat	—
Monounsaturated Fat	8.5 g	Monounsaturated Fat	20.4 g
Polyunsaturated Fat	3.4 g	Polyunsaturated Fat	5.1 g
Cholesterol	197.0 mg	Cholesterol	142.6 mg
Carbohydrate	0.0 g	Carbohydrate	0.0 g
Total Sugars	0.0 g	Total Sugars	0.0 g
Protein	39.1 g	Protein	30.6 g
Dietary Fiber	0.0 g	Dietary Fiber	0.0 g
Sodium	96.8 mg	Sodium	100.2 mg
Calcium	28.9 mg	Calcium	18.7 mg
Iron	8.5 mg	Iron	3.4 mg
Vitamin A, RAE	47.5 mcg	Vitamin A, RAE	107.0 mcg
Vitamin C	3.4 mg	Vitamin C	0.0 mg
Water	105.3 g	Water	86.6 g

DUCK BREAST, SKIN-ON		GOOSE, ROASTED	
Energy	343.0 kcal	Energy	517.9 kcal
Total Fat	17.0 g	Total Fat	35.7 g
Saturated Fat	3.4 g	Saturated Fat	10.2 g
Trans Fat	—	Trans Fat	—
Monounsaturated Fat	8.5 g	Monounsaturated Fat	17.0 g
Polyunsaturated Fat	1.7 g	Polyunsaturated Fat	3.4 g
Cholesterol	230.9 mg	Cholesterol	154.5 mg
Carbohydrate	0.0 g	Carbohydrate	0.0 g
Total Sugars	—	Total Sugars	0.0 g
Protein	40.8 g	Protein	42.5 g
Dietary Fiber	—	Dietary Fiber	0.0 g
Sodium	142.6 mg	Sodium	118.9 mg
Calcium	13.6 mg	Calcium	22.1 mg
Iron	5.1 mg	Iron	3.4 mg
Vitamin A, RAE	—	Vitamin A, RAE	35.7 mcg
Vitamin C	3.4 mg	Vitamin C	0.0 mg
Water	107.0 g	Water	86.6 g

GUINEA FOWL		OSTRICH FILLET	
Energy	268.3 kcal	Energy	246.2 kcal
Total Fat	10.2 g	Total Fat	3.4 g
Saturated Fat	1.7 g	Saturated Fat	1.7 g
Trans Fat	—	Trans Fat	—
Monounsaturated Fat	3.4 g	Monounsaturated Fat	0.0 g
Polyunsaturated Fat	1.7 g	Polyunsaturated Fat	0.0 g
Cholesterol	125.7 mg	Cholesterol	144.3 mg
Carbohydrate	0.0 g	Carbohydrate	0.0 g
Total Sugars	—	Total Sugars	0.0 g
Protein	39.1 g	Protein	47.5 g
Dietary Fiber	0.0 g	Dietary Fiber	0.0 g
Sodium	113.8 mg	Sodium	135.8 mg
Calcium	18.7 mg	Calcium	10.2 mg
Iron	0.0 mg	Iron	3.4 mg
Vitamin A, RAE	47.5 mcg	Vitamin A, RAE	0.0 mcg
Vitamin C	1.7 mg	Vitamin C	0.0 mg
Water	115.5 g	Water	115.5 g

PHEASANT, FARM RAISED		QUAIL (4-OZ PORTION)	
Energy	419.4 kcal	Energy	264.9 kcal
Total Fat	20.4 g	Total Fat	15.8 g
Saturated Fat	5.1 g	Saturated Fat	3.4 g
Trans Fat	—	Trans Fat	—
Monounsaturated Fat	8.5 g	Monounsaturated Fat	4.5 g
Polyunsaturated Fat	1.7 g	Polyunsaturated Fat	3.4 g
Cholesterol	151.1 mg	Cholesterol	97.4 mg
Carbohydrate	0.0 g	Carbohydrate	0.0 g
Total Sugars	0.0 g	Total Sugars	0.0 g
Protein	54.3 g	Protein	28.3 g
Dietary Fiber	0.0 g	Dietary Fiber	0.0 g
Sodium	73.0 mg	Sodium	58.9 mg
Calcium	27.2 mg	Calcium	17.0 mg
Iron	1.7 mg	Iron	4.5 mg
Vitamin A, RAE	96.8 mcg	Vitamin A, RAE	79.2 mcg
Vitamin C	3.4 mg	Vitamin C	2.3 mg
Water	91.7 g	Water	67.9 g

SQUAB, WHOLE ROASTED (SLIGHTLY LARGER THAN 6 OZ)	
Energy	585.1 kcal
Total Fat	45.8 g
Saturated Fat	15.9 g
Trans Fat	—
Monounsaturated Fat	17.9 g
Polyunsaturated Fat	6.0 g
Cholesterol	189.1 mg
Carbohydrate	0.0 g
Total Sugars	—
Protein	35.8 g
Dietary Fiber	0.0 g
Sodium	107.5 mg
Calcium	23.9 mg
Iron	6.0 mg
Vitamin A, RAE	145.3 mcg
Vitamin C	9.9 mg
Water	111.4 g

TURKEY, WHOLE ROASTED	
Energy	288.7 kcal
Total Fat	6.8 g
Saturated Fat	1.7 g
Trans Fat	—
Monounsaturated Fat	1.7 g
Polyunsaturated Fat	1.7 g
Cholesterol	129.0 mg
Carbohydrate	0.0 g
Total Sugars	0.0 g
Protein	49.2 g
Dietary Fiber	0.0 g
Sodium	118.9 mg
Calcium	42.5 mg
Iron	1.7 mg
Vitamin A, RAE	0.0 mcg
Vitamin C	0.0 mg
Water	108.7 g

TURKEY BREAST, ROASTED

Energy	320.9 kcal
Total Fat	11.9 g
Saturated Fat	3.4 g
Trans Fat	—
Monounsaturated Fat	3.4 g
Polyunsaturated Fat	1.7 g
Cholesterol	125.7 mg
Carbohydrate	0.0 g
Total Sugars	—
Protein	47.5 g
Dietary Fiber	0.0 g
Sodium	107.0 mg
Calcium	35.7 mg
Iron	1.7 mg
Vitamin A, RAE	0.0 mcg
Vitamin C	0.0 mg
Water	107.0 g

8

EGGS

HISTORY

By definition the poultry egg is a shelled reproductive structure of a bird containing the ovum and all of the nutritive and protective materials surrounding it. Poultry eggs consist of a yellow yolk, and the albumen or white section. The protein and nutrient value of each section differs but the entire egg, including the shell, possess nutritional value.

No one actually can date when humans or earlier relatives first consumed an egg. Eggs were an easy source of protein and early humans probably stole eggs from nests of a variety of birds. Today we find primates that will supplement their primarily vegetarian diet with eggs. As humans progressed into the Neolithic period poultry domestication occurred for meat but more importantly for egg harvest. Red Jungle Fowl were domesticated for meat and eggs in India and Pakistan over 5,000 years ago. The egg was part of the early Phoenician diet as well as later Egyptian and Roman food culture. In Phoenicia, one of

the world's earliest civilizations, the religious belief about creation was that all things came from the heavens in the form of an egg. In ancient Egypt it was believed the Phoenix comes every 500 years and builds a nest and lays an egg and perishes in its own flames only to be reborn out of the egg, making it immortal. The egg plays a part in Roman and early European culture where it often symbolizes fertility. China, and Asia in general, has a long history of poultry production and eggs are a major part of the cuisine and culture. Chinese poultry and egg domestication and production are well over 3,000 years old. Eggs and chicken were part of the diet found on early Asian and European explorers' ships due to the fact that they provided a renewable protein source.

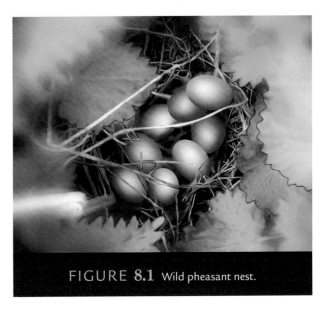

FIGURE 8.1 Wild pheasant nest.

The large ostrich egg shells were once used as water vessels in early Mesopotamia. Due to their size and strength they served as ceremonial goblets. One shell can hold about a quart of water or beer. In the 1600s in Europe, ostrich egg cups were used for drinking alcoholic beverages such as wine or mead.

The Christian celebration of Easter uses the egg to celebrate the resurrection of Christ. Eggs were often used to celebrate spring and the rebirth of the earth in many ancient religions and cultures. The hatching of an egg was considered a miracle in itself and therefore eggs were used in many ancient rituals. It was often colored and decorated.

The ultimate example of the decorated Easter egg was the one produced for the Russian Czar Alexander by the famous jeweler Fabergé in 1885. This world-famous egg has an estimated value of 18–20 million dollars, making it one of the most expensive art objects in the world.

As agriculture spread throughout humanity, the raising of poultry for eggs was integrated into many farms. Eggs provided farmers with an inexpensive, renewable, quality protein and once a flock produced more than the farm household could consume they were sold in markets. Eggs from all sorts of poultry were common in marketplaces worldwide. The domestication of ducks, geese, and chickens resulted in farmers specializing in eggs. As farming became more advanced, grains and feeds were more abundant and poultry production increased. Even today we find eggs being produced in backyard pens all over the world. Raising a few chickens is common in all rural settings worldwide and many small subsistence farmers or hobby gardeners will have a few chickens to help keep pests and insects under control and provide a few eggs as a by-product.

FIGURE 8.2 19th Century ostrich egg drinking vessel.

LARGE-SCALE EGG PRODUCTION

Egg production worldwide, particularly those from chickens, is a gigantic industry. China alone has more than 1.5 billion egg-laying hens that produce over 25 million tons of eggs annually. Today, chicken eggs are a huge commodity product and farms will house thousands of birds. The prolific laying ability of certain chicken breeds allow for as much as 300 eggs per year to be produced by a single hen. The typical breed is the Leghorn which lay the common white egg.

Many large-scale egg farms are vertically integrated systems meaning the entire process is controlled by that farm including the feed milling, hen housing, egg washing, sorting, grading, packaging, and trucking. An *in-line* producer is one that is able to ship eggs directly to market with all of the appropriate packaging directly from the farm/plant, in other words the eggs are shipped without needing any further processing. Feed ration is milled from grains and supplemented with proteins and then piped directly into the layer houses. Most large-scale egg producers will have large grain silos with stored corn ready for milling. It is common to see huge barns with cage operations that contain up to 150,000 hens. Collection is automated and eggs rarely need to be handled. Eggs are separated according to size and color, washed and packaged for transport. They are washed with a detergent at 120°F/49°C and then inspected. Some eggs are rejected due to their small size. These are often broken and separated by machine. Newer technologies can achieve up to 500,000 eggs per hour. Eggs are also separated into yolk and albumen or "white" and trucked out by tanker trailers. The shells are then ground to a fine powder and can be used for other animal feeds or human calcium supplement production.

Laying chickens start as pullets which are raised up to 10 to 15 weeks then placed in stacked cages in the laying houses. During this growth period the birds are vaccinated for a variety of diseases. Photostimulation or altered lighting is used to increase laying. Diet manipulation can also increase egg production. Most laying hens are viable for about two years and then they may be harvested for either very inexpensive meat or rendered. Farmers will force a "molt" or artificial season change to keep the birds producing. This is done with lighting and temperature control.

Many issues have been raised by animal rights advocates against certain practices by the egg industry. First, all of the male chicks of laying breeds are generally culled upon hatching. Also the close quarters of the cages where the chickens are held is considered inhumane by some. California has initiated a law that will be enacted by 2015 that will allow more space per bird and many producers will switch to cage-free systems. In these more open systems, birds are allowed to lay eggs in a more traditional roost. This practice is not to be confused with pasture raised though.

FIGURE **8.3** Many operations use battery cages that enable them to hold large numbers of birds in relatively small space, a practice considered inhumane by some.

The fact that eggs are raised in such volume in enclosed barns results in Salmonella and other bacteria contamination. This has made fully cooking egg dishes a requirement in some kitchens. Antibiotic use for laying hens is restrained to only during times of illness and birds are not fed a steady preemptive antibiotic as are some other meat birds.

FIGURE **8.4** Cage-free layer houses allow the birds to lay eggs in a more traditional roost.

FREE RANGED VS PASTURE-RAISED EGGS

The USDA has no current guidelines or definition for free range eggs. It can be interpreted differently from producer to producer with some stating the eggs are laid by free ranging hens but this may mean access to the outdoors in large dirt pens but not a forage situation. Let the buyer beware when it comes to free range. Take the time to research the producer farm before accepting free range eggs at a higher price.

The European Union has somewhat stricter guidelines of what is exactly a free range egg. The birds must be outside for a certain amount of time each day and must have access to some forage.

Some U.S. farmers are producing eggs in a style that resembles how chickens were raised before large indoor raising facilities became the norm. These tend to be small niche market operations with the goal of creating a higher quality egg. The chickens are typically allowed to roost and all eggs are collected by hand. Birds are outside on a daily basis and allowed to forage. An egg from a true free ranged chicken tends to have more flavor and structure than caged eggs. The bird is eating a varied diet and is naturally digesting greens, insects, wild grains, and more which can elevate the vitamin content of the egg. This can also be done through feed supplements but it is difficult to recreate a pasture-raised flavor in a confined chicken egg. Pasture-raised eggs tend to have less fat and more vitamin A than regular eggs. Depending on its diet the pasture-raised egg will have a much higher Omega-3 fatty acid count as well. The drawback of pasture-raised eggs is the price will be higher due to the labor involved in growing them. There also can be some seasonality depending on where the farm is located. Many chefs today are seeking pasture-raised eggs due to their superior flavor. Be sure to have a steady supply if putting them on the menu.

FIGURE 8.5 Fresh free range eggs.

FIGURE 8.6 Today some farms are using mobile pasture-raised units to efficiently move the birds from pasture to pasture.

Another term previously mentioned is *cage-free* poultry. This is neither free ranged or pasture raised but it does mean birds are not kept in small cages but spread out in larger flat floors with the ability to perch and roost. This type of raising has become more popular as eggs labeled cage free can be sold for a higher price. This system is not as efficient as caging birds but it does offer some freedom of movement for the birds and is considered a more humane treatment.

ORGANIC EGGS

The term "organically raised" egg is defined by the United States Department of Agriculture (USDA) as those eggs produced with organically grown feeds. Chickens can be kept indoors but cannot be caged and must have access to outdoor pens. No artificial molting or false seasons are allowed. No low-level uses of antibiotics are allowed. Here is a quote from the USDA website explaining some of the organic restrictions.

> *"What is organic food? Organic food is produced by farmers who emphasize the use of renewable resources and the conservation of soil and water to enhance environmental quality for future generations. Organic meat, poultry, **eggs,** and dairy products come from animals that are given no antibiotics or growth hormones. Organic food is produced without using most conventional pesticides; fertilizers made with synthetic ingredients or sewage sludge; bioengineering; or ionizing radiation. Before a product can be labeled 'organic,' a Government-approved certifier inspects the farm where the food is grown to make sure the farmer is following all the rules necessary to meet USDA organic standards. Companies that handle or process organic food before it gets to your local supermarket or restaurant must be certified, too."*

Consumer Brochure, USDA National Organic Program

Organic producers also need to adhere to other standards such as waste disposal and humane animal handling practices. Environmental issues such as impact on local streams or waterways are often included in the approval of the farm as certified organic.

FIGURE 8.7 Pasture-raised chickens at Gray Horse Farm in Clinton Corners, New York.

Other certifications such as *Certified Humane: Raised and Handled* attach some of the restrictions of organic but do not require the same feed requirements. Birds are "raised with shelter, resting areas, sufficient space, and the ability to engage in natural behaviors." This certification is approved by the American Society for the prevention of Cruelty to Animals (ASPCA) and enforced by the USDA.

CANDLING

Years ago egg farmers would check to see whether an egg was fertilized before sending it to market. Hens were mixed with roosters and natural breeding occurred. Fertilized eggs were either allowed to hatch naturally with the mother or they were taken and incubated. Unfertilized eggs were shipped out for market. The way to check the egg was to place it in a candler that shines a candlelit lantern device behind the egg to illuminate the contents. The light shines through the shell exposing a fertilized embryo.

Candling also detects any defects or cracks in the shell. There is an air cell in all eggs and candling can determine the size of it for grading purposes. Farmers would hand candle each egg which was a labor-intensive practice.

Today candling is done using sonic testing to detect cracks and evaluation is done at high speed by computerized machines. Sonic testing can judge many of the things the old style candling could such as yolk size, white density, and size of the air cell.

CHICKEN EGG GRADING AND SIZING

Chicken eggs are graded to assign value. The higher the grade the higher the price a purveyor can charge. The USDA grading of eggs is voluntary and is done for producers that are selling in retail stores. Grades are for whole eggs, but have nothing to do with size. Grading examines the shell uniformity, the white, yolk, and air cell of the egg. The air cell is a natural phenomenon caused by the contraction of inner and outer membranes during initial cooling of the egg. There are three basic USDA grades of chicken eggs: AA, A, B. Grades can indicate the initial quality of the egg and also freshness. The older an egg becomes the larger its air cell and the more watery its white. The *chalazae* are strand-like proteins that attach the yolk to the white. They are more prominent in fresher eggs. AA and A graded eggs are typically sold in retail stores and are available to foodservice operators. B grade eggs are typically sent to the egg breaker and sold as bulk eggs for large-scale commercial use.

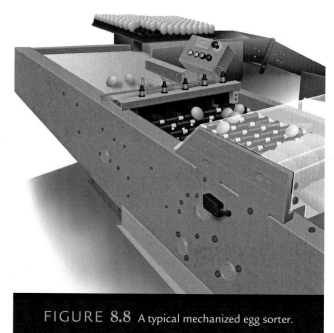

FIGURE 8.8 A typical mechanized egg sorter.

Here is a basic chart explaining the quality differences of egg grades and their typical uses.

CHICKEN EGG QUALITY			
	GRADE AA	GRADE A	GRADE B
Appearance on a griddle or in pan	Does not spread easily, stays in a small circumference	Covers a wider area, somewhat less uniform	Covers a large area, watery, flat and not uniform
Albumen or "White" Appearance	White is relatively firm, relatively cloudy, has prominent chalazae	White is about half firm, chalazae prominent, but smaller	White is transparent, thin, and watery. Chalazae are very small or nonexistent
Yolk Appearance	Yolk is firm, circular, and stands high	Yolk is firm and stands fairly high	Yolk is somewhat flattened and spread out
Shell Appearance	Must have typical egg shape; generally clean, no cracks, some blemishes and texture ridges are allowed		Abnormal shape; some slight stained areas permitted; unbroken; pronounced ridges/thin spots permitted
Usage	Excellent for any use, excellent for presentation such as sunny-side up or poached, whites will whip stiffer	Good for any use, such as poaching, frying, and cooking in shell. Whites may not whip as well but okay	Good for scrambling, baking, and as an ingredient in other foods. Thinner whites may affect some baking recipes negatively

EGG SIZE CLASSIFICATIONS

Chicken eggs are grouped according to size which is determined by their weight. The size of eggs is related to a few factors such as the age, weight, breed, and living conditions of the hen. Overcrowded birds, excessive heat, and poor nutritional rations all will produce small eggs. Some breeds produce larger eggs such as White Leghorns and Plymouth Rocks.

There is also the phenomenon of double yolk eggs. These are a rarity and some companies will isolate them and charge more per dozen.

EGG SIZING, WEIGHT, AND AMOUNT TO MAKE 1 CUP OF EGG INGREDIENT				
EGG SIZE	WEIGHT EACH	WHOLE	WHITES	YOLKS
Jumbo	+2.5 oz	4	5	11
X-Large	+2.25 oz	4	6	12
Large	+2 oz	5	7	14
Medium	+1.75 oz	5	8	16
Small	+1.5 oz	6	9	18
Peewee	+1.25 oz	8	11	22

When using eggs for recipes the size of the egg can alter the recipe. Use this chart for recipes.

SIZE EQUIVALENTS				
JUMBO	X-LARGE	LARGE	MEDIUM	SMALL
1	1	1	1	1
2	2	2	2	3
2	3	3	3	4
3	4	4	5	5
4	4	5	6	7
5	5	6	7	8

Other egg sizes:
Duck egg   70 grams
Goose egg   145 grams
Turkey egg   80 grams
Quail egg   9 grams
Ostrich egg   1.4 kilograms!

There are no USDA grades for other eggs and the purchaser needs to be aware of differences between purveyors. Most eggs taste the same despite the differences between the taste of their meat. The sizes will depend on specific breeds within species as well.

FIGURE **8.9** Chicken egg sizes, left to right: small, large, extra-large, and jumbo.

FIGURE **8.10** Green chicken eggs.

FIGURE **8.11** Duck eggs.

FIGURE **8.12** Goose eggs.

FIGURE **8.13** Left to right: chicken egg, duck egg, goose egg.

FIGURE **8.14** Quail eggs.

FIGURE **8.15** Ostrich egg.

FIGURE **8.16** Left to right: quail egg, chicken egg, duck egg, goose egg, and ostrich egg.

STORAGE AND FRESHNESS

The sooner an egg is used after laying the better. Fresh eggs will be firmer and present better when fresh. Eggs will have a Julian pack date posted on the carton. The pack date indicates the date the carton is packaged at the egg farm/plant.

Eggs should be stored below 40°F/4°C and can last about two weeks. Humidity levels are important also. Storing eggs at about 70 to 80 percent humidity is ideal. Allowing eggs to sweat by placing them in high humidity while cold can allow bacteria to grow on the exterior.

Pre-cracked eggs can be sold frozen and will last about four months. Be sure to use them within one or two days after thawing.

FIGURE 8.17 "Liquid eggs" are mechanically pre-broken and sold in cartons.

PACKAGING

Eggs will come packaged in a variety of protective cartons. The most typical for retail is the dozen count carton. For the foodservice industry, eggs are sold in flats. Egg flats are 30 pieces or 2½ dozen per layer. Eggs are typically ordered in flats for most restaurants. The problem here is they may arrive without pack dates or grades depending on the purveyor. A case of eggs will hold 15 dozen and will be dated. Cases can be purchased as flats or individually packed retail-style dozens.

Bulk eggs already mechanically broken can be sold in large bulk containers for commercial baking uses. The yolks are sometimes separated from the whites and sold in bulk as well.

FIGURE **8.18** Chicken eggs are often packaged in dozen-count cartons.

FIGURE **8.19** In the foodservice industry, chicken eggs are often sold in 30-count flats.

FOOD SAFETY

Like all poultry products, eggs are susceptible to food-borne illnesses. They are high in protein and fats making them attractive for bacteria, especially once the egg is cracked. One problem with eggs is *Salmonella enteriditis* which is very rarely found inside the shell. On rare occasions a laying hen that is infected with this form of Salmonella will pass it into the egg and if the eggs are not stored correctly (namely, above 40°F/4°C), the bacteria will reproduce inside the egg. About 1 percent of commercially produced egg will have Salmonella. By far more Salmonella contamination occurs by mishandling of other meat items such as chicken, turkey, pork, and more. The interior of the egg was once considered sterile but that has been proved false. Even so, if eggs are stored, handled, and cooked correctly they pose little threat. Many breakfast food restaurants will still serve undercooked eggs on a daily basis but people with compromised immune systems should be aware and avoid raw egg.

NUTRITION

Eggs have been a valuable source of digestible protein for many thousands of years. The fact that it is a whole food, containing many valuable nutrients makes it an attractive food even today. But there is one major drawback to eggs and that is the amount of cholesterol found in them. It is plain and simple, eggs are loaded with it. Cholesterol, especially in certain at-risk body types, can be a contributing factor in heart diseases. The question arises, who can eat eggs and how many? Egg producers are quick to explain that cholesterol in eggs if consumed in relative moderation is no concern for most healthy adults. The question arises about what is moderation? Most people considering a low-cholesterol diet should consume no more than 300 mg of cholesterol daily, and one medium chicken egg contains about 200 mg. Eggs have more cholesterol per ounce than any other food. All of the cholesterol in eggs is located in the yolk and whites have none to speak of. For those at risk of coronary heart disease eggs might be something to eat in moderation.

But all people absorb cholesterol differently. Some can eat rich foods loaded with cholesterol without elevating it in their bloodstream. Each person should be aware of their blood cholesterol. Eggs have been consumed for many thousands of years so to say they are a "bad" food is not a true statement for most, but they certainly are for some.

Beyond cholesterol, eggs are an excellent source of easily digestible protein. Two chicken eggs provide about 20 percent of the recommended daily amount of protein for an average person. Eggs have long been consumed by athletes for a protein boost.

Nutrition Facts

Serving Size 1 egg (50g)
Serving per Container 12

Amount Per Serving

Calories 70	Calories from Fat 40

	% Daily Value*
Total Fat 4.5g	7%
Saturated Fat 1.5g	8%
Polyunsaturated Fat .5g	
Monounsaturated Fat 2.0g	
Cholesterol 215mg	71%
Sodium 65mg	3%
Potassium 60mg	2%
Total Carbohydrate 1g	0%
Protein 6g	10%

Vitamin A 6%	•	Vitamin C 0%	
Calcium 2%	•	Iron 4%	• Thiamin 2%
Riboflavin 15%	•	Vitamin B-6 4%	
Folate 6%	•	Vitamin B-12 8%	
Phosphorus 8%	•	Zinc 4%	

Not a significant source of Dietary Fiber or Sugars.

*Percent Daily Values are based on a 2,000 calorie diet. Your daily values may be higher or lower depending on your calorie needs.

	Calories	2,000	2,500
Total Fat	Less than	65g	80g
Sat Fat	Less than	20g	25g
Cholesterol	Less than	300mg	300mg
Sodium	Less than	2,400mg	2,400mg
Potassium		3,500mg	3,500mg
Total Carbohydrate		300g	375g
Dietary Fiber		25g	30g
Protein		50g	65g

Calories per gram
Fat 9 • Carbohydrate 4 • Protein 4

AMOUNT OF NUTRIENTS IN 100 GRAMS OF FRESH EGGS

	DUCK	CHICKEN
Water, g	74.57	70.83
Kcal	185	158
Protein, g	12.81	12.14
Lipids, g	13.77	11.15
MINERALS		
Calcium, mg	64	56
Iron, mg	3.85	2.09
Magnesium, mg	16	12
Phosphorus, mg	220	180
Potassium, mg	222	130
Sodium, mg	146	138
Zinc, mg	1.41	1.44
VITAMINS		
Thiamin, mg	0.156	0.087
Riboflavin, mg	0.404	0.301
Niacin, mg	0.200	0.062

(Continues)

(*Continued*)

VITAMINS

	DUCK	CHICKEN
B6, mg	0.250	0.120
B12, mg	5.395	1.547
A, IU	1328	520

LIPIDS

	DUCK	CHICKEN
Total saturated, g	3.68	3.35
Total monounsaturated, g	6.52	4.46
Total polyunsaturated, g	1.22	1.45
Cholesterol, mg	884	548

AMINO ACIDS

	DUCK	CHICKEN
Lysine, g	0.951	0.820
Methionine, g	0.576	0.392
Cystine, g	0.285	0.289
Threonine, g	0.736	0.596
Isoleucine, g	0.598	0.759
Phenylalanine, g	0.840	0.686

Excerpts from *Properties and Food Uses of Duck Eggs* by Rhodes, Adams, Bennett, and Feeney, 1960.

Eggs do contain some saturated fats especially in the yolk, about 8 percent of the daily required amount, in a single egg. There is a large amount of a variety of B vitamins, phosphorus, zinc, and iron.

Today we are finding companies creating eggs high in Omega-3 fatty acid. The chickens producing these eggs have a diet supplemented with flaxseeds or fish oil that will boost the Omega 3 in the egg.

Another dietary supplement for chickens is carotene. Carotene will make the yolk a deep yellow color. These enhanced eggs are available by many purveyors today but for a premium price.

Besides chicken eggs, duck, goose, quail, turkey, and ostrich eggs all are high in many vitamins, minerals, proteins, and cholesterol. Duck eggs which tend to be a little larger than chicken, also tend to be slightly richer.

An ostrich egg can equal 24 chicken eggs. The ostrich egg has a similar protein, vitamin, and cholesterol makeup. The white tends to be a little more solid than that of a chicken and has more sticking ability in recipes.

Turkey eggs have the highest cholesterol per 100 grams but all eggs are high in it. Cholesterol, vitamin, and protein levels can vary slightly from bird to bird and the diet given to the hens can also change nutrition as well. Wild foraging birds tend to have eggs much higher in Omega-3 fatty acids and lower in saturated fats but again it all depends on diet. Wild turkeys are foraging on wild acorns in the fall therefore the eggs will be high in Omega-3 fatty acid but they are not a commercially available egg.

EGGS AS FOOD

Poultry eggs are an integral part of any chef's ingredient list. Can you imagine the great cookbooks of the world without including the egg? The egg is often used as an ingredient in a myriad of baking and savory recipes and is used for both flavor and texture. It has the ability to bind other ingredients and can be used to add proteins that easily coagulate. Eggs have what are known as globular proteins especially in the whites, which when heated connect together forming a coagulated mass. The longer an egg cooks the more solid the mass becomes. Just think of a hard-boiled egg versus an egg over easy.

Eggs are probably best known as a breakfast food. Eggs are a mainstay on many breakfast menus which includes omelets, scrambled, sunny-side up, over-easy, soft- and hard-boiled, and poached with many variations. A typical breakfast restaurant will feature a favorite dish, Eggs Benedict, that feature poached eggs with hollandaise sauce which contains a large amount of egg as an ingredient. Omelets, basically a folded scrambled egg, are filled with ingredients as simple as plain cheese to complex combinations of vegetables, sausages, cured meats, exotic cheeses, and spices. Other breakfast egg dishes such as frittatas, egg bakes, crêpes, and custards combine ingredients and can vary from culture to culture. The egg is also a main ingredient in other breakfast foods such as pancakes or waffles and acts as a leavening agent to puff up the pancake, making it light and fluffy. Eggs are often found in breakfast muffins and cakes and may be an ingredient in certain breads such as challah. The "French" toast is made by dipping bread slices into an egg batter and then griddling it until golden brown.

Eggs are an integral part of a huge amount of baking recipes. Separating eggs into whites and yolks enables them to be used for different purposes. Whites are used to make meringues which require the albumen to be whipped with sugar to make it firm. When baked, the meringue becomes firm and slightly crisp but very light. The albumen protein is also a quality binder and can be used to secure meat items together or bind sausages. Many meat recipes such terrines, pâtes, galantines, wursts, and blood puddings call for eggs as a binding agent.

Eggs are used to make many sorts of pastas, spaetzles, flat noodles, and dumplings and are used to bind potato pancakes.

The ultimate use of poultry eggs involves another sort of eggs. Hard-boiled eggs are chopped and served with caviar as a garnish.

Commercially available egg powder is often used in large scale baking and processed food recipes. Taking fresh eggs and dehydrating them to make a powder eliminates the dangers of using fresh eggs. Egg powder is available in both whole egg or yolk and white forms. The eggs are pasteurized and the placed in a vertical egg dryer using high, rapid heat and air flow to quickly dehydrate the eggs into a fine powder. Egg whites are fermented to eliminate glucose which would result in the "Maillard" reaction or browning and caramelizing during the heating.

Eggs are often used in savory dishes such as soups and sauces. Egg yolks act as an emulsifier for holding water and fats together. Many salad dressings and classic sauces require an emulsion to stay stable. Hollandaise is one such sauce.

There are also bar cocktails that require egg whites as an emulsifier. The original Whisky Sour is made with a sour mix that uses egg whites to bind lemon juice. Fizzes, flips, and egg creams were once mainstays at the bar and soda fountains and all require eggs as an ingredient. These mixology recipes often would call for raw egg but today we find many bartenders using egg powders.

FIGURE 8.20 Wild goose nest.

PRESERVED EGGS

All sorts of eggs have been preserved for food in a variety of manners. Pickled eggs are hard-boiled eggs that are peeled and placed in a variety of vinegar and salt brines with various spices added. The eggs will last for months but develop a stronger flavor. Some recipes call for beet juice which adds color and natural nitrates. The eggs will turn various shades of pink. Pickled eggs are a typical bar or pub food and it is often speculated that the flavor of them improves with the amount of alcohol consumed.

The "century" or 1000 year egg is an ancient Chinese method of preservation. Also known as a pidan egg, it is dipped in clay, ash, salt, lime, wrapped in rice straw, and then stored for about three months. The result is an edible egg that is a dark greenish color with a distinct flavor that is considered a delicacy. The pH levels of these eggs are drastically changed giving them an alkaline flavor. Today the process is sped up by putting eggs in a brine mixture of salt, calcium hydroxide, and sodium carbonate and the end result is the same as the clay wrap.

Preservation of eggs must be done carefully. Food-borne illness caused by the process can bring an assortment of intestinal distresses. Be sure to follow recipes precisely and be aware of strong sulfur smells that can indicate spoilage.

FIGURE **8.21** A chicken coop on a free-range chicken farm.

FIGURE **8.22** Free-range chickens laying eggs in a small-scale coop.

FIGURE **8.23** Eggs layed in a chicken coop.

POULTRY RECIPES

The recipes of this book are intended to utilize some of the fabrication techniques taught in the other chapters. Although they are all fairly basic they do require some prior cooking knowledge. This is not intended to be a beginner's cookbook in that knowledge of salting, sautéing, grilling, roasting, and smoking will be assumed. As with all poultry cooking, be sure to test temperatures to ensure food safety. If marinades or brines are used do not save them for future reuse. Some recipes are in relatively small portions. If increasing them be careful to adjust accordingly.

Basic Chicken Stock   **202**

Basic Poultry Brine for Enhancing
   Moisture   **203**

Basic Poultry Brine for Curing and
   Smoking   **204**

Frenched Chicken Breast with Fresh
   Basil Sauce   **205**

Apple-Walnut Stuffed Cornish Game
   Hens   **207**

Columbian Chicken Sancocho   **211**

Chicken Paprikash   **212**

Easy Slice Roast Turkey   **213**

Turkey Pastrami   **217**

Roast Goose Grand Marnier   **218**

Smoked Goose Breast with Hoisin
   Glaze   **221**

Duck Magret with Sauce Cassis   **225**

Barbequed Duck Legs   **226**

Spanish Griddled Quail   **227**

Pecan-Stuffed Pheasant   **229**

Duck Saucisse (Sausage)   **233**

Peppered Ostrich Filets with Duck Steak
   Fries   **235**

Foie Gras Fig Newton   **237**

Pan Seared Squab Au Jus   **241**

BASIC CHICKEN STOCK

YIELD: 1 GALLON

Chicken bones	5 lbs/2.27 kg
Water	1 gal/3.84 L
Salt	as needed/as needed
Mirepoix (2 parts chopped onion,	
1 part chopped carrots,	
1 part chopped celery)	3/4 lb/340 g

Sachet d'Espices (tie the following ingredients into a cheese cloth)

Parsley sprigs	3/3
Thyme	1/2 tsp/0.5 g
Bay leaf	1/1
Peppercorns	1/2 tsp/0.85 g
Garlic clove, crushed	1/1
Cloves	2/2
Dill	1/4 tsp/0.25 g

METHOD

1. Add bones, water, and salt to a stock pot. Bring to boil over low heat.
2. Skim off any foam that is created. Cook for 1 hour.
3. Add mirepoix and sachet d'Espices and simmer for 2 or more hours.
4. Strain and chill.

BASIC POULTRY BRINE FOR ENHANCING MOISTURE

YIELD: 1 GALLON

Salt	1/3 lb/151 g
Brown sugar	1/3 lb/151 g
Hot water	1 cup/240 mL
Water	1 gal/3.84 L

METHOD

1. Dissolve salt and sugar into hot water.
2. Pour into remaining water and stir thoroughly.
3. Be sure poultry is submerged in brine. Brine can be injected into poultry for faster reaction.

BRINING TIMES

Small birds or cut parts 2 to 3 hrs
Broiler chicken/pheasants 4 to 5 hrs
Duck/turkey breast 5 to 6 hrs
Turkey 8 to 10 hrs

Chef's Note: Aromatics, spices, or alternative sugars can be used to create different flavors.

BASIC POULTRY BRINE FOR CURING AND SMOKING

YIELD: 1 GALLON

TCM (Tinted Curing Mix) (pink salt)	2 1/3 oz/66 g
Salt	1/2 lb/227 g
Brown sugar	1/3 lb/151 g
Hot water	1 cup/240 mL
Water	1 gal/3.84 L

METHOD

1. Dissolve TCM, salt, and sugar with hot water, then add to remaining water.

BRINING TIMES

Small birds or cut parts 24 hrs
Broiler Chicken, pheasant 24 to 36 hrs
Duck, Turkey Breast 2 to 3 days
Whole turkey/goose 5 days

Chef's Note: After curing poultry may be soaked in cold water to release some of the salt. Spices and aromatics can be added for more flavors. Injecting brine can shorten curing time. Smoking may require poultry to be left at temperatures that could allow for rapid bacteria growth. This brine ensures the poultry will be cured and its proteins denatured helping to preserve the meat and give it a "hammy" tang familiar with cured meats. Cured meats remain pink after cooking. This recipe calls for Tinted Curing Mix which is basically a diluted form of sodium nitrite that accelerates the curing time and prevents against pathogens.

FRENCHED CHICKEN BREAST WITH FRESH BASIL SAUCE

YIELD: 4 SERVINGS

Semi-boneless frenched chicken breast, full skin on	4/4
Salt and pepper	as needed/as needed
Flour	2 oz/57 g
Clarified butter	1 oz/28 g
Shallots, minced	1 Tbsp/15 mL
White wine, dry	1/3 cup/80 mL
Chicken stock	1/3 cup/80 mL
Heavy cream	2 Tbsp/30 mL
Basil, chopped	2 Tbsp/30 mL
Parsley, chopped	1 Tbsp/15 mL

METHOD

1. Season chicken with salt and pepper, dredge in flour.
2. Heat clarified butter in sauté pan and brown chicken until almost cooked through.
3. Place chicken in warm oven to finish.
4. Sauté shallots in the same pan until translucent. Deglaze pan with white wine and reduce by half.
5. Add chicken stock, salt, and pepper to taste. Reduce until slightly thickened.
6. Add cream, basil, and parsley. Reduce a few minutes until it reaches a smooth consistency that will coat spoon.
7. Pour sauce over finished chicken.

APPLE-WALNUT STUFFED CORNISH GAME HENS

YIELD: 4 SERVINGS

Butter	2 Tbsp/28 g
Medium onion, chopped, divided in half	1/1
Garlic clove, minced	1/1
Baking apples, peeled and diced	2/2
Walnuts, chopped	1/2 cup/113 g
Unseasoned bread crumbs	1/4 cup/57 g
Salt and pepper	as needed/as needed
Cornish Game Hens	four 1-lb each/454-g each
Thyme	1 tsp/1 g
Paprika	1 tsp/2 g
Chopped parsley, divided	2 Tbsp/7.6 g
Bacon (optional)	4 slices/4 slices
White wine, dry	1/4 cup/60 mL
Chicken stock	1/4 cup/60 mL

METHOD

1. Heat butter in sauté pan. Sauté half of the onion until translucent. Add the garlic and cook until aromatic.
2. Add apples, walnuts, and bread crumbs. Lightly season with salt and pepper.
3. Reserve and chill slightly.
4. Rinse hens and pat dry, remove any giblets if included.
5. Stuff apple mixture into each hen.
6. Truss each bird closing off back end. Place on rack in roasting pan.

(Continues)

7. Season exterior of hens with thyme, paprika, 1 Tbsp/15 mL parsley, salt, and pepper. Lay bacon strip over top of hen. Place the rest of the onion in the bottom of the roasting pan.

8. Roast at 350°F/177°C. Add white wine to pan when onions are lightly browned, after about 10 minutes. Add chicken stock 10 minutes later.

9. Roast for 1 hour or until internal temp reaches 165°F/74°C. Add extra chicken stock if totally evaporated.

10. Remove hens and degrease the pan sauce. Sauce can be thickened if desired.

11. Serve bird whole with sauce.

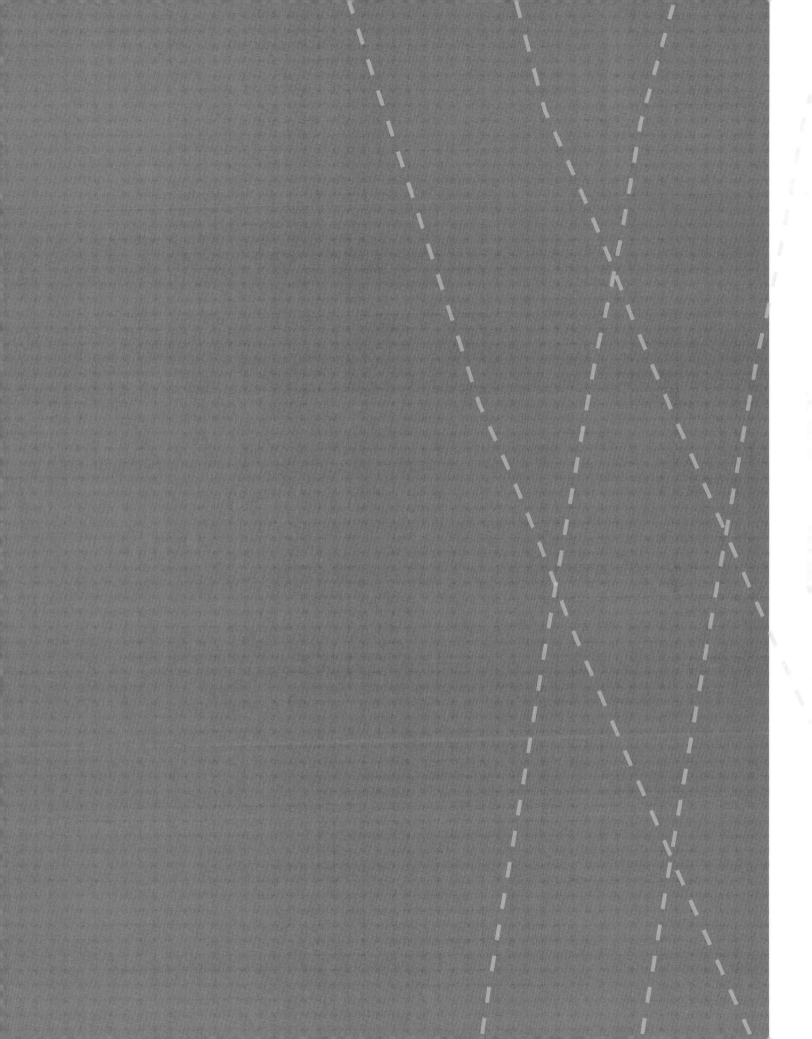

COLUMBIAN CHICKEN SANCOCHO

YIELD: 6 SERVINGS

Chicken legs cut to thighs and drumsticks	6/6
Chicken stock	2 1/2 qt/2.16 L
Garlic cloves, chopped	2/2
Large onion, chopped	1/1
Cumin	1 1/2 tsp/9 g
Paprika	1/2 tsp/1 g
Salt	1 tsp/6 g
Yucca root, peeled and cut into 1 1/2-inch/4-cm cubes (yucca can contain tough center core that should be removed)	2 lbs/907 g
Medium carrots, chopped	2/2
Red potatoes, peeled and cut to 1-inch/3-cm pcs	2 lbs/907 g
Green plantains, peeled and cut on bias into 1 1/2-inch/4-cm pcs	2/2
Cilantro, chopped	1/4 cup/4 g

METHOD

1. Place chicken, stock, garlic, onion, cumin, paprika, and salt in pot and simmer for 15 minutes.
2. Add the yucca and carrots, simmer for 15 minutes more.
3. Add the potatoes and plantains and simmer until tender, about 20 minutes.
4. Add the cilantro in the last 5 to 10 minutes of cooking.
5. Serve as stew in bowls.

CHICKEN PAPRIKASH

YIELD: 6 SERVINGS

Butter	1 Tbsp/14 g
Rendered chicken or duck fat (can use vegetable oil)	1 Tbsp/15 mL
Chicken thighs	12/12
Salt and pepper	as needed/as needed
Flour for dredging	as needed/as needed
Medium onions, chopped	2/2
Garlic cloves, chopped	2/2
Hungarian paprika	3 Tbsp/7 g
Cayenne pepper	1/4 tsp/0.5 g
Chicken stock	16 fl oz/480 mL
Bay leaves	2/2
Sour cream	1/2 cup/120 mL
Chopped parsley	

METHOD

1. In heavy pot or skillet heat the butter and fat, season chicken with salt and pepper, dredge in flour, and brown thoroughly.
2. Remove chicken and reserve.
3. Sauté onions, garlic, paprika, and cayenne pepper until onions are lightly browned.
4. Add chicken back to the pan along with the stock, bay leaves and salt and pepper to taste.
5. Let simmer until chicken is tender, about 30 minutes.
6. Skim excess fat and whisk in sour cream, let simmer for 10 minutes. Adjust salt. Add extra paprika if desired.
7. Sprinkle chopped parsley over after plating.

Chef's Note: Paprikash is often served with spaetzle noodles or potato dumplings.

EASY SLICE ROAST TURKEY

YIELD: 10 TO 12 SERVINGS

Basic Poultry Brine for Enhancing Moisture (page 205)	1 batch/1 batch
Bay leaves	2/2
Peppercorns	1/4 tsp/0.42 g
Garlic clove, crushed	1/1
Turkey, natural (not with phosphate or other additives)	12 to 14 lb/5.44 to 6.35 kg
Chopped onion	1/4 cup/57 g
Celery stalk, chopped	1/1
Thyme	1 tsp/1 g
Coarse ground pepper	1 tsp/2 g
Marjoram	dash/dash
Sage	1/4 tsp/0.18 g
Paprika	1/4 tsp/0.5 g
Kosher salt	as needed/as needed
Garlic cloves, minced	2/2
Butter	2 Tbsp/28 g *or* Smoky bacon *(optional)* 3 slices/3 slices
Chicken stock	1 cup/240 mL (more as needed)

METHOD

1. Mix bay leaves, peppercorns, and garlic into brine mixture. Let stand for 2 hours.
2. Remove giblets from turkey. Bone out turkey by cutting along back (see Turkey chapter). Remove wings and drumsticks, leaving the thigh meat intact. Utilize carcass and parts for stock. Trim off excess skin around neck.
3. Submerge turkey into brine and let stand for 3 to 4 hours under refrigeration.
4. Remove turkey and pat dry.
5. Loosely form turkey into cylindrical shape equally distributing light and dark meat. Tie turkey into roast possibly using trussing needle where needed.

(Continues)

6. Place chopped onion and celery in roasting pan. Mix together thyme, pepper, marjoram, sage, paprika, garlic, and kosher salt and massage onto all surfaces.
7. Place on rack over onions in pan. (Roast can be placed directly on the celery-onion mixture if desired.)
8. Place dots of butter *or* slices of bacon over top of turkey.
9. Roast in 325°F/163°C oven until internal temperature reaches 165°F/74°C, about 2 to 2 1/2 hours.
10. Pour chicken stock into pan 20 minutes after starting to create pan gravy. Add more stock if it fully evaporates.
11. Remove and allow to rest, loosely covered with foil. Scrape pan drippings through sieve into saucepan. Adjust salt and thicken as desired.
12. Remove strings one or two at a time while carving to maintain shape. Can be chilled and served as a sliced cold cut item.

Chef's Note: This recipe is for those serving turkey when presentation of the whole bird is not necessary. The entire bird is boned and rolled into a roast and then carved either hot or cold as a sandwich meat.

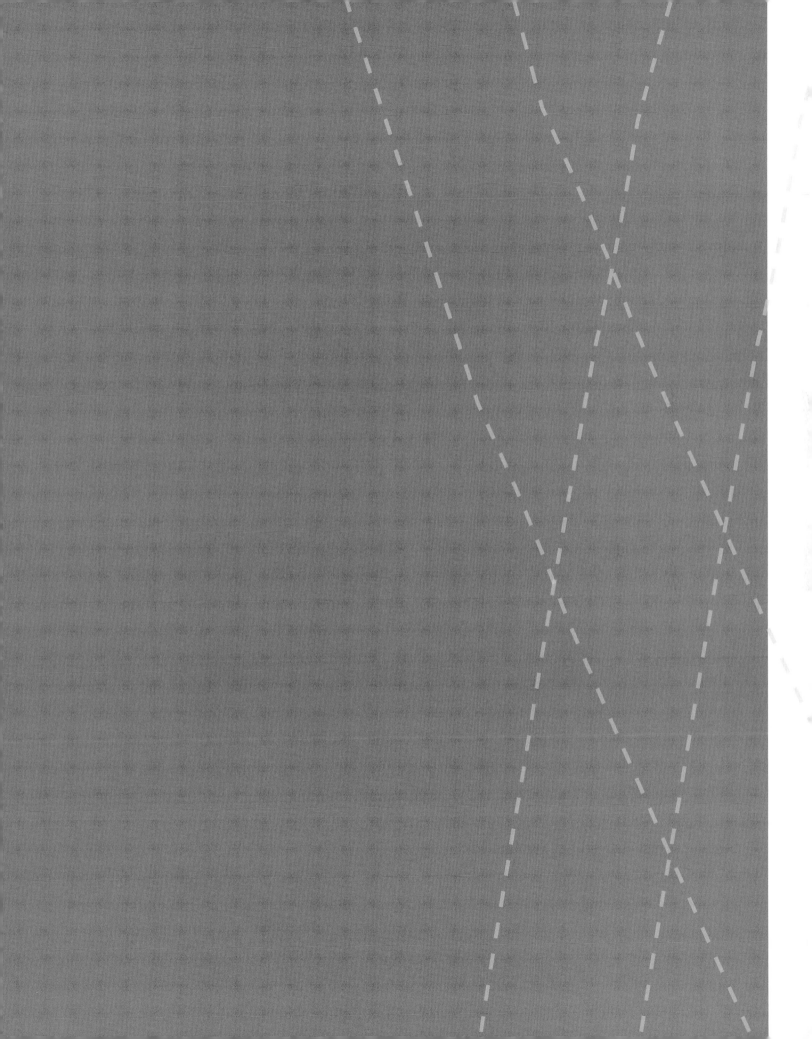

TURKEY PASTRAMI

YIELD: 6 POUNDS TURKEY PASTRAMI

Basic Poultry Brine for Curing and Smoking (page 206)	1 batch/1 batch
Bay leaves	2/2
Garlic cloves, crushed	2/2
Boneless Turkey Breast	5 to 6 lb/2.27 to 2.72 g

SPICE RUB

coriander seeds, coarse ground	3 Tbsp/15 g
Black peppercorns, coarse ground	3 Tbsp/15 g
Garlic cloves, minced	2/2
Sea salt	1 Tbsp/18 g
Brown sugar	1 Tbsp/14 g
Paprika	3 Tbsp/7 g

METHOD

1. Mix brine with bay leaves and crushed garlic. Place turkey in brine and submerge. Store refrigerated for 3 days.
2. Remove and soak in about 2 gallons/7.68 L of cool water for 1 to 2 hours to release excess salt.
3. Place between two pans and top with heavy weight to flatten for 2 to 3 hours under refrigeration.
4. Mix spice rub thoroughly. Pat dry turkey and massage in spice rub on all sides.
5. Heat smoker or grill using wood chips and charcoal. Place in smoker and cook until reaching internal temp of 165° to 170°F/74° to 77°C, about 2 hours. Turkey can be pan smoked and slow roasted if no smoker is available.
6. Once cooked, turkey can be sliced for sandwiches. Breast can be chilled and sliced to re-heat. Pastrami can be stored about 1 week and can be sliced and re-heated as needed.

Chef's Note: Recipe can be made fresh without using curing brine but must be used within 3 days. It will not have the typical cured flavor of true pastrami but will be very flavorful.

ROAST GOOSE GRAND MARNIER

YIELD: 8 TO 10 SERVINGS

Goose, thawed and giblets removed (separate liver)	12 to 14 lb/5.44 to 6.35 kg
Salt and pepper	as needed/as needed
Juice orange, peeled and chopped	1/1
Medium onion, cut into 6 chunks	1/1
Garlic cloves, chopped large	2/2
Chicken stock	3 to 4 cups/720 to 960 mL
bay leaf	1/1
Grand Marnier	1/4 cup/60 mL

METHOD

1. Using a sharp fork, prick goose lightly over breast being sure not to pierce the meat. This will allow some of the excess fat to render off.
2. Truss goose to ensure even cooking.
3. Season goose with salt and pepper on all surfaces.
4. Place giblets (without liver), orange chunks, onion, and garlic in bottom of roasting pan. Place goose on rack over onion mixture.
5. Roast at 300°F/149°C until onions turn light brown and oranges begin to caramelize, about 1/2 hour. Add in 2 cups/480 mL chicken stock ensuring about 1/2 inch/1 cm of liquid on bottom of pan.
6. Roast for about 3 hours adding more chicken stock as needed. Do not let pan cook out dry. Pan sauce should be deep brown but not burnt. Remove when internal temperature reaches 165°F/74°C and wing pulls away easily. Let stand for 15 minutes covered with foil.

(Continues)

7. Pour off pan juices and skim off the large amount of rendered fat and save for future cooking uses. Return pan juices to pan and deglaze. Pour into saucepan through sieve. Heat pan sauce. Add bay leaf, adjust salt and pepper and simmer for 5 to 10 minutes. Use thickener such as roux or arrow root if desired.
8. Disjoint goose and carve breast and thigh. Arrange parts on large platter.
9. Carefully heat Grand Marnier in metal cup. Light Grand Marnier and pour over all of goose engulfing in a blue flame. Be sure not to spill hot alcohol and keep all flammable items away. This can be done tableside or on a buffet line for an exciting presentation! Serve sauce on the side.

Chef's Note: If single portions are desired, carve the goose and serve equal portions of breast and leg. Light a small amount of Grand Marnier for each plate. Be careful!

SMOKED GOOSE BREAST WITH HOISIN GLAZE

YIELD: 2 POUNDS

Basic Poultry Brine for Curing and Smoking (page 204)	1 batch/1 batch
Bay leaves	2/2
Fermented soy sauce	2 Tbsp/30 mL
Small dried red chili pepper	1/1
Full goose breast, unsplit	two 2 lbs/907 g each

GLAZE

Hoisin sauce	1/4 cup/60 mL
Ginger powder	1/2 tsp/1 g
Brown sugar	1 tsp/3 g
Madeira wine	1 Tbsp/15 mL
Orange juice	1 tsp/5 mL

METHOD

1. Add bay leaves, soy sauce, and red chili to brine. Place goose breasts into brine and submerge for 2 days under refrigeration.
2. Remove breasts and soak in cool water for 1 hour to reduce saltiness.
3. Tie breast into two cylindrical roasts and let air-dry under refrigeration for 6 hours or until exterior becomes tacky.
4. Smoke using wood chips in cool smoker until golden brown, about 3 or 4 hours. (Each smoker works differently. Do not over smoke. Do not hot smoke or cook). Remove from smoker and place on roasting rack in pan.

(Continues)

5. Whisk together glaze mixture and brush over goose; reserve any excess.
6. Roast slowly at 300°F/149°C to internal temperature of 165°F/74°C, about 1 hour. Brush on more glaze every 15 to 20 minutes.

Chef's Note: Can be served as an appetizer warm or thin-sliced cold.

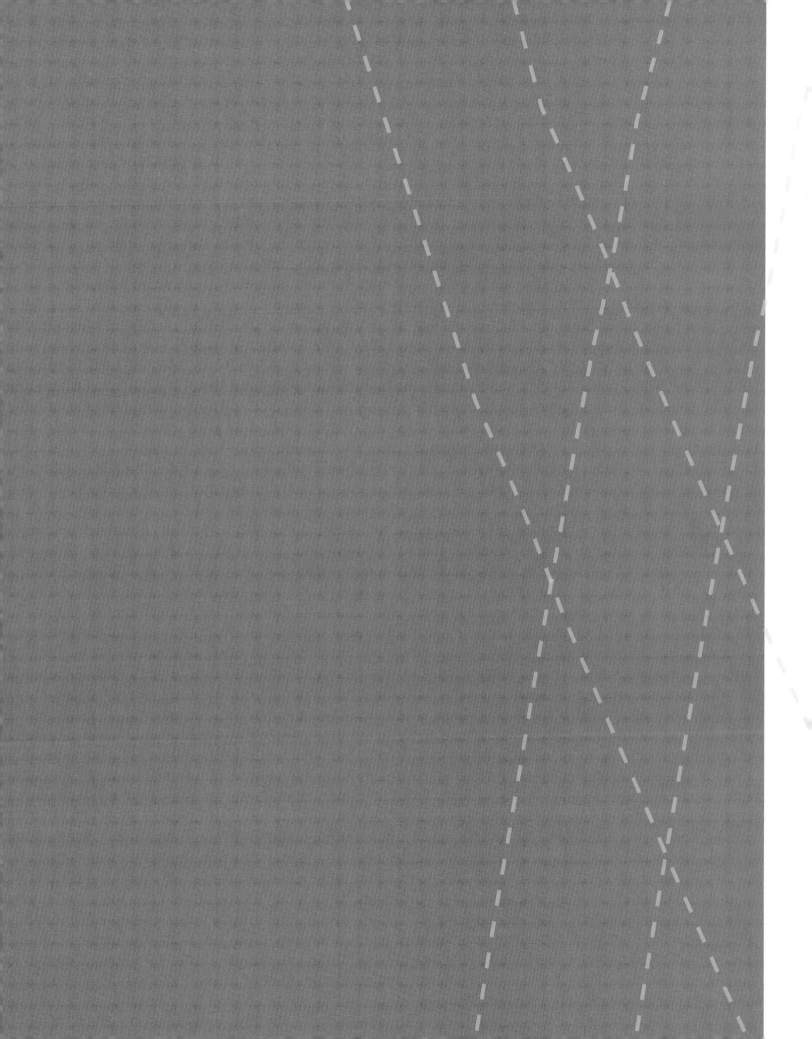

DUCK MAGRET WITH SAUCE CASSIS

YIELD: 4 SERVINGS

Boneless duck breast split to 4 portions, trimmed	2/2
Salt and pepper	as needed/as needed
Cassis syrup	1 1/2 Tbsp/22.50 mL
Cider vinegar	2 Tbsp/30 mL
Brandy	2 Tbsp/30 mL
Brown duck stock (can substitute brown chicken stock)	1 cup/240 mL
Black currants	1/4 lb/113 g *or* currant raisins 1 1/2 Tbsp/14 g
Butter	3 Tbsp/42 g

METHOD

1. Score duck breast skin with crisscross pattern to render fat, season with salt and pepper. Sear in hot skillet skin-side down until well browned. Turn and lightly sear other side.
2. Place in warm oven to finish. Do not overcook breast; it should be pink (145°F/63°C) in the center.
3. In a saucepan heat the Cassis syrup, vinegar, and brandy, reducing to syrupy texture. Stir in duck stock and reduce to desired thickness (about 15 minutes on medium heat); add in fresh currants when almost finished. (If using raisins, add at same time as stock to fully rehydrate.) Reduce heat and add in butter a little at a time to incorporate without breaking sauce. Adjust salt as needed.
4. Slice breast across the grain and on a bias. Sauce may be laid under or over depending on preference.

BARBEQUED DUCK LEGS

YIELD: 6 SERVINGS

Duck legs, whole	6/6

Basic Poultry Brine for
    Enhancing Moisture
    (page 205)
	1 batch/1 batch

BARBEQUE SAUCE

Ketchup	1 1/2 cups/360 mL
Cider vinegar	2 Tbsp/30 mL
Fine minced onion	2 Tbsp/14 g
Fermented soy sauce	2 Tbsp/30 mL
Dark brown sugar	2 Tbsp/
Garlic clove, fine minced	1/1
Spicy mustard	1 Tbsp/15 mL
Tabasco sauce	1 1/2 tsp/7.50 mL
Paprika	1/4 tsp/0.5 mL

METHOD

1. French off ends of legs. Place in brine for 2 or 3 hours. Remove and pat dry.
2. Whisk together and dissolve all Barbeque Sauce ingredients. Grill legs over medium heat. Brush on sauce, turning often to develop crusty exterior. Be sure to cook legs thoroughly to 165°F/74°C internal temperature.

SPANISH GRIDDLED QUAIL

YIELD: 4 SERVINGS

Quail	4 pc/4 pc
Bamboo skewers, soaked in water	8/8
Vegetable oil or duck fat	1/4 tsp/1.25 mL

MARINADE

Black peppercorns, crushed	4–5/4–5
Clove	1/1
Star anise	1/1
Honey	2 Tbsp/42 g
Sherry wine	1 Tbsp/15 mL
Thyme	1/4 tsp/0.25 g
Red pepper flake	1/4 tsp/0.45 g
Salt	as needed/as needed

METHOD

1. Split quail, removing backbone and keel. Cut off wing tips and french the ends of the legs.
2. In bowl, mix Marinade ingredients; add quail halves, coating thoroughly. Cover and let stand for 24 hours under refrigeration. Stir at about 12 hours to ensure even flavoring.
3. Remove and skewer through the meaty sections and press flat.
4. Brush griddle or large heavy skillet with oil or fat, heat until almost smoking. Place quail skin-side down and crisp until golden brown, about 2 to 3 minutes. Turn and crisp other side until brown, about 2 to 3 minutes. Quail will caramelize rapidly. Remove and place in warm oven (250°F/121°C) to finish, about 5 to 6 minutes. Do not overcook. Serve as appetizer or main course.

PECAN-STUFFED PHEASANT

YIELD: 4 TO 6 SERVINGS

Pheasant	1/1
Chopped bacon	2 Tbsp/14 g
Chopped pecans	1/4 cup/27 g
Shallot, fine chopped	1/1
Bread crumbs	1/4 cup/57 g
Egg	1/1
Thyme	1/4 tsp/0.25 g
Ground black pepper	1/4 tsp/0.5 mL
Chopped parsley	1 tsp/1.25 g
Chicken stock	1 cup + 2 Tbsp/270 mL
Salt and pepper	as needed/as needed
Chopped onion	1/4 cup/40 g
Chopped celery	1/4 cup/30 g
Chopped carrots	1/4 cup/30 g
Butter	1 Tbsp/14 g

METHOD

1. Bone out the pheasant breast and legs using the techniques described on pages 40 and 46 being sure not to cut through the skin. Clean out any large tendons in the legs and breast. Pound the legs and breast to about a 1/4-inch/6-mm thickness. Lay the legs out flat over the skin then overlay with the breast.

2. Sauté the chopped bacon until lightly browned, pour off the excess fat and add in the shallots and sauté briefly. Combine bacon, pecans, shallots, bread crumbs, egg, thyme, pepper, parsley, 2 Tbsp/30 mL chicken stock, and salt as needed, into a stuffing. Lay out over the boneless pheasant. Roll into roast and tie into cylindrical shape. Lightly season the exterior with salt and pepper.

(Continues)

3. Place mixed chopped onions, celery, and carrots and butter in small roasting pan, season with salt and pepper. Place roast directly on the vegetables. Roast at 300°F/149°C. After 15 minutes, add remaining chicken stock to pan. Baste the roast often. Add more chicken stock if it all evaporates. Roast until internal temperature reaches 165°F/74°C, about 1 hour. Let stand for 5 to 10 minutes.
4. Slice carefully maintaining shape.
5. Strain pan juices to make a light jus. Season as needed.

DUCK SAUCISSE (SAUSAGE)

YIELD: 6 TO 8 SERVINGS

Boneless duck leg (skin and any large sinews removed)	3 lbs/85 g
Mace	dash/dash
Ground white pepper	1/2 tsp/1 mL
Kosher salt	1 1/2 Tbsp/15 g
Garlic cloves, minced	2/2
Dry white wine	1/4 cup/60 mL
About 6–7 feet/32–35 mm hog casing	

METHOD

1. Cut duck meat into 1-inch/3-cm cubes leaving all excess fat intact.
2. Chill duck meat to almost to the point of freezing.
3. Place in mixing bowl. Mix dry spices and salt; sprinkle over meat. Add garlic and white wine and mix through meat thoroughly.
4. Chill mixture.
5. Grind through a medium 3/8-inch/9-mm die. Mix by hand.
6. Stuff into casing and link to desired size. Typical link is 4 inches/10 cm.

PEPPERED OSTRICH FILLETS WITH DUCK STEAK FRIES

YIELD: 5 SERVINGS

Russet Potatoes	2 Large (50 count)/2 Large (50 count)
Rendered duck fat	2 lbs/907 g
Ostrich Fan portion cuts (about 3/4-inch/2 cm thick)	four 5-oz/142-g each
Coarse black pepper	1 1/2 tsp/3 mL
Canola oil	1 Tbsp/15 mL
Butter	1 Tbsp/14 g
Salt	as needed/as needed
Sea salt	1/2 tsp/3 g

METHOD

1. Peel potatoes and cut into large 3/4-inch/2-cm fries. Soak in cold water to remove excess starch. Remove and pat dry. Heat duck fat in fryer or deep skillet to around 350°F, just below its smoking point. Par cook fries until lightly brown in small batches (do not crowd pan), remove and pat dry. Salt lightly and chill. Reserve duck fat.

2. Season fillet with pepper, pressing deep into steak. In a heavy skillet, add canola oil and heat to almost smoking. Sear fillets until browned and cooked to desired doneness. Reduce heat and deglaze pan with butter. Season steaks with salt and drizzle butter over steaks. (Butter can be eliminated if low-fat serving is desired.)

3. Return fries to reheated duck fat and crisp to desired crispness (deep brown). Pat dry and sea salt. Serve immediately.

FOIE GRAS FIG NEWTON

YIELD: 18 TO 24 PIECES

FOIE NEWTON DOUGH

Butter, soft	1 1/3 cup/302 g
Sugar	3/4 cup/151 g
Vanilla extract	1 tsp/5 mL
Eggs	2 2/3 oz/76 g
Cake flour, sifted	16 oz/454

BRIOCHE DOUGH

Bread flour	8 oz/227 g
Instant dry yeast	1 tsp/3.8 g
Eggs	3 1/4 oz/91 g
Whole milk, room temp	1.6 oz/50 mL
Sugar	1 3/4 Tbsp/22.7 g
Salt	3/4 tsp/4.3 g
Butter, soft but pliable	2/3 cup/136 g

LOBE B OR C GRADE

Foie Gras about 1–1 1/4 lbs/567 g	
Chopped figs	1/3 cup/78 g
Sugar	1/3 cup/67 g
Water	1/3 cup/80 mL
Egg white	1/1

METHOD

1. To make the fig newton dough, in a mixer with a paddle attachment, cream butter and sugar on medium speed. Add vanilla. Gradually, add eggs on low speed until fully incorporated. Add flour all at once, and mix on low speed.

(Continues)

2. Wrap in plastic wrap and rest overnight.

3. To make the Brioche dough, in a mixer with a hook attachment, mix flour and yeast. On a low speed, add eggs, milk, sugar, and salt. Once incorporated, on medium speed, gradually add butter, then, mix on medium speed for 15 minutes, or until dough pulls away from bowl.

4. Rest overnight on a greased surfaced, covered with a damp paper towel, and loosely covered with plastic wrap.

5. To assemble the Foie Gras Fig Newton, devein the foie gras and cut into 1/4-inch/6-mm thick slabs and cut these into 1-inch/3-cm wide strips. (Wide enough to be the center of the "Newton.") Cover with plastic wrap. Form any scrap pieces together to create 1-inch/3-cm wide strips. Foie gras can be passed through a screen to eliminate all fine veins. Freeze formed strips.

6. Combine figs, sugar, and water in a saucepan. Cook over medium-low heat until reduced to a thick jam consistency.

7. Knead both doughs together, to form one pliable mass. Lightly dust a work surface with flour, roll out dough with a rolling pin to 1/4-inch/6-mm thickness. Cut into equal length 1 1/2-inch/4-cm wide strips about 6 inches/15 cm long. Tease dough to ensure consistency. Match enough strips for tops and bottoms of the cookie. Lay jam out 1-inch/3-cm wide down center of bottom sections of dough to 1/4-inch/6-mm thickness. Lay frozen strips of foie over jam. Top with dough and pinch tops and bottoms together securely. Brush with whisked egg white.

8. Bake in 400°F/204°C convection oven until golden brown (Fig Newton color) about 10 minutes. Be sure dough does not separate while baking. Allow to cool completely and cut into 1-inch sections.

Chef's Note: Figs and foie gras go together very well as a flavor combination. The idea of a foie gras "fig Newton" was to create an appetizer/dessert that is fun yet true to the foie. Unlike a seared foie gras or a torchon where the liver is center stage, this dish is more of a meld of flavors. This dish can be made with a lower grade liver or smaller pieces can be mashed into shape. It is a sweet morsel that could be served warm or cold, as an appetizer or as a dessert. The dough is a combination of two doughs to get the proper texture.

PAN SEARED SQUAB AU JUS

YIELD: 4 SERVINGS

Squab, "boned out"	4/4
Canola oil	2 Tbsp/30 mL
Butter	1 Tbsp/14 g
Salt and pepper	as needed/as needed

METHOD

1. In a hot heavy pan, heat canola oil and butter to just below smoking point. Sear squab until golden brown. Press squab, breast-side down with a spatula, or with a smaller frying pan to brown the skin evenly, about 2 minutes. Tilting the pan away from you, carefully flip, and repeat on other side, for another 2 minutes. Rest on a rack in a roasting pan, and repeat with remaining three squab.

2. Once they are all pan seared, finish them in a 400°F/204°C oven for 4 to 5 minutes. Cook medium-rare, based on your preference. (Squab tends to get chewy if cooked past medium rare.)

SQUAB AU JUS

Makes 1+ cup/240+ mL

Medium yellow onion, large diced	¼/¼
Bones from 4 squab, dry	
Canola oil	1 Tbsp/15 mL
Carrot, peel and small dice	1/1
Celery Rib, small dice	1/1
Leek, sliced 1/4-inch/6 mm	½/½
Sachet with 1 garlic clove, 4 coriander seeds	
Dry red wine	1/4 cup/60 mL
Water	2 cups/480 mL
Chicken stock	2 cups/480 mL
Salt and black pepper	as needed/as needed
Thyme sprig	1/1

(Continues)

METHOD

1. Make "onion brûlée" by charring yellow onion in hot pan. This will provide sauce color.
2. Roast bones in 400°F/204°C oven with oil, turning often to brown evenly. Remove bones, then roast carrots, then celery, then leek, until just browned (but not burnt), and remove. These ingredients brown at different times so stagger cooking. Drain off oil. Deglaze pan ingredients with wine.
3. Combine roasted bones, onion, pan ingredients with all drippings, chicken stock, water, sachet, salt, and pepper. Simmer for about 1/2 hour. Strain off liquid and reduce to about 1 cup/240 mL of smooth jus. Add in thyme for last few minutes of cooking.
4. Ladle sauce over birds after plating.

READINGS AND RESOURCES

NAMP Meat Buyer's Guide

CIA Pro Chef

Meat and Muscle Cuts
Nottingham Press

What to Eat
Marion Nestle

The Goose, History, Folklore, Ancient Recipes
Daniela Garavini
Copyright 1996
Bibliotheca Culinaria SRL, Lodi, Italy
English translation:
Copyright 1998
Konemann Verlagsgesellschaft MbH
Bonner Strasse 126, D-50968 Koln, Germany

Web Sites

USDA
http://www.nal.usda.gov

American Egg Board
http://incredibleegg.org
http://www.aeb.org

Sustainable Foods web site
http://www.eatwild.com

Poultry resource web pages
http://www.ithaca.edu
http://www.feathersite.com
http://www.worldpoultry.net
http://www.amerpoultryassn.com
http://www.ansi.okstate.edu

History of poultry
http://www.foodtimeline.org

Game birds
http://www.extension.umn.edu

Egg information
http://ag.ansc.purdue.edu

Industry web sites
http://fossilfarmsostrich.com
http://www.tyson.com
http://www.dartagnan.com
http://www.culverduck.com
http://www.pheasant.com
http://www.mapleleaffarms.com
http://www.joejurgielewicz.com
http://www.perdue.com
http://www.schiltzfoods.com
http://www.rougie-usa.com

GLOSSARY

Airline Breast—Poultry breast with the first wing portion left intact but otherwise boneless.

Anatidae—The family of any number of waterfowl including ducks, geese, and swans.

Avian Influenza/Bird Flu—A variety of strains of influenza affecting a variety wild and domestic fowl. The highly pathogenic strain H5N1 has been the source of concern in recent years in that it has been transferred to humans that come in close contact with the birds.

Broiler—Most typical classification of chicken with an average weight of 2½ to 4½ lbs and about 6 weeks old.

Campylobacter—A genus of bacteria containing some strains that are pathogenic to humans and warm-blooded animals causing infection in the small intestines. Can be found on time-/temperature-abused poultry products.

Canvasback—Breed of wild Mallard duck not grown commercially.

Capon—Castrated male chicken grown to roaster size. Used for dry cooking methods such as roasting or broiling.

Charcuterie—Originally a term to describe the preservation of pork but today can mean any sausage- or ham-like product, often salted and smoked.

Chicken—Domesticated breeds of poultry *(Gallus gallus)* originating from jungle fowl typically used for meat and sold in a variety of weight and age classifications.

Confit—Originally a preservation method for meat, today it is defined as seasoned and salted duck legs that are slow cooked in duck fat to tenderize.

Cornish Game Hen—Small breed of chicken typically sold whole averaging weight of 1 to 2 pounds.

Drake—Mature male duck.

Duck—Domestic breeds of waterfowl in the family Anatidae that are used for food.

Duckling—Young duck usually 6 to 8 weeks old and averaging about 3 to 6 pounds.

Emu—Large Australian ratite or land bird used for meat, feathers, and oil.

Enhanced Poultry—Whole birds or parts injected with a solution of water, sodium phosphate, and salt. Enhanced products may or may not contain spice or flavoring ingredients.

Euro-Quail—A semi-boneless quail, with rib cage and back removed, suitable for stuffing.

Fleshing—Poultry grading feature that judges the overall meat to bone ratio and general conformation, plumpness, and fullness of the meat.

Foie Gras—The fattened liver of a duck or goose.

Forcemeat—Ground, seasoned meat used for stuffing, sausage, terrines, pates, etc.

Free Range—Poultry raised with the unrestricted ability to access areas outside of their grow out house. May or may not have any relationship to the feed type or ingredients added to the poultry.

Frenched Breast—A poultry breast with only the first wing joint intact and the bone of that section exposed. See airline breast.

Fryer—A large broiler chicken typically over 3 pounds.

Game—Traditionally hunted animals not altered in breed from those found in the wild.

Gavage—The method used to fatten ducks or geese to create foie gras. Gavage takes advantage of the bird's natural desire to fatten up before migration.

Giblets—The gizzard, liver, and heart, found packaged together in many poultry items. The neck is often packaged with the giblets.

Gizzard—Part of the digestive tract of various fowl, part of the combination of offal considered giblets.

Goose—Any of a group of waterfowl (Anatidae) between ducks and swans in size, having long necks and webbed feet.

"Grow Out" House—A highly efficient poultry-raising barn that can contain many thousands of birds. Modern grow out houses have automated feed and water lines and are typically ventilated. Due to the close confinement, pathogens can spread easily throughout the population in these environs.

Guinea Fowl—A game bird originating in West Africa known for its robust flavor, about the size of a small chicken.

HACCP—Hazard Analysis Critical Control Points. A system of monitoring critical practices during processing of meat or poultry. HACCP is regulated by the USDA and is mandatory for the poultry industry.

Hen—Adult female of many poultry species typically used for egg production.

Heritage Breed—Any of a variety of traditional breeds of poultry that can trace back to previous historic times. Typically heritage breeds have lost favor with large-scale producers because of slower growth or poorer meat to bone ratios. Heritage birds can offer unique flavors and historic value.

IQF—Individually Quick Frozen products.

Irradiated—Exposing meats to either gamma ray or electronic beam radiation to eliminate pathogens. Also known as cold pasteurization.

Keet—An immature Guinea Fowl.

Listeria—Harmful bacteria found in precooked or processed meats, causing listeriosis.

Magret—The boneless Moulard duck breast typically pan seared similar to steak.

Mallard—Breed of wild duck from which most domestic breeds stem.

MAP—Modified Atmospheric Packaging. A packaging style used for poultry that flushes a loose fitting vacuum bag with a modified atmosphere typically containing an elevated CO_2 level that extends the shelf life of the product.

Moulard Duck—Cross between a Pekin and Muscovy duck used for foie gras production. Also known as a mule duck due its inability to reproduce.

Muscovy—A large nonmigratory duck originating in South America, also known as a Barbary duck.

Myoglobin—Protein containing iron that attaches oxygen to muscle cells. Responsible for the red pigment in meat and poultry.

Ostrich Fan—Large flat very tender muscle found in the Ostrich carcass.

Partridge—Any number of small gallinaceous birds hunted for game. Not domestic to the Americas but now available as farm-raised game. Often referred to as Quail.

Pasture Raised—Poultry raised on at least 20 percent wild forage. Free roaming gives the poultry free natural space to forage.

Pekin Duck—Rapidly maturing Asian white feathered duck. Most popular breed used for meat worldwide.

Pigeon—Mature squab over 3 months old. Can be tough depending on activity and age.

Pinfeathers—The ends of the feather that are left lodged in the skin when a poultry item is not defeathered properly. This feature is considered low quality and will downgrade the poultry.

Poultry—Domestic breeds of fowl used for meat or egg production including chicken, duck, goose, and turkey.

Poussin—Baby chicken about 3 to 4 weeks old.

Quail—A variety of small game known for rapid flight, typically hunted with dogs.

Ratite—A group of large land birds with red lean muscle tissues, for example: Ostrich, Emu, Rhea.

Rhea—Large South American ratite or land bird used for meat and oil.

Roaster—Large mature broiler chicken ranging from 5 to 9 pounds.

Rooster—Mature male chicken.

Salmonella—Genus of enterobacteria, pathogenic to humans and other warm-blooded animals, sometimes found on poultry products. Causes intestinal distress and can be problematic for people with compromised immune systems.

Squab—A young pigeon.

Stewing Hen—Older egg-laying chicken, fowl, typically used in a moist cooking application.

Supreme—Semi-boneless chicken breast, with frenched wing section and skin removed.

Trussing—A variety of methods to tie poultry in order to enhance shape, keep stuffing inside, and maintain moisture.

Turkey—Large North American gallinaceous bird *(Meleagris gallopavo)*, found wild and domesticated.

Turkey Trot—A long turkey drive bringing the birds from farms to city markets. Turkey drovers moved flocks over many miles over weeks.

USDA—United States Department of Agriculture. A government agency that oversees poultry inspection and grading.

WOG—Without giblets. A purchasing spec for poultry.

APPENDIX

POULTRY PURCHASING

Once a foodservice operation decides on a poultry menu item it has to purchase it to create that dish. It is up to the buyer to determine how the poultry should be purchased depending on the ability of the kitchen staff. Some restaurants decide to forego all fabrication and buy precut or even precooked portion items. These eliminate the labor and yield loss involved in producing the cut. The downside of this is the chef will not have any of the by-products that are created by processing the poultry. By-products such as bones can be used for stock.

Another reason to fabricate poultry in-house is unique custom portions can be created. Frenched chicken breasts, glove boned poultry, and other skill-intensive fabrications may not be available from the purveyor.

GOALS OF THE PURCHASER

The goal of the purchaser, whether it's a chef, owner, purchasing agent, or anyone responsible for buying, is to produce the least expensive portion with the highest quality product and stay within the proper food cost for the establishment. Being able to analyze the fabrication skills of the kitchen staff and also the general quantity that will be used will be crucial when deciding how to buy. What may work for one establishment may not for another. Also being able to judge the quality of the products and understanding value is important for the purchaser.

Developing proper poultry specifications for purchasing, even if for precut portions, is very important to the success of the establishment. The purveyor/vendor must understand clearly what is required by the restaurant so they can fill the order correctly. Also the restaurant must have a clear understanding of what is acceptable and what must be rejected. The purchaser and the purveyor must have a good understanding about all the products that might be ordered. Most purveyors will have a list of all the poultry products they can provide. A foodservice establishment should also create a list of everything they might be ordering.

When buying poultry, first an establishment must decide who to buy from. The buyer may be purchasing for a variety of businesses. Most typical would be the restaurant. Also hotels, resorts, cruise ships, casinos, catering services, retail stores, schools, institutions, military operations, and others all buy poultry to be produced into portions. Restaurants can vary in size, cuisine, seasonality, and all sorts of restraints that may help dictate how the restaurant will buy its poultry. A small establishment with a passionate, highly trained chef may be able to buy whole birds and fabricate all portions in-house and utilize everything that comes with the cut. On the other hand, a chef may choose to buy precut portions to free up time to do more complicated foods.

A high-volume restaurant that has a minimally trained crew such as a chain restaurant might not be able to fabricate in-house and would need all poultry cutting to be done offsite by the purveyor. These establishments will establish strict specifications for their portions. Managers will need to check products to be sure specs are adhered to. Many high-volume restaurants will have contracted agreements to ensure a steady flow of product arrives consistently to the restaurant. Some establishments will buy prebreaded or precooked, ready-to-serve items.

VENDOR TYPES

GENERAL FOODSERVICE PURVEYOR

This type of purveyor sells a huge variety of goods of which poultry is just one part. Often the large purveyor has a wide assortment of poultry specs and quality levels. They feature most national brand name items and sell a large variety of pretrimmed breast cuts, wings, legs, and portion cuts. They often have a knowledgeable sales staff who can be helpful in ordering products. Often the general food purveyor is regionally or nationally owned and is part of a larger corporation. This enables the large purveyor to purchase products in huge quantities, therefore offering the best prices.

There are a few drawbacks of purchasing from a large purveyor. They may require a minimum order. In other words, the restaurant would need to buy a minimum dollar amount that might be difficult for a smaller establishment to meet, especially during slower times of the year.

Also a delivery surcharge may be included. Many companies now charge a fuel surcharge. If your establishment is off the beaten path this charge may be substantial. Typically delivery will be once or twice a week by a large semi-trailer truck. Proper forecasting of usage is very important.

Large distributors use a catalog of items. It is very important for the purchaser to understand purchasing specs and check over orders as they are delivered. There may be a charge for returned items.

MEAT PURVEYOR

The meat purveyor is more regional than the large foodservice distributor. They are typically long-established smaller corporations, often second or third generation family owned. They may still fabricate some poultry from whole birds and might be able to provide unique fabrications. Often these establishments are USDA inspected and have their own brand names and labels not available elsewhere. They often sell "naturally" raised, free ranged, air chilled, or certified organic poultry products. They may provide a variety of fresh game birds with consistency.

The true meat purveyor is focused on customer service. They will often deliver multiple times per week. They often feature expert sales staff and have knowledgeable butchers. They can custom package poultry according to the restaurant's needs.

The meat purveyor may be the sole distributor for a specific brand within an area. Brand names such as Tyson, Perdue, FreeBird, Eberling, or Bell & Evans might only be available from a specific distributor. They may also feature special processed pre-seasoned items that can only be purchased from them.

Sometimes prices from a quality meat purveyor can be more expensive. They focus on quality and typically charge for it. They may also charge a delivery fee if beyond a certain mileage range.

RETAIL STORES

Large discount buying clubs will sometimes offer poultry products for less than the purveyors. They are focused on moving a large amount of product with very limited service. Payment is immediate unless a credit card is used. The customer must go to the store to get the products but this eliminates any delivery charges. The range of quality and product type can be limited though. But if the buyer is satisfied with the quality, significant savings can be found.

One thing to be wary of is the fact that your restaurant customers may be shopping there as well. The fact that an establishment is buying discount club meats may down-grade the reputation of that restaurant. The poultry may be the exact same quality grade that the foodservice purveyor offers but customers may not know this fact.

INTERNET SPECIALTY POULTRY SALES

Web sites offer a huge variety of poultry products. Specialty game birds, free ranged or foraged poultry, heirloom breeds, and regional specialties among many other items are all available today. The selection is almost limitless.

The products are often packaged frozen to ensure freshness when delivered. This can compromise quality slightly.

Drawbacks are that the buyer needs to be sure of the products. It may be very difficult to return products especially if there is no problem other than the wrong spec ordered.

Another major issue with Internet sales is the shipping costs involved. Shipping and packaging can be very expensive and may take a few days depending on the carrier. Weather conditions may hamper delivery and cause delays.

SMALL FARMER DIRECT SALES

Some chefs operating near rural areas may prefer to buy local free ranged poultry. This can often lead to buying directly from the small farmer. The local farmer can provide poultry that are grown on local feedstuffs or even foraged. Also some farms are focusing on heirloom breeds that are not available on a large scale. The flavor of small market poultry may or may not be different than what the large farms produce, depending on feed styles and breed.

Most poultry must be inspected by the USDA so the local farmer will need to bring the animal to an inspected slaughter facility. There are exceptions to this rule. Certain game birds such as quail or pheasant may be exempt from USDA inspection but it is a good practice to buy products that are at minimum state inspected.

The local farmer may work with a small processor to produce poultry that is inspected. Often these products are not graded and can vary in size and age. Defects such as pin-feathers or attached hairlike down can be a problem.

Another issue is seasonality. Small farmers might not have animals ready for slaughter all year round. Availability can wane during certain months.

Some farmers, especially those raising heirloom or specialty birds may charge more than standard commercial products. On the other hand a chef serving local poultry can place the name of the farm prominently on the menu and also charge a premium.

INDEX

A

additives, 25, 116–117. *See also* antibiotics
    nutritional value of meat and, 167
Advanced Meat Recovery (AMR) system, 33
Aesop, 88
African geese, 92
airline breasts
    chicken, 27, 42
    guinea fowl, 144
    pheasant, 141, 151
Alsatian roast goose with apples, 87
Ancona ducks, 62
Andalusian chickens, 23
animal rights, 181, 184
antibiotic free poultry, 13
    duck, 58
    egg production and, 181
    geese, 91
antibiotics
    in chicken feed, 19
    in turkeys, 110
antimicrobials, 19
Araucana chickens, 23
Aristotle, 88
arsenates, 19
artificial insemination, 57, 109
Asian White ducks, 57–58
Auburn turkeys, 111
Australian Spotted ducks, 63
avian flu, 8
Aylesbury ducks, 64

B

Barbary ducks, 56, 61
barbequed duck legs, 226
basil sauce, 205
basted poultry, 25
    turkey, 116–117
beef, consumption of, 18
Beltsville Small White turkeys, 111
bird flu, 8
Black Ancona ducks, 62
Black Muscovy ducks, 62
Black turkeys, 111–112
Blue Ancona ducks, 62
Blue Muscovy ducks, 62

boning
    chicken, for galantine, 48–50
    chicken legs, 45–47
    duck breasts, 78–79
    duck legs, 80
    glove, 50–52, 145, 158–159
    goose, 103
    quail, 145, 158–159
    turkey, whole, 127–130
    turkey breasts, 125–126
Bourbon Red turkeys, 112
Brahman chickens, 22
breaded and battered poultry, 25
breeds
    chicken, 20–23, 180
    chicken, for egg production, 185
    definition of, 21
    duck, 60–64, 83
    goose, 92–93
    heritage, 21, 93
    quail, 145
    turkey, 109, 111–115
brines, 201
    recipe for curing and smoking, 204
    recipe for moisture enhancing, 203
    for smoked goose breast, 104, 204
    for turkey, 132
Broad Breasted Bronze turkeys, 112
Broad Breasted White turkeys, 114, 115
broilers, 12, 24
    feed for, 18
    purchasing specifications for, 26–28
Buddhist style duckling, 66, 68
Buff turkeys, 113
bulk packaging, 24

C

Cabot, Sebastian, 108
cage-free poultry, 181, 182
California poulet blue chickens, 22
candling, 184
Canterbury Tales (Chaucer), 4
Canvasback ducks, 56–57, 61
capons, 12, 24, 26, 30
carotene, 195
Cassis sauce, 224–225
cassoulet, 87

Cayuga ducks, 62
century eggs, 197
Certified Human: Raised and Handled, 184
chalazae, 184
Chanticleer the Rooster, 4
charcuterie, 87. *See also* sausages
Chaucer, Geoffrey, 4
chicken, 15–52
    additives in, 25
    boning for galantine, 48–50
    breasts, airline, 27–42
    breasts, boneless, 38–42
    breeds of, 20–23, 180
    classes of, 24
    Columbian chicken sancocho, 210–211
    cutlets, 41
    cutting 8- or 10-piece, 35–38
    domestication of, 16
    eggs, 193–194
    egg sizes, 186–188
    fabrication, 33–52
    feed for, 18–19
    foodservice market forms of, 24–25
    frenched chicken breast with fresh
        basil sauce, 205
    genome of, 15
    giblets, 29, 32
    glove boning, 50–52
    leading producers of, 5, 6–7
    legs, boning, 45–47
    legs, frenching, 44
    in mythology and literature, 4, 16
    nest boxes for, 198
    nutritional value of, 168–170, 171
    origins of, 15
    paprikash, 212
    processed products, 30, 33
    processing, 33–52
    production of, 16–19
    purchasing specifications for, 26–33
    stock, basic recipe for, 202
    trussing, 34–35
    U.S. consumption of, 18
    wings, frenching, 43
"Chicken Little," 4
Chiltz Foods, 92
Chinese geese, 92
Chinese Ringneck pheasants, 140
chitterlings, goose, 95
cholesterol, 165, 192. *See also* nutritional values

chukar, 145–147
classifications, 11–12
    goose, 93
    turkey, 115
Cochin chickens, 22
cock fighting, 16, 20
cold pasteurization, 25, 167
confit
    duck, 55, 71
    goose, 87
cooking
    chicken, 26–29
    critical temperature zones in, 9
    eggs, 192
    nutritional values and, 165, 167
    ostrich, 149
    pheasant, 140, 154
    safety in, 10–11
Cornish chickens, 23
    nutritional value of, 170
Cornish game hens, 12, 24, 26, 30
    apple-walnut stuffed, 206–208
Crescent Duck Farm, 57
critical temperature zones, 9
Culver Duck, 57
curing
    brine for, 204
    duck, 55
    nutritional value and, 167
    turkey, 121
cutlets
    chicken, 41
    turkey, 119, 127
CVP packaging, 24

D

Delaware chickens, 22
domestication, 4
    of chickens, 16
    of ducks, 56–58
    of turkeys, 108
Dominique chickens, 22
Dorking chickens, 23
dove, 147, 148
down
    chicken, 20
    duck, 59
    fill power of, 91
    goose, 91–92
drakes, 60

duck, 55–85
  avian flu and, 8
  breasts, 69
  breasts, boning, 78–79
  breasts, searing, 80
  breeds, 60–64
  classes of, 65
  confit, 55, 71
  dark meat in, 12
  domestication of, 56–58
  eggs, 186, 187, 193–194, 195
  fabrication, 72–83
  fat of, 55, 66, 71, 74
  fat of, rendering, 80, 81
  feed for, 58
  foie gras from, 55, 56, 58, 61, 66, 67, 81–85
  food safety and, 10–11
  history of, 56
  legs, barbequed, 226
  legs, boning, 80
  magret with sauce cassis, 224–225
  nutritional value of, 166
  nutritional values of, 172–173
  peppered ostrich fillets with duck steak fries, 234–235
  production of, 7, 57–58
  purchasing specifications for, 65–71
  sausage from, 71, 72–73, 232–233
  splitting, 76–77
  trussing, 74–75
  undercooking, 10–11
  wild, 139
ducklings, 60, 65, 66–67
Duclair ducks, 60
Dutch Hook Bill ducks, 62

E

Easter, 180
East Indie ducks, 63
eggs, 179–199
  Benedict, 195
  as binding agents, 196
  by-products from, 181
  candling, 184
  chicken, 16, 17
  chicken breeds for, 20–21
  double yolk, 185
  duck, 56, 186, 187
  as food, 195–197
  food safety with, 192
  free ranged, 182

  goose, 92, 186, 187
  grading and sizing, 184–189
  history of, 4, 138, 170–180
  liquid, 190
  nest boxes for, 198
  nutritional value of, 179, 192–195
  organic, 183–184
  ostrich, 149, 186, 188
  packaging, 189, 190–191
  pasteurized, 196
  pasture-raised, 182
  powdered, 196
  preserved, 197
  production of, 16, 17, 180–181
  quail, 186, 188
  size equivalents for, 186
  storing, 189
  turkey, 186
Embden geese, 92
emu, 139, 148–150
  red meat in, 166
enhanced poultry, 25
  turkey, 116–117
environmental issues, 183
Environmental Protection Agency (EPA), 19
Escherichia coli, 8
European Union, 19, 182
Euro-quail, 145, 146

F

Fabergé, Carl, 180
fabrication
  chicken, 33–52
  game bird, 151–158
  goose, 97–104
  ostrich, 149, 160–162
  pheasant, 151–158
  quail, 158–159
  turkey, 122–135
falconry, 139
farmer-direct sales, 250–251
fat
  confit and, 55, 71, 87
  in dark vs. white meat, 165
  duck, 55, 67, 71, 74
  duck, rendering, 80, 81
  in eggs, 195
  goose, 89–90, 96
  nutrition and, 165
  ostrich, 149

fatty acids, 166

FDA. *See* Food and Drug
   Administration (FDA)

feathers
   chicken, 20
   duck, 59
   goose, 91–92
   ostrich, 149

feed
   animal by-products in, 19
   for chickens, 18–19
   for ducks, 57, 58
   effects of on muscle fibers, 12–13
   for egg production, 180, 181, 182
   for foie gras, 83
   game bird, 137
   for geese, 91
   grain in, 13
   nutritional value of meat and, 166
   organic, 183–184
   pheasant, 140
   turkey, 109–110

feet
   duck, 67
   goose, 95

fig newton foie gras, 236–238

fill power, 91

foie gras, 4
   butter, 67
   deveining liver for, 81–82
   duck, 55, 56, 58, 61, 66, 67, 81–85
   fig newton, 236–238
   French style, 85
   goose, 87, 89–90, 92–93, 95, 96
   New York style, 58, 85

Food and Drug Administration
   (FDA), 9–10

food-borne illnesses, 8–9, 117
   in eggs, 192, 197

food safety, 8–10, 201
   cooking and, 10–11
   eggs and, 181, 192
   inspections and, 9–10
   medicated feed and, 19
   packaging and storage in, 10
   turkey and, 117

Food Safety and Inspection Service, 8

food safety guidelines, 8–9

foodservice market forms
   chicken, 24–25

foodservice purveyors, 249

foraged birds
   eggs from, 182, 195
   game birds, 137
   muscle fibers and, 12–13
   nutritional value of meat and, 166

forcemeats, 49

Fosters poultry, 19

fowl, 12, 26

Frankonian geese, 93

free range poultry, 13
   duck, 58
   eggs, 182
   geese, 91

frenching
   chicken breasts, 42
   chicken legs, 44
   chicken wings, 43

French toast, 195

frozen poultry, 10
   chicken, 25
   duck, 65
   eggs, 189
   thawing, 10, 116
   turkey, 116

fryers, 12, 24

G

galantine, chicken, 48–50

game birds, 137–162. *See also* wild birds
   chukar, 145–147
   dove, 147, 148
   emu, 148–150
   fabrication, 151–158
   grouse, 145–147
   guinea fowl, 143–144
   history of, 138–139
   lean meat in, 165
   ostrich, 148–150
   partridge, 145–147
   pheasant, 140–143
   pigeon, 147–148
   quail, 145–147
   squab, 147, 148
   wild turkey, 143

ganders, 92

gavage, 56, 83. *See also* foie gras

giblets
   chicken, 29, 32
   duck, 71
   goose, 95
   turkey, 119

globalization, 5

glove boning, 50–52

goose, 87–104

    boning for pate or sausage, 103

    breast, smoked, with hoisin glaze, 220–222

    breeds, 92–93

    brining for smoking, 104

    by-products from, 91–92

    classes of, 93

    dark meat in, 12

    disjointing, 100–101

    eggs, 186, 187

    fabrication, 97–104

    in farm life, 89–91

    feed for, 166

    foie gras from, 87, 89–90, 92–93

    as guard animals, 89, 90

    history of, 88–91

    lifespan of, 91

    nests, 196

    nutritional value of, 166

    nutritional values of, 173–174

    production of, 7, 91

    purchasing, 94–97

    roast goose Grand Marnier, 218–219

    roasting, tying for, 102

    trussing, 98–99

    as weeder animals, 90–91, 93

"Goose that laid the golden egg, The" (Aesop), 88

grading, 11

    chicken, 33

    egg, 181, 184–189

    foie gras liver, 84

    ostrich, 149

Grand Marnier, roast goose, 218–219

Grey Jungle Fowl, 15

Greylag geese, 92

ground meat

    ostrich, 150

    turkey, 119, 120

grouse, 145–147

grow out houses, 17, 21

growth promotants, 58

guard animals, 89, 90, 143–144

guinea fowl, 143–144, 157

    nutritional values of, 174

H

HACCP. *See* Hazard Analysis Critical Control Points (HACCP)

Hamburg chickens, 23

Harlequin ducks, 63

Hazard Analysis Critical Control Points (HACCP), 10

health issues

    avian flu, 8

    food borne illnesses, 8–9

heirloom breeds. *See* heritage breeds

hens

    chicken, 11, 12, 24

    duck, 60

    turkey, 115

heritage breeds, 21

    duck, 58, 64

    farmer-direct sales of, 250

    goose, 93

    turkey, 111–113

hoisin glaze, 220–222

Holderread Waterfowl Preservation Farm, 64

Hollandaise sauce, 196

hollow boning, 47, 80

Homer, 88

homing pigeons, 147

Hot Wings, 43

Hudson Valley Foie Gras, 58, 83

hunting, 138–139

I

Indian Runner ducks, 62

individually quick frozen (IQF) poultry, 25

individually wrapped packaging, 24

industrialization, 5, 7, 17

injected poultry, 25

in-line producers, 180

inspection, 9–10

    egg, 181

    farmer-direct sales and, 250–251

    of game birds, 140

integrated systems, 5, 18

Internet specialty poultry sales, 250

IQF. *See* individually quick frozen (IQF) poultry

irradiated poultry, 25, 167

isolated soy protein (ISP), 25

ISP. *See* isolated soy protein (ISP)

J

Jersey Giant chickens, 22
Jurgielewicz Duck Farm, 57

K

Kains, M.G., 5
Kansas Ringneck pheasants, 140
keets, 144
Khaki Campbell ducks, 62
kosher laws, 87, 88

L

La Belle Poutry, 58, 83
Langshan chickens, 22
layer hen houses, 17
leather, ostrich, 149
Leghorn chickens, 23, 180, 185
Listeria, 117
literature, poultry in, 4, 16, 88
liver. *See also* foie gras
    chicken, 171
    deveining, 81–82
    duck, 67, 82–85
    goose, 95, 96
    nutritional value of, 171
lutein, 18–19

M

Magpie ducks, 62
magret, 65, 66, 224–225
Mallard ducks, 56, 61, 63
Manchurian cross pheasants, 140
MAP. *See* modified atmospheric packaging (MAP)
Maple Leaf Duck Farms, 57, 58
marinated poultry, 25, 201
    turkey, 116–117
mature poultry
    ducks, 65, 66
    geese, 93
    turkey, 115
meat purveyors, 249–250
medallions, ostrich, 161–162
Melanistic mutant pheasants, 140
migratory birds, 12, 87
Miniature Overberg ducks, 63
Minorca chickens, 23

modified atmospheric packaging (MAP), 10, 24
Moulard ducks, 58, 61, 65, 66, 67, 68, 83
muscle fibers, 12–13, 87
Muscovy ducks, 56, 61, 62
myoglobin, 12, 56
mythology, poultry in, 4, 16, 88

N

NAMP. *See* North American Meat Processors
    (NAMP) Association
Narragansett turkeys, 113, 114
natural poultry, 13
New Hampshire chickens, 22
New Jersey Buff turkeys, 113
nitrates, 167
North American Meat Processors (NAMP)
    Association
    chicken classes, 24
    chicken specifications, 26–29
    duck specifications, 66–67
    goose specifications, 94–95
    grouse specifications, 146
    guinea fowl specifications, 144
    ostrich specifications, 150
    partridge specifications, 146
    pheasant specifications, 141
    pigeon/squab specifications, 148
    quail specifications, 146
    turkey specifications, 118–119
North American Wild turkeys, 114–115
nutritional values, 165–178. *See also* feed
    additives and, 167
    of chicken, 25, 168–170, 171
    of Cornish game hen, 170
    of dove, 171–172
    of duck, 172–173
    of eggs, 179, 192–195
    of eggs, free range, 182
    of goose, 173–174
    of guinea fowl, 174
    of ostrich, 175
    on packaging, 25
    of pheasant, 175–176
    preservation and, 167
    of quail, 176
    of squab, 177
    of turkey, 177–178

O

Ocellated turkeys, 113
Omega-3 fatty acids, 143, 166, 195
Omega-6 fatty acids, 166
open style boning, 45–46
organic poultry
    eggs, 183–184
    natural poultry and, 13
Orpington chickens, 23
osso buco, turkey, 131–132
ostrich, 139, 148–150
    eggs, 180, 186, 188, 195
    fabrication, 160–162
    fillets, peppered, with duck steak fries, 234–235
    nutritional values of, 175
    red meat in, 166
    yield from, 160

P

packaging, 10
    chicken, 24–25, 26–29
    egg, 181, 189, 190–191
    nutrition information on, 25
paprikash, chicken, 212
partridge, 145–147, 158–159
Passenger pigeons, 138
pastrami, turkey, 216–217
pasture raised poultry, 13, 183
    eggs, 182
pate
    goose, 103
paws, duck, 67
pecan-stuffed pheasant, 228–230
Pekin ducks, 57–58, 60, 64, 68
peppered ostrich fillets with duck steak fries, 234–235
"Peter and the Wolf" (Prokofiev), 4
pheasant, 140–143
    fabrication, 151–158
    nests, 196
    nutritional values of, 175–176
    pecan-stuffed, 228–230
    stuffing, 155–158
    yield for, 153
phoenix, 179
pidan eggs, 197
pigeon, 138, 147–148
Plymouth Rock chickens, 22, 185
Polish chickens, 23

Porcelain turkeys, 114
portions
    goose, 95
    nutrition and, 165
    pheasant, 153
Poulet de Bresse chickens, 23
poultry
    classifications of, 11–12
    definition of, 3
    domestication of, 4
    in farm life, 3–4, 16
    muscle fibers in, 12–13
    in mythology and literature, 4, 16, 88
    natural, 13
poultry production
    avian flu and, 8
    cage-free, 181, 182
    chicken, 16–19
    chicken breeds for, 21–23
    duck, 57–58
    eggs, 16, 17, 180–181
    game bird, 137
    goose, 91
    history of, 4–5
    modern, 5–8
    ostrich, 149
    pheasant, 140
    turkey, 109–110
Poultry Products Inspection Act, 9–10
poussin, 12, 24, 26, 30
preservation, 4
    duck, 55
    egg, 197
probiotics, 19
Profitable Poultry Production (Kains), 5
Prokofiev, Sergey, 4
protein, 12, 179, 192. See also nutritional values
pullets, 181
purchasing, 248–249
    chicken, 26–33
    duck, 65–71
    from general foodservice purveyors, 249
    goals in, 248–249
    goose, 94–97
    Internet, 250
    from meat purveyors, 249–250
    pheasant, 141
    retail, 250
    turkey, 116–121
    vendor types, 249–251

Q

quail, 145–147
  eggs, 186, 188
  fabrication, 158–159
  nutritional values of, 176
  Spanish griddled, 227

R

ready to cook (RTC) poultry, 25
recipes, 201–242
  apple-walnut stuffed Cornish game hens, 206–208
  brine, for moisture enhancement, 203
  brine, for smoking and curing, 204
  chicken paprikash, 212
  chicken stock, 202
  Columbian chicken sancocho, 210–211
  duck legs, barbequed, 226
  duck magret with sauce cassis, 224–225
  duck saucisse, 232–233
  egg equivalents for, 186
  foie gras fig newton, 236–238
  frenched chicken breast with fresh basil sauce, 205
  goose breast, smoked, with hoisin glaze, 220–222
  pecan-stuffed pheasant, 228–230
  quail, Spanish griddled, 227
  roast goose Grand Marnier, 218–219
  squab, pan seared, au jus, 240–242
  turkey, easy slice roast, 213–214
  turkey pastrami, 216–217
Red Jungle Fowl, 4, 15, 179
retail stores, purchasing from, 250
Rhea, 149
Rhode Island Red chickens, 22
roasters, 24, 26, 30
  breasts, 27
roasting
  chicken, 34–35
  goose, 102
  goose, Grand Marnier, 218–219
  turkey, whole boneless, 127–130
roasting ducks, 65, 66
Rock Cornish hens, 26
roosters, 11, 12, 24
Rouen ducks, 61
Rougie, 83
Roxarsone-4-hydroxy-3-nitrobenzenearsonic acid, 19
Royal Palm turkeys, 114
RTC. *See* ready to cook (RTC) poultry
Runner ducks, 62–63

S

Salmonella, 8, 117, 181, 192
salumi, 87
saucisse, duck, 232–233
sausages
  chicken, 30
  duck, 71, 72–73, 232–233
  goose, 87, 88, 103
Saxony ducks, 62
seared squab, 160, 240–242
seasonality, 251
seasoned poultry, 25
show birds, 20, 21
Silky ducks, 63
Silver Appleyard ducks, 62, 63
Silver Muscovy ducks, 62
Smithfield market (London), 4–5
smoked poultry
  brine for, 104, 204
  duck, 55, 69
  goose, 87, 94, 97, 104
  goose breast, with hoisin glaze, 220–222
  pheasant, 141
  turkey, 121
sodium nitrite, 204
Sonoma County Poultry—Liberty Ducks farm, 57
Spanish griddled quail, 227
squab, 147, 148, 160
  nutritional values of, 177
  pan seared, au jus, 240–242
squeakers, 148
steak fries, duck, 234–235
steroids, 58
stewing fowl, 24, 26, 30
storage, 10
  critical temperature zones in, 9
  egg, 189
  of goose, 94
strains, 21. *See also* breeds
Strickland, William, 108
stuffing
  pheasant, 155–158
  turkey, 122–124
supremes, 42
Sussex chickens, 23
Swan geese, 92
swans, 8

T

Teal ducks, 64
tenderloin, ostrich, 161–162
thawing poultry, 10, 116
Tinted Curing Mix, 204
toms, 115
tongue, duck, 67
Toulouse geese, 92–93
trussing
   chicken, 34–35
   ducks, 74–75
   goose, 98–99
   turkey, 122–124
turkey, 107–135
   boning whole, 127–130
   breasts, boning, 125–126
   breeds, 109, 111–115
   brining, 132
   carving, 133–135
   classes of, 115
   consumption rate of, 109
   easy slice roast recipe, 213–214
   eggs, 186, 195
   fabrication, 122–135
   feed for, 109–110
   history of, 108–109
   legs, removing, 124
   nutritional value of, 166
   nutritional values of, 177–178
   osso buco, 131–132
   pastrami, 216–217
   processed cooked products, 121
   production of, 7, 109–110
   purchasing, 116–121
   raw products, 116–120
   trussing, 122–124
   wild, 5, 139, 143
   yield from, 135
turkey trots, 109
Tyson, John, 5
Tyson Corporation, 18, 19

U

United States Department of Agriculture (USDA)
   chicken inspections, 33
   on chicken production, 17
   egg grading, 184–185
   food safety guidelines, 8–9
   on free range eggs, 182
   game bird inspections, 140
   grading by, 11
   inspections by, 9–10, 251
   on organic eggs, 183–184
USDA. *See* United States Department of
   Agriculture (USDA)

V

varieties, 21. *See also* breeds
vendors, 249–251. *See also* purchasing

W

water fowl. *See* duck; goose
weeders, geese as, 90–91, 93
Whisky Sour, 196
White Holland turkeys, 114, 115
wild birds
   duck, 56, 61, 64
   game cocks, 20
   geese, 92
   turkey, 5, 108, 109
Woodland Duck Farms, 58
World Health Organization (WHO), 8
World Ostrich Association, 149
Wyandotte chickens, 22

Y

yield
   from ostrich, 160
   from pheasant, 153
   from turkey, 135
young poultry
   chickens, 11
   geese, 93
   turkey, 115

PHOTO CREDITS

BEN FINK

Pages 28, 29, 30, 31, 32, 33, 68, 69, 70, 71, 84, 85, 96, 97, 98, 101 (Fig 4.10F), 104, 116, 117, 120, 142, 143, 144, 146, 147, 148, 153, 208, 211, 212, 217, 218, 222, 225, 226, 230, 233, 234, 236, 238, 214, 242

KEITH FERRIS

Pages 34, 35, 36, 37, 38, 39, 40, 41, 42, 43, 44, 45, 46, 47, 48, 49, 50, 51, 52, 72, 73, 74, 75, 76, 77, 78, 79, 80, 81, 82, 99, 100, 101 (Fig 4.10D, E), 102, 103, 122, 123, 124, 125, 126, 127, 128, 129, 130, 131, 132, 133, 134, 135, 150, 151, 152, 153, 154, 155, 156, 157, 158, 159, 160, 161, 162, 185, 189, 190, 191, 192, 193, 199, 200, 201

CIA CONVERSION CHARTS

TEMPERATURE, WEIGHT AND VOLUME CONVERSIONS

TEMPERATURE CONVERSIONS

32°F = 0°C	205°F = 96°C	380°F = 193°C
35°F = 2°C	210°F = 99°C	385°F = 196°C
40°F = 4°C	**212°F = 100°C**	390°F = 199°C
45°F = 7°C	215°F = 102°C	395°F = 202°C
50°F = 10°C	220°F = 104°C	**400°F = 204°C**
55°F = 13°C	**225°F = 107°C**	405°F = 207°C
60°F = 16°C	230°F = 110°C	410°F = 210°C
65°F = 18°C	235°F = 113°C	415°F = 213°C
70°F = 21°C	240°F = 116°C	420°F = 216°C
75°F = 24°C	245°F = 118°C	**425°F = 218°C**
[room temp]	**250°F = 121°C**	430°F = 221°C
80°F = 27°C	255°F = 124°C	435°F = 224°C
85°F = 29°C	260°F = 127°C	440°F = 227°C
90°F = 32°C	265°F = 129°C	445°F = 229°C
95°F = 35°C	270°F = 132°C	**450°F = 232°C**
100°F = 38°C	**275°F = 135°C**	455°F = 235°C
105°F = 41°C	280°F = 138°C	460°F = 238°C
110°F = 43°C	285°F = 141°C	465°F = 241°C
115°F = 46°C	290°F = 144°C	470°F = 243°C
120°F = 49°C	295°F = 146°C	**475°F = 246°C**
125°F = 52°C	**300°F = 149°C**	480°F = 249°C
130°F = 54°C	305°F = 152°C	485°F = 252°C
135°F = 57°C	310°F = 154°C	490°F = 254°C
140°F = 60°C	315°F = 157°C	495°F = 257°C
145°F = 63°C	320°F = 160°C	**500°F = 260°C**
150°F = 66°C	**325°F = 163°C**	505°F = 263°C
155°F = 68°C	330°F = 166°C	510°F = 266°C
160°F = 71°C	335°F = 168°C	515°F = 268°C
165°F = 74°C	340°F = 171°C	520°F = 271°C
170°F = 77°C	345°F = 174°C	**525°F = 274°C**
175°F = 79°C	**350°F = 177°C**	530°F = 277°C
180°F = 82°C	355°F = 179°C	535°F = 279°C
185°F = 85°C	360°F = 182°C	540°F = 282°C
190°F = 88°C	365°F = 185°C	545°F = 285°C
195°F = 91°C	370°F = 188°C	550°F = 288°C
200°F = 93°C	**375°F = 191°C**	

WEIGHT CONVERSIONS

For weights less than 1/4 oz: use tsp/tbsp for U.S. measure with gram or mL equivalent
(see specific conversion tables).

Formula to convert ounces to grams: number of oz $\times$ 28.35 = number of grams (round up for .50 and above)

1/4 ounce = 7 grams	
1/2 ounce = 14 grams	
1 ounce = 28.35 grams	
4 ounces = 113 grams	
8 ounces (1/2 pound) = 227 grams	
16 ounces (1 pound) = 454 grams	
32 ounces (2 pounds) = 907 grams	
40 ounces (2 1/2 pounds) = 1.134 kilograms	

VOLUME CONVERSIONS

Formula to convert fluid ounces to milliliters: number of fluid ounces $\times$ 30 = number of milliliters

1/2 fl oz = 15 mL	20 fl oz = 600 mL
1 fl oz = 30 mL	24 fl oz = 720 mL
1 1/2 fl oz = 45 mL	30 fl oz = 900 mL
1 3/4 fl oz = 53 mL	**32 fl oz = 960 mL [1 qt]**
2 fl oz = 60 mL	40 fl oz = 1.20 L
2 1/2 fl oz = 75 mL	44 fl oz = 1.32 L
3 fl oz = 90 mL	**48 fl oz = 1.44 L [1 1/2 qt]**
3 1/2 fl oz = 105 mL	64 fl oz = 1.92 L [2 qt]
4 fl oz = 120 mL	**72 fl oz = 2.16 L [2 1/2 qt]**
5 fl oz = 150 mL	80 fl oz = 2.4 L
6 fl oz = 180 mL	96 fl oz = 2.88 L [3 qt]
7 fl oz = 210 mL	128 fl oz = 3.84 L [1 gal]
8 fl oz = 240 mL [1 cup]	1 1/8 gal = 4.32 L
9 fl oz = 270 mL	1 1/4 gal = 4.8 L
10 fl oz = 300 mL	1 1/2 gal = 5.76 L
11 fl oz = 330 mL	**2 gal = 7.68 L [256 fl oz]**
12 fl oz = 360 mL	3 gal = 11.52 L
13 fl oz = 390 mL	4 gal = 15.36 L
14 fl oz = 420 mL	5 gal = 19.20 L
15 fl oz = 450 mL	10 gal = 38.40 L
16 fl oz = 480 mL [1 pt]	20 gal = 76.80 L
17 fl oz = 510 mL	25 gal = 96 L
18 fl oz = 540 mL	50 gal = 192 L
19 fl oz = 570 mL	